Plastic Sovereignties

Incitements

Series editors: Peg Birmingham, DePaul University and Dimitris Vardoulakis, University of Western Sydney

An incitement is a thought that leads to a further thought or an action that solicits a response, while also testing the limits of what is acceptable or lawful. The books in this series, by prominent, world class scholars, will highlight the political import of philosophy, showing how concepts can be translated into political praxis, and how praxis is inextricably linked to thinking.

Editorial Advisory Board

Étienne Balibar, Andrew Benjamin, Jay M. Bernstein, Rosi Braidotti, Wendy Brown, Judith Butler, Adriana Cavarero, Howard Caygill, Rebecca Comay, Joan Copjec, Simon Critchley, Costas Douzinas, Peter Fenves, Christopher Fynsk, Moira Gatens, Gregg Lambert, Leonard Lawlor, Genevieve Lloyd, Catherine Malabou, James Martel, Christoph Menke, Warren Montag, Michael Naas, Antonio Negri, Kelly Oliver, Paul Patton, Anson Rabinbach, Gerhard Richter, Martin Saar, Miguel Vatter, Gianni Vattimo, Santiago Zabala

Available

Return Statements: The Return of Religion in Contemporary Philosophy
By Gregg Lambert

The Refusal of Politics
By Laurent Dubreuil, translated by Cory Browning

Plastic Sovereignties: Agamben and the Politics of Aesthetics
By Arne De Boever

From Violence to Speaking Out: Apocalypse and Expression in Foucault, Derrida and Deleuze
By Leonard Lawlor

Forthcoming

Agonistic Mourning: Political Dissidence and the Women in Black
By Athena Athanasiou

Plastic Sovereignties

Agamben and the Politics of Aesthetics

Arne De Boever

EDINBURGH
University Press

Edinburgh University Press is one of the leading university presses in the UK. We publish academic books and journals in our selected subject areas across the humanities and social sciences, combining cutting-edge scholarship with high editorial and production values to produce academic works of lasting importance. For more information visit our website: edinburghuniversitypress.com

© Arne De Boever, 2016

Edinburgh University Press Ltd
The Tun – Holyrood Road, 12(2f) Jackson's Entry, Edinburgh EH8 8PJ

Typeset in Bembo
by R. J. Footring Ltd, Derby, UK, and
printed and bound in Great Britain by
Gomer Press Ltd, Llandysul SA44 4JL

A CIP record for this book is available from the British Library

ISBN 978 0 7486 8497 7 (UK hardback)
ISBN 978 1 4744 2299 4 (US hardback)
ISBN 978 0 7486 8498 4 (webready PDF)
ISBN 978 1 4744 1797 6 (paperback)
ISBN 978 0 7486 8499 1 (epub)

The right of Arne De Boever to be identified as the author of this work has been asserted in accordance with the Copyright, Designs and Patents Act 1988, and the Copyright and Related Rights Regulations 2003 (SI No. 2498).

Contents

Acknowledgments

I decided it would be worthwhile publishing this book partly in response to some comments I received on my books of literary criticism, comments that suggested the theoretical focus of those books – and in particular their political theoretical focus – was underdeveloped. Indeed, the writerly project of the books of literary criticism was to work out as much as possible the theoretical references so as to let the literary works do that thinking *and more* for us, as literary-political thought. Over the years, however, it has also begun to seem useful to me to articulate the political theoretical focus of my work in literary criticism in the form of a book, as a way of clarifying my position in a time when it has come to seem less and less fashionable but more and more meaningful.

Rather than providing the reader with a chapter-by-chapter narrative outlining the progressive argument of the book, I have tried to weave the major concerns that are addressed in the following chapters into my first chapter. Some parts of this book were written as early as 2005, and sections from most of the chapters have appeared in journal articles or book chapters (some difficult to access, some only available in French) that I have published since then: in the journals *Azimuth* and *Cahiers du Post-Diplôme: Volume 3* (Chapter 1), the edited collection *The Work of Giorgio Agamben* (Edinburgh; Chapter 2), the journals *Journal of Aesthetic Education* and *Cahiers du Post-Diplôme: Volume 1* (Chapter 3), the journal *Law & Critique* (Chapter 4), the journals *Foucault Studies* and *Cahiers Simondon* (Chapter 5), the journal *Image[&]Narrative* (Chapter 6), the journal *Philosophy Today* (Chapter 8), and the journal *Parrhesia* (Chapter 9). All of the previously published work reappears here in an entirely different context and as a result has been thoroughly revised. Embarrassing mistakes have been edited out – but I'm sure many remain.

This book has been "in progress" for a long time, and during all the years that I have been at work on it I have been blessed with a great number of interlocutors, many of them critical readers of Agamben. I would like to extend my thanks, as always, to Bruce Robbins, Stathis Gourgouris, and Patricia Dailey at Columbia University; the students and faculty of the second Seminar in Experimental Critical Theory (SECT) at the University of California, Irvine, in particular Imogen Bunting and Anna Kornbluh (thanks also to Anna for inviting me to present a part of Chapter 8 in the InterCcECT group in March 2015); the students and faculty of the summer 2006 School of Criticism and Theory (SCT) at Cornell University, in particular my seminar leader, Eric Santner, and Maria Boletsi, Brent Edwards, Anne-Lise François, Nick Heron, Alysia Garrison, MLE Wilbourne, and Hiie Saumaa; and the participants of the 2007–8 Paris Program in Critical Theory, in particular its director, Samuel Weber, as well as Laura Reagan and Crina Archer.

None of this would have been written without the generous support of the Belgian American Educational Foundation, the Francqui Foundation, and Columbia University's Graduate School of Arts and Sciences (GSAS). I am grateful to GSAS for the two years of summer funding that enabled me to attend SECT and SCT, and for the 2007–8 Reid Hall Fellowship that made it possible for me to participate in the Paris Program in Critical Theory.

This book was completed while I was teaching in the School of Critical Studies at the California Institute of the Arts, one of the few places in the United States where theory is still very much alive. I am particularly grateful to my colleague Martín Plot, first-rate theorist of the aesthetico-political, as well as to the students who worked through Agamben's writings with me in my undergraduate (!) and graduate seminars on Agamben, biopolitics, and the care of the self. Judith Butler's residency in the MA Aesthetics and Politics program at CalArts provided a late inspiration for the completion of the manuscript.

I owe a special thanks to Eduardo Cadava and Brent Edwards, who joined my dissertation committee for the defense and suggested I bring my thoughts on sovereignty together under the title "contesting sovereignties" – it is this suggestion that ultimately lead to the central concept of this book; to Catherine Malabou, for discussing plasticity and Agamben's work with me in Paris, Los Angeles, and at UC Berkeley; to Jason Smith, for inviting me to present some of my thoughts on Rancière at the Art Center College of Design; to Érik Bullot, for inviting me to present my work on Agamben at the European School for Visual Arts in Angoulême; to Jean-Hugues Barthélémy, for supporting and translating my work on Agamben and Simondon; to my co-editors at *Parrhesia: A Journal of Critical Philosophy*, Alex Murray, Jon Roffe, and Ashley Woodward, for welcoming me into the philosophical fold.

I can only hope that you won't hold the wildness of this book against me.

Abbreviations

B   "No to Biopolitical Tattooing" [2004], available at: <http://www.ratical.org/ratville/CAH/totalControl.html>.

C   *Qu'est-ce que le commandement?* Trans. Joël Gayraud. Paris: Bibliothèques Rivages, 2013.

CC   *The Coming Community.* Trans. Michael Hardt. Minneapolis: University of Minnesota Press, 1990.

HP   *The Highest Poverty: Monastic Rules and Form-Of-Life.* Trans. Adam Kotsko. Stanford: Stanford University Press, 2013.

HS   *Homo Sacer: Sovereign Power and Bare Life.* Trans. Daniel Heller-Roazen. Stanford: Stanford University Press, 1998.

IH   *Infancy and History: On the Destruction of Experience.* Trans. Liz Heron. New York: Verso, 2007.

IP   *Idea of Prose.* Trans. Michael Sullivan and Sam Whitsitt. Albany: SUNY Press, 1995.

IS   "Image and Silence." Trans. Leland de la Durantaye. *Diacritics* 40.2 (2012), 94–8.

K   *The Kingdom and the Glory: For a Theological Genealogy of Economy and Government.* Trans. Lorenzo Chiesa (with

Matteo Mandarini). Stanford: Stanford University Press, 2011.

MWC	*The Man Without Content.* Trans. Georgia Albert. Stanford: Stanford University Press, 1999.
MWE	*Means Without End: Notes on Politics.* Trans. Vincenzo Binetti and Cesare Casarino. Minneapolis: University of Minnesota Press, 2000.
N	*Nudities.* Trans. David Kishik and Stefan Pedatella. Stanford: Stanford University Press, 2011.
O	*The Open: Man and Animal.* Trans. Kevin Attell. Stanford: Stanford University Press, 2004.
P	*Potentialities: Collected Essays in Philosophy.* Trans. Daniel Heller-Roazen. Stanford: Stanford University Press, 1999.
PR	*Profanations.* Trans. Jeff Fort. New York: Zone Books, 2007.
RA	*Remnants of Auschwitz: The Witness and the Archive.* Trans. Daniel Heller-Roazen. New York: Zone Books, 1999.
S	*Stanzas: Word and Phantasm in Western Culture.* Trans. Ronald L. Martinez. Minneapolis: University of Minnesota Press, 1993.
SE	*State of Exception.* Trans. Kevin Attell. Chicago: University of Chicago Press, 2005.
SR	*Signatura Rerum: Sur la méthode.* Joël Gayraud. Paris: Vrin, 2008.
TR	*The Time That Remains: A Commentary on the Letter to the Romans.* Trans. Patricia Dailey. Stanford: Stanford University Press, 2005.
WA	*What is an Apparatus? And Other Essays.* Trans. David Kishik and Stefan Pedatella. Stanford: Stanford University Press, 2009.

WM   "The Work of Man." Trans. Kevin Attell. In: Calarco, Matthew and Steven DeCaroli, eds. *Giorgio Agamben: Sovereignty and Life*. Stanford: Stanford University Press, 2007. 1–10.

Prologue: The Future of Sovereignty

Why keep the word, then? (Jacques Derrida, *Sovereignties in Question*)[1]

[W]e should discard the essentialist idea that some institutions are by essence destined to fulfill one immutable function. (Chantal Mouffe, *Agonistics*)[2]

I have, in the past, strongly defended the right of young movements to their amorphous structures – whether that means rejecting identifiable leadership or eschewing programmatic demands. And there is no question that old political habits and structures must be reinvented to reflect new realities, as well as past failures. But I confess that the last five years immersed in climate science has [sic] left me impatient. As many are coming to realize, the fetish for structurelessness, the rebellion against any kind of institutionalization, is not a luxury today's transformative movements can afford. (Naomi Klein, *This Changes Everything*)[3]

Cutting Off the Head of the King

The period after the Second World War is often associated with the end of national sovereignty.[4] In light of Michel Foucault's notorious remark in the first volume of *The History of Sexuality* that in political thought and analysis, we are yet to cut off the head of the king,[5] one could interpret post–Second World War developments such as human rights declarations or European integration as stages in a process of sovereign decapitation that began with the French Revolution. Many have recognized and welcomed these developments. Some have recognized but resisted them.[6] More recently, some have also begun to question Foucault's remark and the political reality it assumes. To those latter critics (and I count myself among them), the contemporary moment seems to provide proof of a revival of sovereignty, making necessary a reversal of Foucault's question: shouldn't political thought and analysis at the very least catch up with sovereignty's afterlife instead?[7]

Thirty years after Foucault's death in 1984, it is undeniable that sovereignty has been a key concept in the analysis of three recent political events: the September 11 terror attacks; the 2008 economic crash and the rise of Occupy; and the Arab Spring. If the first of those three events perhaps cast further doubt on the politics of sovereignty due to the United States' response to 9/11 – "heightened nationalist discourse, extended surveillance mechanisms, suspended constitutional rights, and developed forms of explicit and implicit censorship," as the American philosopher Judith Butler summarized it[8] – the second has had some critics draw attention (perhaps naïvely so) to the positive possibilities of sovereignty as a political power separate from economic power,[9] capable (at least in theory) of forcefully regulating the force of the economy (even if, of course, those economic agents causing the crash could also be referred to as "petty sovereigns," and even if a certain concept and practice of sovereignty is obviously also under attack in the Occupy movement).[10] In the third case, the Arab Spring, might the concept of sovereignty be capable of naming ongoing attempts at self-determination in response to tyranny (an abusive form of sovereignty)?[11] Could sovereignty be a name for the rebirth of popular power that is movingly documented, in its Egyptian instantiation and in all of its complexities, in Jejane Noujaim's documentary film *The Square*?

If we could, then, agree on sovereignty's continued importance, not just in theory but also in practice, it seems important to ask – before the fashionable call for the end of sovereignty is simply (and blindly) renewed – what kinds of sovereignty we are talking about in those different situations. What kind of sovereignty is imagined by those who turn to sovereignty as a political power that could keep the economy in check? What kind of sovereignty is imagined by those who cast the agents of the economic crash as "petty sovereigns" ("petty sovereignty" as opposed to *what*?)? It seems important to ask whether a horizontal, flat under-standing of sovereignty – a sovereignty of Occupy – is possible, and desirable; whether sovereignty *can* apply as a name for the popular, anti-tyrannical uprisings in the Arab world (a question that needs to be translated from post-colonial studies, in which the importance – and pitfalls, to recall Frantz Fanon – of the politics of sovereignty for anti-colonial resistance has been given ample attention, into the contemporary moment); whether if tyranny is *abusive* sovereignty, there is a *non-abusive* sovereignty that may be worth holding onto; and also, for example, whether sovereignty can really be said to have "ended" with the Universal Declaration of Human Rights or with European integration. Might these developments also continue a politics of sovereignty in disguise? What sovereignty? Asking these questions does not add up to an "unholy alliance" against sovereignty, as the editors of *Politics Without Sovereignty* put it.[12] They do not necessarily show that the concept of sovereignty and the politics it enables are in decline. Rather, these are part of a critical attempt to rethink sovereignty as a key term in contemporary politics – a rethinking that does not necessarily have the negative implications it is often assumed to have.

In each of the situations where there is allusion to a sovereignty that is ending, it is clear that a certain kind of sovereignty is being imagined – and the question is whether it would be doing us any good to let the ending of that particular kind of sovereignty take all other kinds of sovereignty down with it. For example, when the period after the Second World War is associated with the end of sovereignty due to developments such as human rights declarations or European integration, it is clear that the sovereignty that is being targeted here is that of the nation-state, which is being overcome by international (between nation-states), transnational (superseding the nation-state), or even post-national (after the nation-state) developments. Traditionally conceived, sovereignty does after all name supreme authority within a territory – the territory occupied by the nation-state. However, if sovereignty is traditionally conceived as supreme power over a territory, that same tradition also defines it as the guarantor of the rule of law over that territory. Presumably, those who enthusiastically welcome declarations of human rights and European integration as well as the end of sovereignty they bring would much less enthusiastically welcome the end of sovereignty's guarantee of the rule of law? In the last case, the end of sovereignty risks coinciding with "diminished political possibilities throughout the world"[13] – and indeed, the already mentioned book *Politics Without Sovereignty* shows that this is the case. As the editors of that book point out, the end of sovereignty risks meaning the end of organization, authorship, and accountability, for sovereignty "articulates the idea that human beings are the authors of their own destiny."[14] Sovereignty operates in their vision in close relation to autonomy. Humans give themselves their own law (auto-nomy). They need a political power – sovereignty – to guarantee it. If that power disappears, the force of their law is diminished, and their self-determination is challenged. Before we blindly call for the end of sovereignty, we must imagine the end of the politics that risks coming with it.

Now jump to the 9/11 terror attacks and the US response to them. In this situation, we are no longer dealing with sovereignty as it is traditionally conceived, as the supreme power over a territory and guarantor of that territory's rule of law. Instead, sovereignty operates as the supreme power to decide on what political theorists call "the state of exception": a situation or state in which the normal rule of law is suspended in the name of a national emergency or security situation. After all the declarations about the end of sovereignty, sovereignty reappears here, in Judith Butler's characterization, as an anachronistic, zombie-like power that operates in a deterritorialized fashion and for which the law is merely a tactic to take life or make it. To many, that appears to be the afterlife of sovereignty today, the spectral but living realization of its "post." When those critics renew the call for sovereignty's end, it is that exceptionalist sovereignty they have in mind: sovereignty not as the guarantor but as the suspender of the rule of law.

Finally, those two positions – guarantee and suspension of the law – must also be brought together, for it is obvious that sovereignty's power to guarantee the law is not unrelated to its power to suspend it. Both assume a transcendental (in this context, specifically theological) relation to the law that enables sovereignty to both make the law or take it away (this relation of sovereignty to the law is one of the aspects of what has been called "theologico-political" understandings of sovereignty). To argue against the sovereign power to suspend the law risks meaning to argue against the sovereign power to guarantee it. To argue for the sovereign power to guarantee the law risks meaning to argue for the sovereign power to suspend it. Given that these two operations of sovereign power are inseparable, positive and negative – pharmacological – aspects of the same power, this raises the promise of having done with sovereignty and its infernal dialectic of guarantee and suspense in order to consider other concepts of the political and other politics instead (by "other," I do not mean that these concepts and politics would necessarily be "absolutely positive" – let's not be naïve!). Yet here, sovereignty's promise of organization, authorship, and accountability – evoked by sovereignty's defenders – remains in the balance, as well as those defenders' warning that a politics without sovereignty may amount to a politics without … politics.

The choices are probably not quite as stark; indeed, it seems obvious that forms of political organization, authorship, and accountability – autonomy – are possible outside of "sovereignty," for example outside of the dialectic of guarantee and suspense (if we consider this to be the defining aspect of sovereignty). But if the aim really is to dismantle problematic aspects of sovereignty, why wouldn't we continue to call these other forms of organization – critical of, for example, the dialectic of guarantee and suspense – sovereign? Wouldn't that be the most powerful dismantling of the concept? Not simply to leave it intact, and oppose to it something else (that will have its own problems), but to dismantle within it that from which it is ailing?[15] Wouldn't that be the properly critical and political task?

Not to run to an elsewhere that is not necessarily better, but to change from within? Otherwise, what are the guarantees that we will have truly understood the problems of sovereignty as it currently exists? Otherwise, how can we preserve the political gains that sovereignty – or, for that matter, any other of our political concepts that are under siege – has brought? Those minor victories that should not be forgotten when we consider the bigger picture – even if it may look dismal?

Giorgio Agamben and the Ontology of Sovereignty

While a consideration of sovereignty's capacity to guarantee and suspend the law is one consideration of political philosophy (one that I turn to in the third part of this book), theories of sovereignty have also emphasized the ontological dimensions of such philosophical work, and this has added an important element to the consideration of sovereignty as guarantor/suspender of the rule of law, and to the consideration of those "alternate" forms of political organization, authorship, and accountability that critics of sovereignty seek to consider. In his analysis of theologico-political sovereignty, the Italian philosopher Giorgio Agamben – whose work will be the focus of this book – has tied the infernal dialectic of guarantee and suspense to an ontological reflection about a divided sense of life that informs the operation of sovereignty.[16] Going back to classical times, Agamben observes that the Greeks had two words for life: "zoe," which refers to the simple fact of living as shared by animals, humans, and gods; and "bios," which refers to ethical and political forms of life.[17] Agamben's argument is that the separation of these two kinds of life structures the operation of sovereign power, whose essential activity is the production of a third kind of life: bare life. Bare life, mere life, or naked life comes about when *bios* is either violently stripped away from *zoe* – as in the case, for example, of those who are being held in the Guantánamo Bay detention center – or violently forced onto it – as in the case of Terri Schiavo who, in her persistent vegetative state, became part of a legalo-political battle about her life.[18] Read through the lens of Agamben's philosophy, these examples indicate that *zoe* – the simple fact of living – only becomes part of an ethical or political community – *bios* – by being internally excluded or excepted from it, because *zoe* itself is never enough to constitute an ethical or political community. Thus, *zoe* becomes politicized as bare life – as the internally excluded or excepted element of the community.

Agamben's claim that the production of bare life is the essential activity of sovereignty is evidenced for example by Thomas Hobbes's theory of sovereignty, in which human life's "animal" side is internally excluded or excepted from the political community. Indeed, Hobbes's political community defines itself through the internal exclusion or exception of the animal and operates "as if" this dimension can be surgically separated from human life. At the same time, however, Hobbes knows very well that such a separation is impossible – and hence he theorizes an all-powerful sovereign whose fearful being would prevent the internally excluded or excepted animal from returning.[19]

If Hobbes is an obvious example in this context, consider that Agamben makes the same argument about so-called universal human rights.[20] Originally conceived (during the time of the French Revolution) as the rights of "man and the citizen," the confusion of "man" and "citizen" that their original title realizes – and that raises the question of whether human beings, separately from being citizens, have rights – actually continues in the later declaration of universal human rights, because the category of the "human" raises the question of whether one needs to be considered "human" in order to have "rights." What about, indeed, those who (for whatever reasons) aren't recognized as such, and as a result risk falling outside of the protection offered by human rights? Agamben's argument is that virtually, all of us are in that position – for none of us definitively live up to the category of the "human." Instead, and once again in Judith Butler's parlance, the human is "a differential norm"[21] that is forever shifting, and is granted and retracted depending on the situation. Given such an unstable attribution, "human" rights can only provide a very precarious form of protection indeed.

It is important to see, in this ontology, that the solution to the separation of *zoe* and *bios* and the bare life that it separates is not to take *bios* away and call for a community that would be rooted in the simple fact of living, *zoe* – such a move is in fact one example of the exceptionalist politics that Agamben criticizes. Let me explain: if the problem is that ethically and politically, life is never valued as such, the issue is not to turn biological existence into an ethical and political value – again, that would constitute an example of the exceptionalist (and potentially racist or sexist) politics that Agamben criticizes (in the case of Terri Schiavo, for example, in which *bios* is violently forced onto *zoe*, the point is not to insist on the ethical and political value of *zoe* alone). At the same time, the solution cannot be to move into a denial of the simple fact of living (*zoe*) either – a complete swing of the pendulum toward *bios* – for such a conception of ethics and politics would deny human beings their biological existence (in the case of the Guantánamo Bay detainees, for example, where *bios* is violently taken away, the point is not to insist on the ethical and political value of *bios* alone for that would deny the biological life of the detainees[22]). Indeed, if Agamben calls for a community of "life as such," it is neither the simple fact of living nor ethical and political life that he has in mind – neither the biological matter of life nor its symbolic form – but what he calls a "form-of-life"[23] in which life's biological matter and symbolic form would become inseparably hyphenated – *contracted* – into a new ontological and politico-philosophical category.

Form-of-life thus offers nothing less than a new political contract based in an ontological rethinking of contraction itself. Think of it as a new ontology of contract theory, one that would be beyond the logic of abandonment (which Agamben uses, after Jean-Luc Nancy and with reference to Martin Heidegger, as a synonym for exception[24]) that according to Agamben operates in contract theory as we know it.

It is, I argue, from the ontological fusion of matter and form in Agamben's work that a new political community is born. Put negatively, it is from the ontological fusion of matter and form that sovereignty – or at the very least a particular ontology of sovereignty – is targeted in his work. Indeed, if sovereignty's essential operation is the production of bare life through the separation of *zoe* and *bios* – of the biological matter and symbolic form of life – then it is this hylomorphic (matter/form) ontology of sovereignty that needs to be rethought in order for another politics of sovereignty to come about.[25] This amounts to a rethinking of the philosophical category of difference: if, to return to the example of Thomas Hobbes, "difference" is figured in Hobbes's theory of sovereignty as the material, biological animal that the symbolic form of the Leviathan wants to exclude, what Agamben's reading of Hobbes exposes is that such material difference is always internally excluded or excepted from the Hobbesian political form, thus rendering this political form strangely material (indeed, the Leviathan itself as a name for a gigantic sea monster marks this animalistic – if you will – material difference; seen from the other side, that "animalistic," material difference is therefore also never entirely separate from the Hobbesian political form). In Agamben's reading of Hobbes, form and matter thus become fused and he moves from the hylomorphic understanding of sovereignty that Hobbes wants to put forward into a different ontology of politics, a different thinking of difference – matter – and its relation to the Hobbesian sovereign – form.

One of the characteristic features of the history of sovereignty is that it has been difficult, if not impossible, to think of this changed difference *as* sovereign. Instead, it has been theorized as sovereignty's opposite, its other. While sovereignty's formation of matter is traditionally considered to be indivisible, this in-divisibility is conditioned by the form/matter difference by which indivisible sovereignty remains haunted (sovereignty's indivisibility assumes an ontological difference or division by which it remains haunted). Changed difference targets indivis-ibility on this count by unworking the exceptionalist difference that conditions it.

The guarantor/suspender problem of sovereignty (already evident in the work of one of Agamben's main influences, Carl Schmitt) needs to be tackled in close relation to the ontological problem of sovereignty that Agamben – writing after Schmitt, and partly relying on one of Schmitt's interlocutors, Walter Benjamin – has exposed, namely the *zoe*/*bios* separation that produces bare life (a notion that Agamben borrows from Benjamin). Indeed, the guarantor/suspender pair, which produces the pair rule of law/state of exception, relates to the *bios/zoe* pair, which produces the pair citizen/bare life (in parallel to guarantor/suspender). Bare life is the life that is produced in the state of exception. In the same way that we must see the relation between the state of exception and the normal rule of law, we must see the relation between bare life and the life of the ordinary citizen. While on the surface, they appear different, Agamben's work exposes their undeniable, foundational relation.

Any consideration of sovereignty, then – of the politics of sovereignty and its possible alternatives – will have to consider these insights of political philosophy and ontology. It is worth noting, in a final movement, that both the politico-philosophical reflection about the guarantor/suspender problem and the ontological reflection about *zoe/bios* involve the issue of representation that is central to Agamben's thought. As guarantor/suspender of the rule of law, the sovereign – whether an individual or a collective – represents by its sovereign body[26] the bodies of the people living on the territory that it rules over (this is powerfully visualized in the frontispiece to Hobbes's *Leviathan*). The law is the expression of the people's collective will, and so is (ideally) the state of exception (the sovereign decides, as a representative of the people, on whether a situation or state qualifies as a state of exception). In Hobbes's vision, of course, the body of the sovereign and the body of its people become one – and he insists (in fear of the Civil War he was philosophizing against) that this is not a metaphorical but a real unity. However, the unity is evidently never total, and in a situation like a revolution or even in the more innocent contemporary situation of voting its foundational, representational split always lies exposed. The sovereign is, and is not, the people; when all is well, the sovereign is – when not, the sovereign is not. While it is important to insist on the former to ensure political unity, it is probably equally important not to forget about the latter, in order to preserve politics and the particular difference it fosters. The question of the sovereign's representation thus mirrors the ontological form/matter issue that I laid bare above. At the level of the sovereign representation, too, it is a question of navigating the relation between matter and form, and seeing that a "healthy" sovereignty would not be one of total unity, in which form has completely domesticated matter, nor of total disintegration, in which matter would have utterly defeated form. Instead, the fusion of matter and form would enable a new ontology of sovereignty to come about. Hobbes cannot afford to think this, even if there is much in his writing that points in this direction (it is of course only normal, in view of the Civil War, that he comes down more heavily on the side of form).

Within the ontological perspective itself, and specifically within the *zoe*/*bios* separation that produces bare life, the question of representation is also crucial. Indeed, *bios* – ethical and political life – can be read as a representation of *zoe* – the simple fact of living – with the form of symbolic life (*bios*) representing the matter of biological life (*zoe*).[27] In such a reading, bare life is produced by the relation between the matter of biological life and the form of symbolic life, between *zoe* and *bios*. To think what Agamben calls a "form-of-life" that would be the "healthy" sovereignty I tried to capture above would mean to disrupt this logic of representation, where symbolic life is added to biological life in order to enable ethical and political community. Instead, symbolic life (form) would become hyphenated – contracted – with material, biological life to realize a symbolic, formal dimension of material biology and a biological, material dimension of symbolic form – something that, in my view, much recent critical theory has sought to achieve. We now know, for example, that whatever we mean by material biology is also a symbolic form that always inevitably fails to arrive at the "material" or "biological." At the same time, we know that our symbolic forms have a material dimension to them that, in the case of "material biology" for example, brings this symbolic form in close proximity to the "material" realm it seeks to capture. These developments have involved changes in our thinking of language's relation to difference, in the same way that in political philosophy, deconstructing the form/matter distinction has involved changes in our thinking of ethical and political community's relation to difference.

This is where we get to the heart of the matter, because it shows either that in our relation to language, we reproduce the politico-philosophical and ontological structures of sovereignty; or that the politico-philosophical and ontological structures of sovereignty are shaped by our relation to language. Indeed, if human beings are in language, and if the human being's relation to language is arguably at the origin of its ethical and political community, then language becomes a crucial component in the politico-philosophical and ontological critique of sovereignty that I am developing. Language is entirely caught up in the structures of representation, which separate between biological and symbolic life, matter and form, referent and sign (sign = signifier/signified) – a separation that is the characteristic work of sovereignty. It is indeed in our relation to language that a certain kind of sovereignty operates. To target this kind of sovereignty will therefore also mean to target this relation to language, and transform it.

To once again avoid a naïve confusion that could be produced by these statements, let me clarify that the aim of such a project would not be to focus entirely on the material dimension of language, that is: to focus entirely on language's matter (the referent), and thus to forget about its symbolic form (the sign); and neither would it be to focus entirely on the symbolic form (the sign) and forget entirely about language's matter (the referent). The point would be, rather, to bring these two perspectives together in a contracted arrangement through which the sign would become its own referent – once again outside of the vulgar formalism of a uniquely sign-oriented linguistic approach – and, vice versa, the referent its own sign – in this case outside of the vulgar materialism of the anti-representational. How might such an approach to language be realized? The question is crucial, given the implication of this linguistic problem in the ontological and politico-philosophical problems of sovereignty.

If, generally speaking, the procedure here can be characterized as the deconstruction of binaries – a characterization that would only tell part of the truth, as my remarks about deconstruction in the next section of this chapter will reveal – one binary of sovereignty that will also be deconstructed along the way, even if it will not play a central role in my argumentation (others have already paid it plenty of attention), is the friend/enemy distinction that Carl Schmitt perceives to be crucial to his sovereign conception of the political. Some might argue that this distinction is essential to sovereignty, and that to cut off the head of the king means to have done with this distinction too, once and for all. However, as will become clear in the very last chapter of this book, I think it would be a mistake to limit political antagonism to the friend/enemy distinction and reject the positive possibilities of political antagonism on the basis of this limitation. If the friend/enemy distinction that structures theologico-political sovereignty amounts to the existential negation of the enemy in war, the sovereignty I theorize here revolves around other figures of antagonism – those that would emerge from the notion of a "conflictual peace of the living" that, in the final chapter of this book, I oppose to the "perpetual peace of the dead" evoked at the beginning of Immanuel Kant's essay on perpetual peace. Our imagination of political antagonism cannot be limited to sovereignty as we know it; sovereignty *as we know it* cannot be the only conceptualization of what Schmitt, in a memorable formulation, already called the political *pluriverse*.

In what follows, I take Agamben's ontological criticism of sovereignty as my central concern, and I pursue it in three major areas of his thought: aesthetics (I develop an aesthetic approach to language, storytelling, and translation; Part I of this book), economy (bare life, technology, and work; Part II), and politics (I develop a political, an aesthetic, and a poetic approach to the state of exception; Part III). Art and aesthetics – the theory of sensing, feeling, perceiving – will, for reasons that will be clarified in Chapter 1, take up an important role throughout, even if aesthetics is a contested term in Agamben's work. My aim is, indeed, to retrieve from a focused engagement with Agamben's work a politics of aesthetics that would dismantle the ontology of sovereignty. Drawing from my research on the work of Gilbert Simondon – characterized by Muriel Combes as a philosopher who "avoids any formalist conception of the constitution of the collective by contract, and even any thinking in terms of sovereignty, whose sole concern is to guarantee the legitimacy of the subsumption of society within the State"[28] – I characterize this new aesthetico-political perspective as ontogenetic, that is: as capturing a process rather than a principle of what I will continue to call (at odds with the dominant interpretation of Agamben and, I guess, Simondon) "sovereignty."[29] The underlying argument here is that a hylomorphic approach to sovereignty – one that would seek to explain the genesis of sovereignty starting from a theory of the union of matter with form – acts out what Agamben argues to be the foundational distinction of any "sovereign" operation (the separation of matter from form, *zoe* from *bios*, which generates an individual and collective that internally excludes or excepts its dynamic condition), and thus fails to account for true genesis.

As Combes's presentation of Simondon as an anti-sovereign thinker reveals, in the eyes of many "sovereignty" is irreconcilable with an ontogenetic approach – for what defines it is precisely the hylomorphic ontology of matter/form. But such a criticism, while valuable, only goes so far, because it continues to oppose – all too easily, in my opinion – "sovereignty" to its "other" (in Dimitris Vardoulakis's recent account, "democracy"[30]). However, such a criticism is relativistic because it ultimately leaves sovereignty intact – it merely opposes a "bad" politics of sovereignty to a "good" politics of, for example, democracy. As I see it, the task of dismantling the ontology of sovereignty needs to occur within sovereignty itself rather than place its bets on sovereignty's "other"; it needs to intervene within the ontology of sovereignty so as to transform the theory of sovereignty into an ontogenetic one. This would not only dismantle sovereignty from the inside (an approach that hasn't always characterized Agamben's politics, as I discuss in Chapter 1), but also enable us to preserve what is valuable about sovereignty – for example, sovereignty's association with organization, authorship, and accountability, "the idea that human beings are the authors of their own destiny," that they *make* their own history even if they may not make it just as they please. This idea is not irreconcilable with genesis. An ontogenetic approach would draw out the fact that the "life" formed by "sovereignty" is always already formed; and, vice versa, that sovereignty's form is always already materialized, and part of life. It would also enable one to account for sovereignty's energetic conditions, for what in Simondon's vocabulary one could call sovereignty's "metastability." If sovereignty has traditionally (in Hobbes, for example) been presented as "stable," it is also evident from Hobbes's text (as I show in the final part of this book) that it is really a metastable entity through which political genesis continues. To dismantle sovereignty means to wrest it away from its ontological, hylomorphic, and stable articulation so as to free up in it the dynamic metastability that is characteristic of an ontogenetic – and, in my view, truly political – perspective. *We are yet to think a truly political sovereignty.* As I already said, one can understand why Hobbes, in view of the historical situation in which he was writing, may not have been particularly keen on such an approach, even if it lies dormant in his text. Today, however, as new political movements are on the rise and *struggling to be politically effective*, it seems important to remember that not all metastability equals "Civil War," and more importantly that not all politics of dissensus are anti-sovereign. It is time to move away from sovereignty's traditional opposition to life, and restore the living dimension of this political concept. More importantly, sovereignty can bring to dissensus the organization, authorship, accountability of political efficiency that the left, according to some of its most perceptive analysts,[31] is lacking today.[32]

It will be obvious (and I will readily grant) that such a perspective – intervening within sovereignty rather than rejecting it – is not necessarily reconcilable with how Agamben has been received, or even with Agamben's work. There is thus something of an incitement that is at work in this book. In Agamben scholarship, attempts to hold on to traditional notions of political thought – sovereignty, law, rights, or the state, for example – are generally unconvincing because they do not tackle in any serious way the ontology that informs these terms. However, I do think there is value in the attempt to hold on, on the condition that what is being held on to is radically transformed. In fact, I will draw out throughout this book some moments – they are, admittedly, rare – where Agamben himself seems to hold on to sovereignty, to another conception of sovereignty than the one he criticizes. In an early article I wrote about Agamben's work (and that reappears here in a drastically revised form as the final chapter of this book), I pointed out that there appear to circulate two states of exception in Agamben's writings: one "bad" state of exception (catastrophe), which he criticizes relentlessly as the paradigm of our contemporary political condition; and one "good" state of exception (redemption), which becomes the site in his work for political reinvention. The same is arguably true for sovereignty. By way of Hölderlin, whose famous line of poetry about the darkest hour in which a saving grace also grows circulates here, Jessica Whyte has recently identified this close connection between catastrophe and redemption in Agamben's work as a weakness – and she must, of course, given that she presents Agamben as a non-sovereign thinker and thus cannot think a pharmacology of sovereignty. However, it seems to me, even if I find Whyte's illuminating study convincing otherwise, that the adjective "non-sovereign" simply cannot do to characterize Agamben's thought, even if Agamben himself may claim it does (and Whyte certainly backs up her own use of "non-sovereign" with plenty of evidence). In this sense, the proximity of catastrophe and redemption in Agamben's work may not only be a weakness, but an indicator that the engagement with sovereignty that his work develops is not simply one of "negation," of opposing sovereign politics to non-sovereign politics.

Consider, for example, Whyte's claim, which I footnoted earlier on, that there is a growing attachment to national sovereignty in a time of austerity measures "which are commonly characterized as an abrogation of national sovereignty."[33] This is one example of the continued importance of sovereignty, as a political power that could keep economic power (of course often enacted by sovereign power, a political power that, in this case, would have been overtaken by economic concerns) in check. Whyte notes, correctly, that such an attachment to national sovereignty "has been premised on a supposed opposition or antagonism between sovereignty and economic government"[34] – an opposition that not only no longer holds today, but that Agamben in his work – in particular in his book *The Kingdom and the Glory* – has drawn into question. There, Agamben shows that sovereignty and economic government are part of a single power-machine. However, Whyte's attempt to then claim this connection between sovereignty and economic government as part of her characterization of Agamben's politics as "non-sovereign" immediately produces a problem, since she mentions a public intervention that Agamben made in the context of the austerity measures in which he appears to back up the very opposition of sovereignty to economic government that, elsewhere, he criticizes.[35] Whyte has no other choice than to leave this intervention aside as an anomaly, and she focuses on *The Kingdom and the Glory* instead to trace the contours of what she calls "an alternative non-sovereign conception of politics that would simultaneously contest both economic government and sovereign power."[36] As I see it, however, the problem here is: what kind of sovereignty and economy is Whyte talking about?

Another way to ask this question would be to inquire into the force of the verb "contest" in my last quotation: does a "*contested* economic government and sovereign power" amount to a *non*-economic government and a *non*-sovereign power? As this question, I think, immediately makes clear, it probably doesn't: while the flip from sovereignty to non-sovereignty may still be imaginable, it is much harder to imagine a flip from economy to non-economy. The question in the case of economy is evidently one that must be asked *within* the realm of this term, since it would be difficult to imagine any kind of human collectivity outside of economy – it's simply an issue of bettering the economic reality from within.

Why is it so difficult for us to adopt the same approach with sovereignty? Is it perhaps another lure of sovereignty that it seems to demand a sovereign decision on its own being – for or against – thus making those who oppose sovereignty to its other act out a certain kind of sovereignty, giving sovereignty the last word in their attempt to end it? Cutting off the head of the king is, after all, a very sovereign gesture. Why is it nearly impossible for critics to consider that when Agamben appears to be backing up sovereign power against economic government, he may have had another sovereign power in mind than the theologico-political one whose ontology he criticizes relentlessly in his work? Is our imagination of sovereignty *that* limited?

Indeed, when it comes to the positive politics that Agamben proposes in response to the problems of sovereignty he diagnoses, one arguably finds what could be referred to as "remains" of sovereignty – leftovers from a dismantled sovereignty that are playfully used for the material formation of a coming community, founded in whatever being, and a new linguistic experience. Agamben's thought of this coming community, which overcomes sovereignty's separation of *zoe* from *bios* and the production of bare life that it entails through the enigmatic notion of a form-of-life, has developed over several works, but has received its most elaborate articulation so far in a book titled *The Highest Poverty*. In that book, as I will show, Agamben has moved from a criticism of sovereignty, the highest power that separates *zoe* from *bios*, to the proposition of the highest poverty as a form-of-life that would *contract zoe* and *bios* into a new ethical and political community. In Agamben's development of the notion of the highest poverty, it is clear, however, that it is not entirely removed from the sphere of sovereignty (which, etymologically, means "the highest" power, from the Latin "superanus") – even if, of course, it drastically transforms it. There is a moment in his book where he associates the life of the highest poverty with sovereignty. Given such an association, doesn't this indicate – against all odds – that the intervention in sovereignty that we confront in his work does not simply seek to oppose sovereignty to its other, but transform it from within? Again, the majority of the evidence would answer "no" to this question. But I am suggesting that it may be useful in view of recent political developments, to hold on to those moments in Agamben's work that would contradict this answer, both to see how they may make his criticism of sovereignty more efficient and how they may open up future forms of sovereignty – beyond sovereignty's mere afterlife.

Catherine Malabou and the Politics of Plasticity

Does sovereignty have a future? It seems that today, while the 9/11 window is closing and new political movements such as

Occupy and the revolutions in the Arab world are on the rise, this question must be asked. As I already noted, the concept of sovereignty can and has played multiple roles in the analysis of both movements: as the target of Occupy's "horizontalism"; as the political power that could potentially keep the economic power; as a name for the popular organization against tyranny (abusive sovereignty) – as both an enemy and an ally. It thus seems that sovereignty, in spite of its claim to indivisibility, is in reality divided across a spectrum of concepts of the political and politics that nevertheless all have the value of organization, authorship, and accountability (in short, the idea that one can write one's own destiny) in common.[37] This is not a relativist statement. Instead, it reveals that it is possible to single out one or several problematic aspects of sovereignty and dismantle them from within the concept of sovereignty itself, without giving up on sovereignty's positive accomplishments. Such a *pluralism*, rather than a *relativism*, resists the all too easy escape from sovereignty into its other. As I see it, sovereignty's pluralization raises the bar for its critics, for one can no longer simply reject sovereignty wholesale and move on. Finer distinctions are needed.[38]

My question about sovereignty's future echoes a question that the French philosopher Catherine Malabou asked, by now already a number of years ago, about G. W. F. Hegel, namely whether there was a future in Hegel's philosophy.[39] Malabou points out that asking this very question puts her at odds with traditional Hegel scholarship, which reads Hegel as the philosopher in whom history is ending. Malabou is thus confronting the dominance of a certain Hegel, and separating another Hegel from it. I pursue here a similar project with respect to sovereignty. Now, where does Malabou find the future of Hegel? She finds it in his notion of plasticity, developed in

Hegel's *Aesthetics* and intimately related to the Hegelian dialectic, which Malabou (contra other interpreters, specifically Gilles Deleuze) understands as evidence for Hegel's "preoccupation with 'fluidifying solidified thinking.'"[40] If Deleuze, who was a reader of Simondon, would perhaps have opposed Simondon to Hegel (and indeed, Simondon himself indicates that his theory of individuation is not a dialectic), Malabou transforms Simondon and Deleuze's understanding of the dialectic, showing instead that Hegel may be closer to Simondon than had been thought.

Whatever the case may be – I am not interested here in settling it – the notion of plasticity is worth considering in this context because it enables us to bring together the various kinds of life that Agamben's ontology of sovereignty singles out – as well as their contraction, associated above with the ontogenetic criticism of a certain kind of sovereignty – as part of a single system. When defining plasticity after Hegel, Malabou points out that it has three dimensions: it can receive, give, and explode form. Clay, for example, is plastic because it can receive the form that a sculptor gives to it; the human body is plastic because it can receive the form given to it by a plastic surgeon. Plasticity also names the activity of this sculptor or surgeon, in other words: the giving of the form that the clay or the human body receives. Third, plasticity refers to an explosive substance that evokes the annihilation of all form, something that Malabou has pursued in her works *Ontology of the Accident* and *The New Wounded* in which she has discussed personality–destroying neural disorders.[41]

Now, I would like to suggest that these three dimensions of plasticity can be made to correspond to the three kinds of life that are central to Agamben's criticism of sovereignty: *zoe* (matter that can receive form; clay, the human body), *bios* (the giving of form; sculpting, plastic surgery), and bare life (the biopolitical matter produced through the explosion of form, either its violent taking away or its violent implementation; in Malabou's work, an advanced Alzheimer's patient, for example). To see this enables one to bring together *zoe*, *bios*, and bare life into a plastic concept of sovereignty. However, and this is why such a thinking together of Malabou and Agamben is worthwhile, it should also be noted what Malabou aspires to with her plastic rethinking of form – for Agamben's work cannot be mapped onto Malabou's without this piece of the puzzle. In *Ontology of the Accident*, she points that she is interested in what she calls (in another text titled "Grammatology and Plasticity") "the formation of form":[42]

> It is not form that is the problem; it's the fact that form can be thought separately from the nature of the being that transforms itself. The fact that form is presented as skin, vestment or finery, and that one can always leave without an alteration in what is essential … as if in the evening, form could be left hanging like a garment on the chair of being or essence.[43]

In the (Simondonian) terms that I used earlier on, the perspective that is presented in these lines is an ontogenetic rather than an ontological one: it is in the notion of plasticity that sovereignty's form/matter distinction explodes. To rewrite Malabou's lines about the formation of form in the context of Agamben's work on sovereignty:

> It is not bios that is the problem; it's the fact that bios can be thought separately from the zoe of the being that transforms itself. The fact that bios is presented as skin, vestment, or finery, and that one can always leave without an alteration in what is essential … as if in the evening, bios could be left hanging like a garment on the chair of zoe.

Indeed, this is the ontological separation of sovereignty that Agamben criticizes and that Malabou evidently also challenges with her theory of plasticity – even if sovereignty has not appeared as a central concern in her work so far.

What is particularly interesting is that plasticity enables us to see the three kinds of life that Agamben theorizes as part of a *single* system that, as per Malabou's reading, ontogenetically criticizes the ontology that it also lays out. In other words (and as I have been suggesting above): the ontogenetic criticism of the ontology of sovereignty already lies contained within that ontology itself. It is plasticity – which contracts the matter/form distinction – that enables one to see this. Of course, this sounds like good old deconstruction, and indeed, Malabou is a student of Derrida's. However, in "Grammatology and Plasticity," she also labors hard to distinguish her theory of plasticity, and the formation of form that it seeks, from Derridean deconstruction, pointing out that the formation of form entails "a power to shape meaning that exceeds [the] graphic displacement"[44] that is central to deconstruction and that is perhaps most memorably captured by Derrida's notion of "différance," a neologism that marks through a difference that is visible/written yet not audible/spoken (the famous "a" instead of the "e" of "difference") a displacement or deferral of meaning. Even though Malabou obviously does not deny such graphic displacement, she evidently also wants more – and thus she arrives, I would argue, from Derrida's deconstruction of sovereignty (marked by his theory of graphic displacement) at the future of sovereignty. Not the old sovereignty, whose ontology Agamben so powerfully exposes, but one that has been ontogenetically rethought – one that has passed through plasticity's explosion of the form/matter distinction. A new experience of language rather than mere graphic displacement.

In this context, it is probably also worth noting Agamben's complicated relation to Derrida and deconstruction:[45] it is perhaps most powerfully captured by Agamben's rereading of Kafka's parable "Before the Law" in *Homo Sacer*.[46] Whereas deconstruction, in Agamben's view, endlessly negotiates with the law – in a manner reminiscent of Malabou's characterization of graphic displacement – Agamben reads the waiting of the man from the country as a patient strategy to have the door of the law "shut." What does this reveal within an ontological perspective? If the man from the country is *zoe*, and the law is *bios*, and if deconstruction thus marks the logic of sovereignty that would place *zoe* in perpetual negotiation with *bios*, Agamben reads the life of the man from the country as a strategy to close the door of the law. The material life of *zoe* thus takes on – *contracts* – the formal, symbolic traits of *bios*. At the same time, if the *bios* of the law appeared to be a symbolic form in which the matter of life could enter, its closing decidedly materializes this symbolic form (matter gets contracted into it). The point of Agamben's reading is not, I think, to propose a "non-legal" perspective; shutting the door of the law does not amount to destroying the law, as he has insisted elsewhere. Instead, what is dismantled here is material, biological life's relation to the symbolic life of the law – a relation of theologico-political sovereignty, as Agamben's work has enabled us to understand; instead, matter and form, biological and symbolic life, are contracted into each other at which point another understanding of life and law can emerge. Kafka's story thus becomes a scene of plasticity, even if Agamben does not name it such.

Here, Simondon's famous example of the brick also comes to mind: the brick breaks down a hylomorphic conception of the individual because it is evident a brick does not come about as the union of a matter with a form. Instead, the brick's matter is always already preformed (like clay or the human body in Malabou's examples) and the brick's mold (its form) is always already materialized (like the molds that sculptors and plastic surgeons use).[47] Simondon thus begins to think the plasticity that Malabou will lay out later as the central element of her own philosophical system, and both of them make major contributions to the ontogenetic criticism of sovereignty's ontology that Agamben's work demands. As I have already indicated, Muriel Combes has uncovered this criticism of sovereignty in Simondon's work. In Malabou's oeuvre, this political dimension is less evident: in her most political book, *What Should We Do With Our Brain?*, her opponent seems to be neoliberal flexibility – the eternal transformability that characterizes our contemporary economic condition, a transformability she opposes to plasticity and refers to as "plasticity minus its genius."[48] While several of Malabou's works have strong connections to politics – *The New Wounded*, which mentions the post-traumatic stress disorder of soldiers or also her article on Darwin,[49] which explicitly calls for a political reading of plasticity in Darwin – she has not yet developed any positive politics on the basis of her work on plasticity. However, in recent years, she has given the occasional lecture on sovereignty, engaging precisely the problematic ontology of sovereignty that, following Agamben, I have laid out here, and interestingly she has mobilized Agamben's thought in this context.

In a lecture titled "Sovereignty and Biology,"[50] Malabou tackles the question of sovereignty, beginning with Foucault's claim about cutting off the head of the king. "Have we, after Foucault" – and she adds: after Derrida and after Agamben – "cut off the King's head?" "My answer, here, is 'no.'"[51] As will be clear from what I wrote at the beginning of this Prologue, I do not think a position that questions the end of sovereignty is difficult to justify: sovereignty remains a key concept for the analysis of contemporary political events. But Malabou is interested specifically in what she calls the "structure"[52] of sovereignty, one that she shows to be continuing even within those very discourses that claim to attack it. Here she focuses on the example of biopolitics which, as a "new form of power" that is "absolutely incompatible with relations of sovereignty,"[53] is presented in Malabou's text as a deconstruction of sovereignty, as a power that challenges sovereignty's structure. But does it?

Malabou doesn't think so. First of all, biopolitics operates in part "behind the traditional ideological mask of sovereignty,"[54] for example through laws or rights that, while belonging in the realm of sovereignty, actually practice the (biopolitical) normalization of life. Secondly, and more importantly, Malabou questions the role of biology in biopolitics, and in philosophical discourse at large. Biology, she posits, "always appears, for philosophers, as an instrument of power, never as an emancipatory field or tool. There can't be any *bio*logical resistance to *bio*power."[55]

> This means that biology – the biological determination of life – has to be transgressed. As if there were always two concepts of life in life. For the philosophers I am talking about here [Foucault, Derrida, Agamben], there exists a non-biological definition of life that transgresses or exceeds the scientific, objective one. This surplus of life is symbolic life. Symbolic life as opposed to biological life. This symbolic life appears as the resource of the potentiality of resistance.[56]

Malabou finds this structure – biological life and the surplus of non-biological, symbolic life – in each of the three philosophers she mentions: Foucault, Derrida, and Agamben. What she uncovers here is something I have also insisted on above, namely not just the difference in Agamben's work between the simple, biological fact of living – *zoe* – and *bios* – symbolic, ethical and political life – but also between the simple, biological fact of living – *zoe* – and "bare life": "Bare life … dwells in the biological body of every living being," Agamben writes, and Malabou quotes this line to reveal that in Agamben, there is a symbolic life – identified with bare life by Malabou – within biological life – *zoe* – "a body within the body," in Agamben's work.[57]

It is perhaps counterintuitive to think of bare life as a symbolic life, given that it marks a more extreme version of *zoe* – it seems to me to be more of an impoverished biological life, a biological life as surplus, rather than the excessive surplus of what a symbolic life is usually considered to add to biological life – but this is because Malabou seems to offer two different understandings of the symbolic. On the one hand, she writes (in the passage that I've just discussed) that bare life *is* symbolic life. Further on in her lecture, however, she indicates that by symbolic, she means "the structural spacing" that *separates* bare life from the biological body.[58] "Symbolic life" thus seems to be both the spacing and the other kind of life it produces, and this doubleness risks generating serious problems for Malabou, given her critique of the deconstructive splitting of life in Agamben and others. I will address this point in detail in my first chapter.

Let's focus for now on the central argument: what Malabou finds in the split between biological and symbolic life is the ancient tradition of thought that has proposed the king has two bodies. This, she argues, is the structure of sovereignty: it is this doubleness – which is already a deconstructive discourse, as she notes – that needs to in its turn be deconstructed if we want to challenge the structure of sovereignty: "The time has come to free continental philosophy from the rigid separation it has always maintained between the biological, hence the material, and the symbolic, that is the non material, or the transcendental."[59] Such a deconstruction of deconstruction happens in "plasticity," more precisely in the plasticity of the particular "difference" she seeks to think in her work by taking recourse to recent developments in biology, genetics, and neuroscience. In these disciplines, "plasticity" refers to a domain not so much beyond as within the determinism that is traditionally considered to characterize these disciplines, revealing that what "until recently [appeared] as irreversible or unchangeable – the genetic code, cellular differenciation, the phenotype in general – is currently described as plastic, that is, mutable and reversible."[60] In her view this "opens up a new perspective on the relationship between the symbolic and the biological": "Their dialectic interplay is inscribed within the body, not outside of it, putting an end to the logic of the two bodies, but consequently also challenging the structure of sovereignty inherent in this philosophical discourse."[61] It is thus from biology, the very site where no philosopher could distinguish a possibility of resistance against biopolitics, that the deconstruction of the structure of sovereignty begins to take place. Until now, it seems that we have always needed the two bodies of the king to kill (the two bodies of) the king: this is what one could call the *sovereign lure* or the *cunning of sovereignty* – the fact that it seems to require a sovereign decision on its end, thus effectively perpetuating itself in the very decision on its ending.[62] Malabou's approach interrupts this sovereign cunning. (Here we see how the fact that there are two meanings for symbolic life in her text risks subverting her own argument, appearing as a trace of sovereignty to the reader ...)

Interestingly, Malabou does not draw any "positive" political conclusions from this argument in "Sovereignty and Biology." She lays out her critique of sovereignty, based in biology, showing how recent developments in biology challenge the two-body model that she considers to be the structure of sovereignty. She seems to accomplish, in other words, an effective deconstruction of sovereignty – of the deconstructive lure of sovereignty's two bodies. But there is no reflection here on the practical consequences of this deconstruction for sovereignty as a political power. Does this deconstruction mark the end of sovereignty? Or only of sovereignty as we know it? Is a sovereignty outside of Malabou's deconstruction of sovereignty possible? Is there such a thing as a one-body sovereignty – a plastic sovereignty that would not be split between the biological and the symbolic, the material and the transcendental? A one-body sovereignty that would in that sense be different from the one-body sovereignty that Hobbes insists on and that, in Hobbes's theory, is in fact always split between two, as deconstructive readings have revealed? But also: a new sovereignty beyond the sovereignty of this graphic displacement of deconstruction?

These questions must concern Malabou to a certain extent, for they return in her lecture "Odysseus' Changed Soul,"[63] where she seems to develop a theory of non-sovereign sovereignty. From the get-go, this lecture is focused on politics – the part that is missing in "Sovereignty and Biology" – and much of the lecture is spent on a reading of "The Myth of Er" from Plato's *Republic* (a political text). The myth deals with a question of central interest to Malabou, namely if we were given the choice to live our lives over again, would we choose the same lives? She is interested here in the figure of Odysseus, who appears in the myth she is reading, because unlike what most of us would likely choose – that is: the *same* life – he chooses a *different* one: he chooses a banal, uninteresting, normal life away from the crowds, and limited to the private sphere. Malabou reads this as "a very profound example of what relinquishing sovereignty might mean": "In choosing to become a private man who minds his own business, Odysseus seems to dismiss or relinquish his sovereignty."[64]

However, it is immediately clear from her formulation – she expresses the relinquishing of sovereignty through the verb "choose," which resonates with Schmitt's decisionist definition of the sovereign as "whoever decides"[65] – that the relinquished sovereignty of Odysseus may not be *entirely* beyond sovereignty. Of course, one can understand Malabou's reading: to deconstruct sovereignty, if we take Odysseus as a model,

> implies the interruption of self-foundation, of self-sufficiency, of, again, the relation of the sovereignty's self to itself defined as the origin of all limits or boundaries, as that which decides of the interior and the exterior, the inclusion and the exclusion, the rule and the exception.[66]

Yet, Odysseus still "chooses" this, he still *decides* on this interruption – even if that decision may not be the same kind of decision as the "sovereign" ones he took in his previous life. If we substitute "self" for "sovereign" for a moment in the argument, it is clear that while Odysseus abandons a certain kind of self, he does not abandon himself altogether – there is an Odysseus that remains, even if it is a changed Odysseus. As will be clear from the above, I wonder about such a remainder of sovereignty in this book – and it seems that Malabou does as well in her lecture.

For after Malabou has rehearsed her discussion of Agamben, familiar to those who have read "Sovereignty and Biology" –

she repeats the argument about the structure of sovereignty as being split between a biological and symbolic body and makes the case for a "unity between symbolic and biological life" that would constitute an "emancipation from sovereignty"[67] – she comes to write of "the threat of tyranny that is immanent to sovereignty," thus distinguishing between a tyrannical sovereignty and a sovereignty that exists in addition to or around such a threatening sovereignty.[68] There is, in other words, a two-body problem that is introduced here, for a distinction seems to be made between tyrannical sovereignty and another sovereignty (a distinction that seems to resonate with a passage in Agamben that Malabou criticizes, where Agamben writes of a bare life within the biological body). And it is, in fact, the suggestion of this split – Malabou's flirtation with this deconstruction, which appears like a sovereign lure – that triggers the last part of her argument.

The life chosen by Odysseus, she argues, is not so much a life that leaves sovereignty behind but interrupts it from within – at least for a moment: for as readers familiar with the Odysseus story will know, Odysseus does not entirely disappear within the sphere of the private. In fact, he reappears within the sphere of sovereignty in disguise, as a beggar (a poor person; one should note here the affinities between this figure and the figure of the monk in Agamben's *The Highest Poverty* – I will return to this in Parts II and III of this book). This disguise, Malabou argues, is not a disguise that furthers sovereignty's two-body structure, but one that draws sovereignty and in particular the threat of tyranny that it always contains into an impoverished sovereignty, a poor sovereignty – at least for a moment. Odysseus appears in the sphere of sovereignty not as a mask that confirms the old sovereignty but as its "ontological displacement."[69] Of course, it is only momentary, and we know that Odysseus then reveals himself to be Odysseus, kills off his wife's suitors, and thus violently restores the old order. But Malabou's question seems to be about the possibility that opened up with Odysseus' disguise as a poor beggar. She suggests that as such, Odysseus was the figure in which *zoe* and *bios* came to coincide, in Agamben's terms a figure of "whatever being" that constitutes not only a counterpart to what Agamben calls "bare life" but also – as I will argue in this book – a model for another, poor, plastic sovereignty, one that in Agamben's work is associated (as Malabou points out) to Herman Melville's enigmatic scrivener Bartleby (whom I will discuss in detail in the last chapter of this book). Indeed, this leads Malabou to conclude with the questions: "How to remain sovereign in a non-sovereign way? What model or sample of life is to be chosen for such a return?" From the question about "relinquishing sovereignty" we have moved to the question of "remaining sovereign in a non-sovereign way."[70]

Plastic Sovereignties takes place in-between these two questions, starting with Foucault's call to cut off the head of the king and developing along its different chapters a theory of a poor, plastic sovereignty that would remain sovereign – but beyond the structure (ontological, linguistic, political) that I consider to inform the concept of sovereignty. By pursuing such a project at the crossroads of Catherine Malabou and Giorgio Agamben's thinking, I aim to accomplish two things: first, I want to show that Agamben arguably does not fully abandon sovereignty in his thought but invites us to begin to think, instead, a plastic sovereignty that, however, he has some difficulty naming – and Malabou can help us on this count; second, I show that while Malabou thinks the effective deconstruction of sovereignty, supplementing that project with Agamben's work – a thought that she is very critical of, as am I – enables one to articulate a "positive" politics starting from her work, using the more developed understanding of sovereignty that can be found in Agamben. Thus, taken together, Agamben's and Malabou's thoughts yield a theory of plastic sovereignty that, from the field of aesthetics (plasticity) deconstructs the political structure of sovereignty (its two-body problem). My central concept – plastic sovereignties – should thus be understood as a single term rather than as two: plural, it nevertheless splices the bodies of Agamben's and Malabou's works into one, overcoming the sovereign distinction between the symbolic (in this case, Agamben) and the material (in this case, Malabou), and effectively accomplishing a unified body of both – and thus, *both* a deconstructed, aesthetic sovereignty *and* a plasticity that is more politically robust.

Notes

1   Derrida, *Sovereignties*, 117.
2   Mouffe, *Agonistics*, 101.
3   Klein, *This Changes*, 158.
4   For a critical overview of this "politics without sovereignty," see Bickerton et al., *Politics*.
5   Foucault, *History*, 88–9.
6   This resistance has taken several forms. Some have defended sovereignty in response to the call for its ending. Michael Hardt and Antonio Negri, on the other hand, have proposed the terminology of empire and multitude to replace the terminology of sovereignty and the people, arguing that the pair empire/multitude enables them to more precisely name the organization of power and life in the contemporary neoliberal era. See Hardt and Negri's trilogy *Empire – Multitude – Commonwealth*.
7   I write "at the very least" because my project will obviously not simply be to "catch up"; it is also to intervene within sovereignty and enable other sovereign futures.
8   Butler, *Precarious Life*, xi.

9 This may be one reason (in addition to others that have been developed, for example by Alex Galloway and Eugene Thacker) why Hardt and Negri's terminology of empire and multitude should be resisted: because these terms, which seek to capture the contemporary economic condition, do not sufficiently articulate a mode of political organization, authorship, and accountability that would be separate from the economy. In other words, the terms are not sufficiently sovereign. As will be clear, I make this criticism not in the name of traditional sovereignty, that is: in the name of going back to sovereignty's past, but in view of a future of sovereignty at a critical distance from economic power. It seems worthwhile, today, trying to separate the political from the economic spheres, and sovereignty could be a weapon in that battle.

10 In this context, Jessica Whyte mentions an attachment to national sovereignty in particular in a time of austerity measures "which are commonly characterized as an abrogation of national sovereignty": Whyte, "'The king,'" 144.

11 In this last case as well, Hardt and Negri's terminology does not seem appropriate.

12 Bickerton et al., *Politics*, 8.

13 Ibid., 12. To draw this conclusion would of course mean to operate within a certain conception of politics, namely politics in relation to law, as guaranteeing the rule of law – as the law's "muscle," so to speak. But such a conception of politics already hyphenates the political with the legal into the legalo-political and prevents one from thinking a politics separate from the law. It is worth reflecting here, as I will do in this book, about the consequences of such a limitation to political imagination and practice.

14 Ibid., 1.

15 To be clear, by "dismantling" I do not mean "separating out" the element of sovereignty that appears problematic. That would mean to apply the logic of sovereignty to sovereignty, by internally excluding or excepting its problematic element – one that, inevitably, will continue to steer it. "Dismantling" refers here to a more radical intervention, one that would thoroughly transform sovereignty's operation.

16 Matthew Abbott and Jessica Whyte have each drawn out the ontological aspects of Agamben's political philosophy in their recent books on Agamben. See Abbott, *Figure*; Whyte, *Catastrophe*.

17 The following summarizing discussion of Agamben's work is mostly based on my reading of Agamben, *HS*.

18 See Santner, "Terri Schiavo."

19 It's a model that, years later, Freud will repeat in psychoanalysis – but the insight he took from it, namely that "everybody's weird," was of course drastically different. It's no coincidence, I think, that some of the most enthusiastic readers of Agamben work in psychoanalytic theory.

20 See Agamben, *HS* and *MWE*.

21 Butler, *Frames*, 76.

22 Interestingly, Agamben himself has been charged with this by Geoffrey Hartman. Hartman argues that in his ethical work on Auschwitz, where he proposes the "Muselmann" as the ultimate witness, Agamben gives in too much to a figure of silence, thus denying survivors' actual testimony. Hartman takes on Derrida as well in this context as focusing too much on the spectral aspects of testimony. See Balfour and Comay, "Ethics."

23 See Agamben, *HS*, *MWE*, and also *HP*.

24 See Agamben, *HS*.

25 A key reference for my thinking in this context is Jane Bennett's book *Vibrant Matter: A Political Ecology of Things*. Following Gilbert Simondon, Bennett criticizes the hylomorphic model (56) and urges her readers to think of matter as alive.

26 This sovereign body is obviously already split between a biological and a symbolic body, as Ernst Kantorowicz has pointed out.

27 I take this distinction in part from Eric Santner's book *The Royal Remains: The People's Two Bodies and the Endgames of Sovereignty*.

28 Combes, *Gilbert Simondon*, 48.

29 I return to Simondon's work as well as Agamben's use of it in Chapter 5.

30 See Vardoulakis, *Sovereignty*.

31 On this, see also Chapter 9.

32 See, for example, Srnicek and Williams, *Inventing*.

33 Whyte, *Catastrophe*, 144.

34 Ibid.

35 See ibid.

36 Ibid., 145.

37 I return to this in Chapter 8, where I develop an aesthetic approach to the state of exception, focusing on what I call, after Hito Steyerl, "sovereignty's glitches."

38 Here, I will easily grant that "pluralization" is not traditionally associated with sovereignty, the indivisible power of the one. A pluralized sovereignty is, to some, no doubt closer to a non-sovereignty – and it is precisely this proximity that I will be pursuing; but without giving up sovereignty altogether. See my discussion of Malabou's "non-sovereign sovereignty" at the end of this Prologue.

39 See Malabou, *Future*.

40 Malabou, "Who's Afraid?," 117.

41 Malabou, *Ontology*; Malabou, *New Wounded*.

42 Malabou, *Changing Difference*, 63.

43 Malabou, *Ontology*, 17.

44 Malabou, *Changing Difference*, 63.

45 This is the subject of a new book that was published too late for me to consider it here: Attell, *Giorgio Agamben*.

46 See Agamben, *HS*, 58.

47 See Simondon, *Du mode d'existence*.

48 Malabou, *What Should We Do?*, 12.

49 Malabou, "Darwin."

50 Malabou, "Sovereignty." I would like to thank Catherine Malabou for letting me quote from this manuscript.

51 Malabou, "Sovereignty," 1.

52 Ibid., 3.

53 Foucault qtd. ibid., 2.

54 Ibid., 3.

55 Ibid., 4.

56 Ibid.

57 Ibid.

58 Ibid., 6.

59 Ibid., 5.

60 Ibid., 5–6.

61 Ibid., 6.

62 Derrida has argued something similar about the death penalty, intimately related in his thought – and also in the thoughts of Foucault and Agamben – to sovereignty. Calling for the end or death of the death penalty seems to be a secret advertisement for the death penalty. War to end war, et cetera.

63 Malabou, "Odysseus." I would like to thank Catherine Malabou for letting me quote from this manuscript.

64 Ibid., 6.

65 Schmitt, *Political Theology*, 5.

66 Malabou, "Odysseus," 7.

67 Ibid., 9.

68 Ibid., 11.

69 Ibid., 14.

70 Ibid., 16.

Part I: Aesthetics

1

An Experiment with Language

From Athens to Auschwitz

On 10 January 2004 the Italian philosopher Giorgio Agamben published a short text in the French newspaper *Le Monde* in which he explained why he had cancelled a class he was supposed to teach at New York University in March of the same year.[1] The reason was a new regulation that required "whoever wants to go to the United States with a visa" to be "put on file" and "leave their fingerprints when they enter the country." "Personally," Agamben writes, "I have no intention of submitting myself to such procedures," which have "long been imposed on criminals and political defendants." His criticism is not simply about these procedures being imposed on the latter class of human beings: "If it were only that, we would certainly be morally able to share, in solidarity, the humiliating conditions to which so many human beings are subjected." The problem is, rather, that the new regulation marks a shift in "the juridical-political status … of citizens of the so-called democratic states in which we live," a shift through which we have come "to accept as humane and normal dimensions of our existence, practices of control that had always been properly considered inhuman and exceptional."

Agamben characterizes this as a "bio-political shift" through which we have gone "one step further in what Michel Foucault called the progressive animalization of man which is established through the most sophisticated techniques." The word "animalization" is used here to capture the fact that this regulation aims to "fil[e] away … the most private and incommunicable aspect of subjectivity: I mean the body's biological life." When "humanity itself has become the dangerous class" that is subjected to "techniques" and "devices" that were invented for criminals and political defendants, the birthplace of Western democracy – the *polis*, the Greek city-state – has effectively been transformed into a *camp*. Noting that his comparison of the states in which we are living to Auschwitz is "obviously a philosophical thesis, and not a historical recital" ("one could [sic] not confuse phenomena that it is proper, on the contrary, to distinguish"), Agamben concludes by stating that the biopolitical tattooing to which those entering the US with a visa are subjected is similar to the tattooing that happened in the camps. *From Athens to Auschwitz*: that is how Agamben summarizes Western democracy's trajectory.

Agamben's text is provocative, and as a way into some of the central concerns of this book, I propose to briefly review a number of objections that can be raised against it. Let me begin with the most obvious one: even if Agamben states that his comparison of the visa regulation to the camp is a philosophical and not a historical one, many would likely still take issue with it. Indeed, given that "electronic devices such as credit cards or cell phones" are mentioned in Agamben's text as further indicators of his underlying thesis – defended at greater length in his book *Homo Sacer: Sovereign Power and Bare Life* – that the camp is the model according to which modern political life needs to be understood, one begins to wonder whether this kind of comparison isn't simply giving the critical practice of "comparison," and more generally "philosophy" or what in the United States goes by the name of "theory," a bad rap. Once again, the theorist has his head in the clouds (to recall Aristophanes' characterization of Socrates), and is drawing conclusions on the basis of superficial comparisons that no serious (grounded) historian or political thinker or even philosopher of technology – for technology is clearly also under attack in Agamben's short text[2] – could possibly accept.

One imagines that the objections to Agamben's thesis would not only be based on an (in my view, equally problematic) insistence on Auschwitz's incommensurability, on the fact that the Holocaust *cannot* be compared;[3] they would likely also target Agamben's comparison of Auschwitz to a new visa regulation, and the link he establishes between Auschwitz and credit cards or cell phones. Could the Holocaust possibly become more "banal," to loosely recall an expression – "the banality of evil" – of one of Agamben's major influences, the political thinker Hannah Arendt?[4]

If Auschwitz would likely warrant a categorical rejection, matters seem to be different with a technical object such as the cell phone, which falls instead within the logic – or perhaps better, the dynamic – of what Jacques Derrida in his reading of Plato[5] has called the "pharmakon": a cure that is also potentially a poison, a means of emancipation that is also potentially a means of oppression.[6] French philosopher of technology Bernard Stiegler (to whom I will return in Chapter 5) has pursued this track throughout his work.[7] Although understanding the camp as *both* a thanatopolitical *and* a biopolitical site demands that we inscribe it into this dynamic – one must understand how the camp was *both* a site where (Jewish) life was put to death *and* another kind of life (Aryan) was being fostered – this inscription can no longer hold from our perspective. We are left with mere poison (in Stiegler's parlance, the absolute negativity of the pharmakon). With the cell phone, however, the case appears to be different still: an art project like Ricardo Dominguez's *Transborder Immigrant Tool* – a phone app that uses GPS technology to help immigrants find water stations as they are crossing the border from Mexico into Southern California – or books like Manuel Castells's *Communication Power* or *Networks of Outrage and Hope* reveal the necessity to also consider the emancipative role that technological objects such as the cell phone have played, for example in democratic elections or also in progressive radical politics.[8] To simply forgo a careful investigation of the differences between Auschwitz and the cell phone would mean to side with a radically immature anti-modernity that blindly equates modernity with fascism without asking about its emancipatory dimensions.[9]

Education, Abandonment, Animalization

The comparison of the visa regulation to Auschwitz is by no means the only aspect of Agamben's text that can be criticized. Consider also his call at the beginning of the *Le Monde* text for "other European intellectuals and teachers" to follow his example, and cancel their studies, research, and classes in the US in response to the new regulation. Even though the political situations under consideration are obviously very different, my response to this echoed literary critic and theorist Bruce Robbins's analysis of Susan Sontag's essay "A Lament for Bosnia: 'There' and 'Here'" (republished in *Where the Stress Falls* as "'There' and

'Here'").[10] As Robbins points out, Sontag's "harshest words" in the essay "are reserved for the intellectuals, who have become 'morosely depoliticized.'"[11] Frustrated by people's general disinterest in the aftermath of the Bosnian peace agreement in her experiences in Sarajevo – a city which, as she explains in her text, she has visited nine times – Sontag criticizes those who are "a creature of 'comfortable upper-bourgeoisie apartments and weekend country houses,'" and "loath to leave them."[12] Instead, she wishes intellectuals would act: like George Orwell or Simone Weil (who is a major, though largely overlooked, influence in Agamben's work), they should get involved – not just from the comfort of their homes, through their writing or teaching, but *on site*.

While Robbins appreciates Sontag's criticisms and takes the question that her essay raises – why is it that today, "only domestic political commitments seem plausible?"[13] – as the starting point for his book *Feeling Global: Internationalism in Distress*, he also takes issue with Sontag's words, pointing out that "very few" of Sontag's readers "are likely to enjoy the time, the personal autonomy, and the disposable income necessary for even one or two trips to Sarajevo, let alone nine": "Sontag suggests it is the poor who go and the rich who stay home. But her ethics presupposes a very different sociology: everyone must act, she implies, as if they were as free and as privileged as I am."[14] Very few of Agamben's readers – myself included; I was a European pursuing graduate studies in the US at the time when his text was published – were likely to enjoy the freedom and the privilege he had, namely to cancel a class they were assigned to teach at a major US university, and return to the comfort of another academic position at home. This is not to say that Agamben's text does not raise an important question; but it does make one think a little more critically about the "sociology" (Robbins's term) that his call for action assumes.

Also worth noting is an important difference between Sontag's and Agamben's calls to action: whereas Sontag is urging her readers to *go to* Sarajevo, Agamben is urging his readers to *leave* the US. Both could arguably be valid responses to a situation of political emergency. But one must wonder, in Agamben's case, what good it would do for European intellectuals and teachers to abandon their American students and the American educational system in order to return to Europe. Wouldn't it be more effective to actually stay on and attempt to insert a difference within the political system through education, by introducing generation after generation of students to critical thinking? What guarantees do we have, in fact, that Europe is less saturated with biopolitics than the US? Can Agamben's home country, Italy, really present a valid political alternative?[15] One might want to recall, in this context, the notion of "educative violence" that Walter Benjamin – who is with Arendt and Foucault probably Agamben's third most important influence – mobilizes in his text "Critique of Violence," as a form of divine violence that can break the link between violence and law that Benjamin takes on.[16] Given that this text is central to Agamben's work, one wonders what light it might cast on Agamben's decision to abandon his American students, and his call on his European colleagues working in the US to do the same.[17]

Agamben's short text in *Le Monde* appears problematic from the standpoint of his own work for at least one other reason. I have in mind his uncritical use, supposedly after Foucault, of the term "animalization" to capture the effects of biopolitics on human beings. The phrase "progressive animalization of man" ("une animalisation progressive de l'homme," in the translated

French), which Agamben seems to quote (without giving an actual reference) from the third volume of Foucault's *Dits et Écrits*, is translated in the introduction to Agamben's book *Homo Sacer* as "bestialization of man."[18] Readers of Jacques Derrida's seminars on *The Beast and the Sovereign* might want to apply some pressure to the distinction between the animal and the beast that haunts these translations: are the animal and the beast the same? If not, how are they different? And how might this difference matter not only for our naming, but also our understanding, of the effects of biopolitics on human life? That the problem shows up at all, however, is surprising: Agamben's own work has done much to break down the ways in which the difference between humans and animals has been constructed, and how human and animal life have been defined. Attempting to "jam" what he calls (with reference to Furio Jesi) "the anthropological machine"[19] that is continuously generating the gap between humans and animals, Agamben has introduced a third kind of life into the debates: "nuda vita" (naked life, also translated as mere life or bare life), a notion that he borrows (once again) from Benjamin's "Critique of Violence."[20] Naked life is not the same as animal life; it is located in a zone of indistinction between human life and animal life, as an inhuman kind of life to which *both* human and animal life are reduced in a state of exception (a situation or state in which the normal rule of law is suspended in the name of an emergency or security issue).[21] It is therefore highly surprising, to say the least, that in his pamphlet against biopolitical tattooing, Agamben appears to reproduce precisely the distinction that his work has done so much to break down, by capturing the effects of biopolitics on human life as an "animalization."[22] Actual animals may have much less to do with biopolitics than this figuration suggests.

Positive Politics

All these issues – the camp, political action, the animal – are important and have been central in the developing criticism of Agamben's work. One can think of the essays collected in Andrew Norris's book *Politics, Metaphysics, and Death: Essays on Giorgio Agamben's* Homo Sacer, or of Matthew Calarco and Steven DeCaroli's edited collection *Giorgio Agamben: Sovereignty and Life* as good examples. Although I too will have occasion to return to these issues in what follows, I consider the approach of this book to be closer to works such as Catherine Mills's *The Philosophy of Giorgio Agamben*, Leland de la Durantaye's *Giorgio Agamben: A Critical Introduction*, or David Kishik's *The Power of Life: Giorgio Agamben and the Coming Politics*. This is for two reasons, one of which is stated clearly in the introduction to another collection, edited by Clemens et al., *The Work of Giorgio Agamben: Law, Literature, Life*:[23] in order to understand Agamben's political project, one must tie it to his work on aesthetics and poetics, which continues to resonate in his writings on politics.[24] If the early edited collections on Agamben's work still largely ignored his writings on aesthetics, the consensus in the more recent scholarship has been that an engagement with Agamben's aesthetic thought is indispensable in any discussion of his political writings, and this has of course also produced the other extreme of the swing of the critical pendulum: William Watkin's *The Literary Agamben: Adventures in Logopoiesis*, which seeks to separate aesthetics and poetics from politics in Agamben's work.[25] In what follows, I treat the political and the aesthetic/poetic (the difference between the latter two will be clarified in a moment) in tandem, in order to reveal their intimate connection.

The second reason why I consider this book to be closer to these more recent studies of Agamben's work, is because *Plastic Sovereignties* tries to articulate Agamben's political project in positive terms – in other words: in terms that go beyond the negative criticism of his work that I developed in the previous paragraphs. Although I think the negative criticism is useful, and in fact makes up a large part of Agamben's own project – one that revolves, crucially, around a passive politics of withdrawal that can be contrasted with, for example, Sontag's positive call for action in her text on Bosnia – my feeling is – and this goes against what many have suggested – that there actually is an affirmative politics that can be found throughout his writings: a power *of* life, to work within the terms developed by David Kishik, that is mobilized against the power *over* life that Agamben in texts like "No to Bio-Political Tattooing" criticizes.[26] In this respect, Agamben's work might actually be closer to the work of his colleague Roberto Esposito – whose name is most prominently associated with the phrase "affirmative biopolitics" – than has been acknowledged.[27] However, such a power of life will name only one dimension of what I call plastic sovereignty – a concept that, as I indicated in my Prologue, ultimately exists at a critical distance from Agamben's thought. (The more obvious association is between Agamben and radical politics.)

But let us stick for the moment with the short text that was published in *Le Monde*, and that has received little attention in Agamben scholarship so far:[28] what, if any, *is* the positive politics that Agamben articulates there? The text suggests that it revolves around the privacy and incommunicability of the body, the human being's biological life. That is, at least, what Agamben considers to be violated by the new visa regulation. We could focus here on Agamben's emphasis on the body, or biological life, and criticize – as Catherine Malabou has been doing in her most recent work – the understanding of biology that circulates in Agamben's writings (Malabou also takes on Foucault and Derrida in this context, as I explained in my Prologue).[29] But my suggestion would be that in order to understand Agamben's positive politics, one should focus not so much on the body, or biological life, but on the notion of the *privacy* of the body, and more specifically that of its *incommunicability*, which he also mentions.[30] Given the negation that haunts these terms – privacy, incommunicability – some work will need to be done in order to clarify how they can be part of a positive politics, and I will get to this in a moment, through a discussion of a text from Agamben's early book *Infancy and History*, titled "Preface: *Experimentum Linguae*."[31] For now, let me simply note that if the issue with respect to the body, the human being's biological life, is indeed privacy, and specifically the body's incommunicability, then biopolitics – the attempt to make the body communicable – clearly becomes an issue of *communication*, a *poetic* issue related to the question of the sayable and the unsayable. One could even propose, somewhat controversially given Agamben's own criticism of the term,[32] to use the word *aesthetic* instead of *poetic* in this context,[33] given that the issue is not simply one of articulation, of what *can* and what *cannot* be said, but rather of the *separation* or *distribution* between the sayable and the unsayable *itself*: of the very *faculty* of language that precedes it (the fact that human beings "have" language), and that as such poses a challenge to our capacities of apprehension.[34] As I see it, there is thus an *aesthetic* question that takes precedence over the link between poetry and politics in Agamben's work, and it is this question that *Plastic Sovereignties* is ultimately interested in. Hence my slightly unorthodox use of the phrase "Politics of Aesthetics" in my subtitle.[35]

Experimenting with Language

As a way to explain the aesthetic dimension of Agamben's work in a little more detail, and to develop an example of how closely politics and aesthetics are connected in it, I propose to turn to a text that is part of a book that was originally published in 1978, *Infancy and History: On the Destruction of Experience*. The book's subtitle reveals its indebtedness to the work of Walter Benjamin, and indeed, Benjamin's essay "The Storyteller" – which I discuss in detail in Chapter 2 – appears at the very beginning of the book, in the first chapter after the preface. In what follows, I will be looking at the book's preface, a short text titled *"Experimentum Linguae"* (Latin for "the experiment of language") that lays out what could be called Agamben's politics of language, and his politics of aesthetics more generally.

The text is not only a preface in name: it also reflects on the status of the preface, casting the entire book that is to follow as merely a "prologue," which is a kind of preface itself, "of a work never penned" and "remaining stubbornly unwritten."[36] We thus find ourselves in the space of the *parerga*, of those works (*erga*) that exist next to (*para*) the actual work – those bits of text that accompany and supplement the body of the text, but that are strictly speaking not fully part of it (the title, an opening motto, a dedication, a preface, the footnotes, et cetera). The text that is left over after the main body of the text is taken away. This status of the preface is closely connected to the book's central concept, infancy. "If every thought can be classified according to the way in which it articulates the question of the limits of language," Agamben writes, "the concept of infancy is then an attempt to think through these limits in a direction other than that of the vulgarly ineffable."[37] With the notion of infancy, which refers to an incapacity to speak, a not-yet of speaking – a not-yet that resonates, of course, with the status of a pre-face or a pro-logue, of a work that pre-cedes the actual work – Agamben is not interested in what he calls "the vulgarly ineffable."[38] The question of the limit of language is not just that of what can be said, and what cannot be said. "The concept of infancy, on the contrary, is accessible only to a thought which has been purified ... 'by eliminating the unsayable from language.'"[39] Language must signify, he concludes, "not something ineffable but something superlatively sayable: the *thing* of language,"[40] our very capacity for speaking itself (our potentiality not-to speak). The preface accomplishes something similar in its relation to "the book."

Agamben's clarifications about infancy are crucial, for they indicate that with the concept of infancy, we are not simply dealing with the separation of the sayable from the unsayable, and the ineffable as it would be defined according to this distribution. Instead, we are dealing with the *separation* of the sayable from the unsayable *itself*, and the supremely sayable thing that it has occluded: the *thing* of language. With the notion of infancy, Agamben is interested in the experience of language itself. To recover this experience, and by extension experience at large (as per Benjamin's essay on storytelling – see Chapter 2), does not mean to recover the said, or even to recover what cannot be said; it means to recover infancy, the faculty of language, the thing of language that our focus on the sayable versus the unsayable has tended to eclipse.

If we tie this to Agamben's concern with communication that we uncovered in the short text on biopolitical tattooing, the parallel argument would be that Agamben is not interested in the difference between what can and what cannot be communicated. Instead, he is interested in the communication of communication itself – in the thing of communication, the experience of com-munic*ability*. The challenge is to translate this point to Agamben's concern (in his more explicitly political work) with the body, with the human being's biological life. Here too, he is not so much interested in what the body means, or does not mean, does or does not do; instead, he theorizes a body that would be its own meaning and doing, a biological life that would not need another meaning or doing to be added to it in order to be valuable. What we have lost, he argues, is the experience of biological life itself, of the *thing* of biological life – of a body as faculty, as pure means rather than a means towards an end.[41] We are not valued, politically, for just being. Instead, another identity – a political, symbolic life; a form of life (*bios*) – always needs to be added to the simple fact of our living (*zoe*) in order for our lives to become valuable.[42] As soon as this logic kicks in, Agamben argues, we are lost: as soon as this logic is at work, we become part of a political community *only by virtue of ultimately being excluded from it*. For what makes us part of the community is merely a symbolic identity that was added to our biological life. In such a world, "just being" is never enough; the simple fact of our living only becomes valuable through the addition of a symbolic surplus. Such a surplus can at any point be stripped away – flip over into "life as surplus" (mere, bare, or naked life), to recall the title of Melinda Cooper's brilliant book.[43] Political life should be liberated from this vicious oscillation between surplus (more) and lack (mere). Agamben's project, both with respect to the body and with respect to language, is to appreciate the "thing" of life. It needs nothing more than what it is in order to be of value. Just language is intimately connected to just being.[44]

With language, which is so much caught up in the separating structure of meaning – a word always refers to something else, it is never just what it is – this project begins to feel like a radical transformation. For the challenge would be to stop treating language as a window, through which one attempts to see something else, something added to language. Instead, Agamben wants to redirect our gaze to language itself – not just to its vulgar material dimension, of course, but to the *faculty* of language, its gestural[45] dimension – in order to show how much of the logic of our use of language has been translated into our political life. In politics, we treat life like we treat language: life itself never suffices; it always needs something in addition to what it is. It needs to become communication. Politics, like language, is thus caught up in practices of reading and interpretation, in a certain understanding of communication according to which communicability itself is never enough. One can see how the project of reading differently – something that Agamben's work demands from us – thus becomes politically meaningful, when dealing with human beings' biological lives.[46]

"I Love Art"

I would now like to discuss, in a second step, some of Agamben's writings dealing with art and aesthetics so as to show that there is a close connection between the politics of language that Agamben lays out and the way in which he understands art to be political. I would like to begin to approach the issue by way of a detour, through another text that is apparently unrelated to Agamben's oeuvre.

In 2003, Belgian art theorist Frank Vande Veire published a by now notorious pamphlet about contemporary art titled "I Love Art. You Love Art. We All Love Art, This is Love" in the Belgian newspaper *De Morgen*.[47] The pamphlet was controversial, but (as Vande Veire himself pointed out in a follow-up publication) for the wrong reasons: because Vande Veire had mentioned a few important contemporary artists and curators whose work and/or persona he considered to exemplify the malaise he perceived, everyone ended up focusing on those names rather than on the pamphlet's general argument – a pity, because the case that Vande Veire was making remains an important one that pertains to the political status of art today and that can put us on the track of Agamben's aesthetic politics.

"I Love Art" was triggered by a postcard Vande Veire received in the mail: sent out by S.M.A.K., the city of Ghent's museum of contemporary art, and signed by one of the city's political leaders, the postcard read: "In the twenty-first century, art wakes up those who are sleeping." On the other side of the card, there was a photograph of the artist couple Marina Abramović and Ulay (Uwe Laysiepen), their faces very close to each other, screaming. The issue that Vande Veire has with the postcard is that it exemplifies the appropriation – political, given that the card was signed by a political leader; but also "aesthetic," given that it was sent by a museum of contemporary art – of art's critical potential, art's crisis. Clearly, everyone receiving the postcard can continue sleeping, for they already belong to the community of those who are awake (the postcard preaches to the choir). And they can sleep soundly, because being awake has the full approval of our aesthetic and political institutions: it is *good* to be awake.[48] We all *love* being awake. What conception of wakefulness – of criticality – can remain in a society where being awake has become the aesthetico-political norm?

Such a situation not only reflects the contemporary status of art. It also affects the status of art criticism. Art criticism, Vande

Veire writes, has turned into a fetish: "as long as we can keep talking," we are satisfied. Needless to say, this is not a convincing model of criticism. Such a conversation, in which everyone holds back from saying what they really want to say in order to instead exchange ideas endlessly in a world that resembles that of Bill Gates's "frictionless capitalism," actually masks what Vande Veire calls a "taboo" of criticism. In contemporary art criticism, everything is allowed, as long as no one gets offended. With reference to G. W. F. Hegel, Vande Veire characterizes such a situation as the end of art criticism, and – by extension – of art. Critical consciousness has been hollowed out; criticality has been fetishized into a commodity that can be safely carried around in one's pocket until the next opportunity to show it off arrives.

Like Hegel, however, Vande Veire does not think that art and art criticism have really ended. There *can be* poetry after Auschwitz, to recall Theodor Adorno's statement in "Cultural Criticism and Society" – but it will have to be *another kind* of poetry.[49] In a follow-up article, Vande Veire clarifies that the art of the future can actually be the same art, but better – more lucid. As Adorno puts it in his follow-up article to the cultural criticism text, titled "Commitment": "I have no wish to soften the saying that to write poetry after Auschwitz is barbaric; it expresses in negative form the impulse which inspires committed literature."[50] It is a question about what kind of art – and ultimately, about whether any art – has the right to exist; and about "whether regression is not inherent in the concept of committed literature because of the regression of society."[51] For Vande Veire, art's commitment is its crisis; and its crisis, as he points out, is receding.

Ultimately, and this is the conclusion I draw from the names that Vande Veire mentions towards the end of the pamphlet, it seems that Vande Veire's concern is not so much with art or art criticism, but with the people who practice them. From where Vande Veire is standing, it appears that their practice has become appropriated by political and curatorial visions, by an idea of art as something that fits into society, and has beneficial effects on it. Art is *therapeutic*, it practices some kind of *good*, isn't that why we *love* it? But what about, Vande Veire asks, art that does *not* fit: art as misfit, as failure, as something that does not belong and therefore poses a limit to the curatorial and political visions that want to subsume it? What about, to put it in different but related terms, "just" art rather than art that is "just"? What about an idea of justice that would coincide with a notion of "just" art? If we were to pursue such a vision of art, Vande Veire argues, art would be forced to confront itself, at a distance from curatorial and political visions (a distance that would be different from the one that has become the norm – Vande Veire associates the latter with the figure of the dandy, of the critical artist who, dressed only in black, always keeps her- or himself at a distance, in a "critical" state of disengagement).

At first sight, this seems nothing new. Whereas art was, for centuries, caught within the sphere of the beautiful, the avant-garde definitively liberated it from that burden. However, Vande Veire argues that since the 1980s, the critical legacy of the avant-garde has itself entered into a crisis, and become the norm: "Criticism, provocation, alienation, and disturbance have become normalized notions." Art has become legitimate *because* it is critical. In other words, art's critical function has become defused. This puts the legacy of the avant-garde in a peculiar bind: it forces one to reinvent criticism, to practice a *critical* criticism that would be critical of the crisis in which criticism has landed. It would be a criticism squared, so to speak;

a squaring that would break the circle in which criticism has been caught. As his follow-up text indicates, Vande Veire is in fact trying to invent a future for the crisis of art, for art's critical function. What he considers to be "proper" to modern art – its criticality – needs to be saved from its own crisis/needs to be returned to its own crisis (which differs from the crisis that has become the norm).

Politics of the Uncanny

In his follow-up article, titled "Men Neemt de Kunst Haar Crisis Af" ("Art's Crisis is Being Taken Away"), Vande Veire at several points comes close to linking art's critical function – the *malaise* or *Unbehagen* that its crisis can also bring – to Sigmund Freud's notion of *das Unheimliche*, the uncanny.[52] Art's critical function is uncanny; with art's crisis, its uncanny dimension has gone lost. If we state this position positively rather than negatively, this means that Vande Veire is in fact developing a plea not simply for a return of art's critical function, but also for its uncanny dimension.

Such a plea puts Vande Veire's pamphlet in line with the theory of "aesthetics"[53] that Agamben develops in the first chapter of his first book, *The Man Without Content*, which (like Vande Veire's texts) also deals with the end of art in the modern era. Titled "The Most Uncanny Thing," the chapter opens with a discussion of Friedrich Nietzsche's criticism (in the third essay of *On the Genealogy of Morals*) of Immanuel Kant's theory of aesthetics, developed in the *Critique of the Power of Judgment*. As Nietzsche points out, Kant's analytic of the beautiful only understands art from the perspective of the spectator. For

Nietzsche, however, the spectator's experience can hardly exhaust our understanding of art: the point would be precisely to "[filter] out the αἴσθησις [aisthesis], the sensory involvement of the spectator, and thus to consider art from the point of view of its creator."[54] Thus, "the aesthetic dimension … is replaced by the creative experience of the artist."[55] Further down on the same page, Agamben characterizes this move, rehearsing Kant's definition of beauty as "purposiveness without purpose," as a "turn from the idea of disinterested beauty as a denominator of art to the idea of happiness, that is, of an unlimited growth and strengthening of the vital values."[56]

In the conflict between Nietzsche and Kant, Agamben appears to side with Nietzsche. He associates Nietzsche's position with Plato's *Republic*, pointing out that Plato famously banned poets from his ideal city – the *kallipolis* – because he thought they were dangerous. They dealt in second-hand truths (shadows of shadows, representations of a reality that is itself already merely a shadow) and risked messing with the city's neat distribution of classes through their skills at imitation. And Agamben points out that "[e]ven before Plato … a condemnation of art, or at least a suspicious stance towards it, had already been expressed"[57] by Sophocles, in his drama *Antigone*:

> After characterizing man, insofar as he is the one who has τέχνη [techne] (that is, in the broad meaning the Greeks gave this term, the ability to pro-duce, to bring a thing from nonbeing into being), as the most uncanny thing there is, the chorus continues by saying that his power can lead to happiness as easily as to ruin.[58]

In the *Republic*, art is thus quite literally condemned as something that is *politically* risky, for it poses a risk to the *polis*. Given that

Plato's position is connected to Nietzsche's critique of Kant, this puts a political spin on Agamben's embrace of Nietzsche as well.[59] Although Agamben in this early text appears to still take it up for art's dangerous dimension, for the potentially disturbing dimension of technology, his later work will reveal a much more conservative take on technology (as I discuss in Chapter 5).

The point of the argument in the early text appears to be that today, art has lost its politically subversive function: it is "[o]nly because art has left the sphere of interest to become merely interesting" that we "welcome it so warmly."[60] To this, Agamben opposes (after Nietzsche) the experience of the artist:

> For the one who creates it, art becomes an increasingly uncanny experience, with respect to which speaking of interest is at the very least a euphemism, because what is at stake seems to be not in any way the production of a beautiful work, but instead the life and death of the author, or at least his or her spiritual health.[61]

To make art is a question of such extreme risk that to speak of interest in this context becomes almost meaningless. It is not a mere question of interest; instead, it is a question of life and death. To practice art means to revisit life in such a way that it comes in close proximity to death. It is along those lines that art needs to be rethought today. To echo Nietzsche's words quoted at the end of Agamben's chapter, we need "an art for artists, for artists only!"[62] An art for the creator, with all the dangers that this entails.

To be sure, to say that Agamben "embraces" Nietzsche in this context is probably to say too much: for we already know, with Vande Veire, that the figure of the interested artist becomes hollowed out over time and ultimately amounts in that of what Vande Veire calls the critical, disengaged artist – dressed only in black. Agamben, too, traces this hollowing out in *The Man Without Content* and while it would be too much to say that he strives for a return to the interested artist with all the problems that this figure entails, he is certainly thinking and writing against this figure's self-absorption in order to oppose to it another politics of art.

Now, let me consider Nietzsche's theory of art next to my discussion of Agamben's "*Experimentum Linguae.*" Doing so enables one to understand that Agamben's "experiment of language" is not simply about passively receiving the thing of language (aesthetically experiencing it); it is *also* about actively (poetically) producing it. How can we produce language so that it does not merely refer to the world that lies behind it, but is capable, instead, of speaking its own world, the sign of its own being, of the faculty of language? How can we foster a language that would speak the supremely sayable experience of language itself? A language of infancy? And how can we – extending the argument to Agamben's political work – ultimately *live* in this way?

Indeed, if language, like art, falls within the domain of the human being's uncanny *technical* capacity to bring something from nonbeing into being, then Agamben's point about language is that it is a technical object that has become entirely forgotten – that has become eclipsed by the world that it attempts to name. Such a logic familiarizes language to the point where it risk disappearing. If Agamben's *political* point about art is that it risks subverting the *polis*, then the same goes for the art of language, for the technical object of language: it too risks subverting the *polis*; it too possesses an uncanny quality that poses a danger to politics. The precise way in which it does so requires some discussion, as I have shown; but the general point here is that this political potential of language has become forgotten. What I have analyzed here as Agamben's "thing" of language thus becomes connected not only to art, but also to art's uncanny, political dimension. Not as something that would be added onto art, but that would be marked by art as it is – "just/mere" art, but situated on the far side of what Agamben (after Benjamin) calls "bare/mere" life.

Vande Veire does not discuss language as such in his pamphlet, but the relations between Agamben's theory of art and his own are clear. Like Vande Veire, Agamben also involves criticism in the problem: in the introduction to his book *Stanzas*, he calls for a criticism that would be able to expose the thing of language,[63] and one could argue that Agamben's own writing intends precisely to pull off this feat (in this, his work comes remarkably close to that of Benjamin, whose writing realizes something similar). Like Vande Veire, Agamben is highly skeptical of the "I Love Art" attitude that prevails in an art world that promotes an art for the spectator as opposed to an art for artists, and has produced the figure of the self-absorbed artist. In such a world, art's aesthetic and political crisis has gone lost. It is this situation that both Vande Veire and Agamben criticize. The originality of Agamben's work is marked by the site where he finds this crisis: in language's infancy, in the supremely sayable "thing" of language. His first answer to this situation is neither silence nor speech but the faculty of language. It is only in a second moment that a poetry of such a faculty can be produced.

Reading Politics

By now, readers familiar with Sontag's work will have guessed why I included a brief discussion of Robbins's critique of Sontag above. Indeed, Sontag's classic essay "Against Interpretation" resonates, one could argue, with Agamben's work and articulates several of the concerns I raised above as a practice of reading – a political practice of reading (though I am not convinced Sontag grasps what she is saying in this way – ultimately, she insists on an "erotics of art," thus establishing the connection between the issue of reading/interpretation *and* art that I have also tried to draw out here).[64] Consider, however, what Sontag has to say about interpretation: "a conscious act of the mind which illustrates a certain code, certain 'rules' of interpretation,"[65] interpretation "erected another meaning on top of the literal one" ("old style") or "excavates, destroys; it digs 'behind' the text, to find a sub-text which is the true one" ("modern style").[66] She associates the work of both Marx and Freud with these logics. In Freud's work, to which I will return in the following chapters, "[a]ll observable phenomena are bracketed … as *manifest* content. This manifest content must be probed and pushed aside to find the true meaning – the *latent* content – beneath"; "individual lives … are treated as occasions for interpretation."[67] In Marx, the same happens with "social events like revolutions and wars."[68] For Sontag, however, the "merit" of literary works, and of art in general, "certainly lies elsewhere than in their 'meanings.'"[69] "What matters in [Alain Resnais's film] *Marienbad* is the pure, untranslatable, sensuous immediacy of some of its images, and its rigorous if narrow solutions to certain problems of cinematic form."[70] In other words: *Marienbad* does not say anything other than what it says; interpretation does not do justice to it. The "modern" way of "understanding something … is based on the highly dubious theory that a work of art is composed of items of content."[71] But this approach "violates art," Sontag argues; "it makes art into an article for use, for arrangement into a mental scheme of categories."[72]

Although it ultimately does not go quite as far, Sontag's criticism of interpretation can be brought in line with Agamben's experiment of language, and with its political articulation, in particular the critique of biopolitics that I have discussed above. Indeed, one might consider "interpretation" to be the mode of operation of modern politics, which is always on the look-out for some kind of latent content behind the manifest appearance.[73] One's mere life is never enough; instead, some kind of surplus, symbolic identity must be added to it in order for one to become part of the political community. Ultimately, this means that life is always at risk of being considered a surplus, *not* enough, a *left-over*. While Sontag's argument leads in this direction, her ultimate plea for an "erotics" of art risks ultimately focusing too much on the vulgar, material side of language – whereas Agamben, of course, is interested in infancy rather than the vulgar, material side of language (an approach that entails its own understanding of "eros").[74]

It is through his work on language, now closely tied to his work on aesthetics – and specifically through his focus on the supremely sayable thing of language as the interruption of the theory of signification – that Agamben exposes an ethical and ultimately political problem in the treatment of life. Life tends to be treated "like" language, specifically in the way in which language is treated in signifying theory. Ethically and politically, one's mere life is never enough; instead, some kind of surplus or symbolic identity must be added to it in order for one to become part of the community. Ultimately, this means that life is always at risk of being considered a surplus, not enough, a left-over. It means, for Agamben, that "community" is continuously in the process of being reduced to "society," as he indicates in a short text titled "Tiananmen." Part of his positive political project – which is intimately aesthetic and linguistic, as should by now be clear – is to pave the way for the community that is coming: the community of just being, just language, just art.

It is perhaps for this reason that Agamben develops a fondness for the left-over, for what remains, in his work, as the basis from where the coming community can be thought. For to love what is left over, to love what remains would be one way of working through the pernicious interpretative and political logic by which something is always separated from what it is.[75] Such a separation produces, inevitably, a left-over, which tends to be valued as less. In other words, in order to be valued as more, one tends to pay a very high price: the virtual reality of being potentially valued less.[76]

More recently, Jacques Rancière has in his work on the politics of aesthetics challenged the work of Sigmund Freud, which operates – as Sontag already laid bare – according to a vertical logic that always assumes a hierarchy, a relation of a superstructure to a substratum, a position of mastery. In an interview with Gabriel Rockhill (to which I will return in Chapter 3), Rancière explains that he has always tried to work against such a logic.[77] His work resonates, in this respect at least, with that of Agamben. Of course, both Sontag and Rancière could not be more different from Agamben as far as their politics goes, in the sense that both have a much more active understanding of politics than Agamben. Agamben's political hero – or anti-hero – is Herman Melville's scrivener Bartleby: a passive, disengaged character who troubles his employer and colleagues at a Wall Street law office through his preference not to execute any and all tasks that are assigned to him. Bartleby's politics resonates with Agamben's call to leave the US in response to a new visa regulation; it is a politics of withdrawal, that does not really call on one to positively act. Compare and contrast this to Sontag, who urges her readers to get politically engaged in Bosnia; or to Rancière, who always locates politics in a subjective challenge to the distribution of the sensible – in a kind of blasphemous, impossible political act combining two worlds into one.

It may be, as I will suggest in the second part of this book, that Agamben's choice for a politics of passive withdrawal as resistance is a left-over of the Italian political critique of work, associated with the writings of contemporary theorists and activists such as Franco "Bifo" Berardi. Berardi speaks in his work of a politics of exhaustion in the face of the pressures of contemporary life, which aims to put human beings to work all the time, regardless of the fact that machines should have opened up more leisure time, more time for play, education, art-making.[78] It is here that Agamben's politics of potentiality, and specifically of a potentiality that would not immediately flip over into actuality (what he calls "a potentiality not-to"), becomes evident – and that, as a consequence, the greatest challenge to my presentation of his "positive politics" as a technique of the self emerges. For how can such a politics of passive resistance ever be part of a positive politics of the self?

A similar conundrum arises in Foucault's essay "What is Enlightenment?," where Foucault, in a section where he attempts to articulate positively what the stakes of the Enlightenment project are, ends up saying it has to do with the capacity to "no longer be, do, or think, what we are, do or think" (I will turn to

Foucault's essay in Chapter 5; but it should be noted that none of these imperatives sound particularly "positive" at first sight). The task is, in other words, to be, do, or think "otherwise," that is: to break with the actualizations of being, doing, or thinking through which we are governed. For Foucault, such a task is ultimately linked to a reconstructive project, to a project of rebuilding – through partial transformations – the self. It is about regaining a certain degree of sovereignty over oneself so as to ultimately also begin to transform larger sovereign structures, such as the ones that can be found in politics. As I argue throughout this book, I consider this to be the project of Agamben's work as well (and his most recent publications have started to develop this more clearly): although Agamben develops a strong, and violent even, critique of sovereignty, the task that he ultimately poses to his readers is not to destroy it – he is quite explicit on this count. Instead, it is to begin to practice it otherwise, beyond the logic of exception that his work associated not only with biopolitics, but also with certain practices of language, and of reading and inter-pretation – in the aesthetico-political space of their *désoeuvrement* (I will return to this term in Chapters 6 and 8). If this risks leading away from what many perceive to be Agamben's radical politics, I show in the final chapter of this book that such a politics is not incompatible with Agamben's hero, Bartleby – more specifically with Melville's story "Bartleby," whose politics does not exactly coincide, of course, with that of the actual scrivener: otherwise there would most likely not have been a story at all.

Notes

1   See Agamben, *B*, for an unauthorized English translation.

2 Further proof for this claim is provided by Agamben's later essay "What is an Apparatus?," to which I turn in Chapter 5.

3 See Robbins, "Comparative."

4 See Arendt, *Eichmann*.

5 See Derrida, *Dissemination*.

6 This double dynamic is characteristic of the Enlightenment. As will become clear, I am partly rethinking Agamben's work here through the lens of Michel Foucault's essay on the Enlightenment, titled "What is Enlightenment?" My suggestion, developed at length in Chapter 5, is not only that Foucault's essay is crucial for our time, but also that it can help readers appreciate the contemporary stakes of Agamben's work.

7 The most pertinent reference is perhaps Stiegler's book *Ce qui fait que la vie vaut la peine d'être vécue: De la pharmacologie*.

8 Castells, *Communication Power*.

9 On this count, Agamben and one of his other influences, Michel Foucault, could not be further apart. For Foucault, also a thinker of the apparatus, the question of technology sounds decidedly different. Consider, for example, Foucault's text "What is Enlightenment?," in which he asks: "How can the growth of capabilities be disconnected from the intensification of power relations?" (Foucault, *Politics*, 116). This question inscribes technology into a dynamic, rather than identifying it with the logic of the camp.

10 Robbins, "Internationalism." For Sontag's essay, see Sontag, "'There' and 'Here.'" Sontag's title is a reference to a film by Jean-Luc Godard, to whom I turn in Chapter 3.

11 Sontag qtd. Robbins, "Internationalism," 11.

12 Sontag qtd. ibid., 13.

13 Sontag qtd. ibid., 12.

14 Robbins, "Internationalism," 13.

15 Agamben raises this very question – about whether there really is an elsewhere where one might go – in an interview with the French journal *Vacarme*, stating that for him, "it's a question of thinking a flight which would not imply evasion: a movement on the spot, in the situation itself" (Smith, "'I am sure,'" 121). In view of this theoretical position, Agamben's actual decision to flee the US becomes all the more troubling.

16 For a detailed discussion of Benjamin's essay, including the notion of educative violence, see Chapter 2.

17 More recently, some of these questions have been revitalized in the debates about the Boycott, Divestment and Sanctions (BDS) movement against

Israel, and its support by the American Studies Association. Robbins was involved in this as well.

18 Agamben, *HS*, 3. Here too, no reference is given. Jeffrey Nealon solved the mystery of this attribution for me in a brilliant footnote to his book *Plant Theory: Biopower and Vegetable Life*, where he indicates that this quote from Foucault exists only as quoted in Hubert Dreyfus and Paul Rabinow's *Michel Foucault: Beyond Structuralism and Hermeneutics* (Chicago: University of Chicago Press, 1982). Nealon shows that Agamben's Italian reveals he is translating the Foucault quote from the French translation of Dreyfus and Rabinow's book (Nealon, *Plant Theory*, 127–8).

19 Agamben, *O*, 26.

20 See Chapter 2.

21 My reading of Yann Martel's novel *Life of Pi* draws out exactly these issues. See Boever, *States of Exception*, ch. 1.

22 See Agamben, *B*.

23 This book includes a version of Chapter 2.

24 I have developed this point at some length in my review of William Watkin's *The Literary Agamben*.

25 Watkin's excellent second book on Agamben, *Agamben and Indifference: A Critical Overview*, instead takes into account the full, comparative perspective of Agamben's thought.

26 Alex Murray makes the same point in his *Giorgio Agamben*, 2, 4.

27 Other references that could be mobilized here to characterize such a power of life are the work of Friedrich Nietzsche and Gilles Deleuze. In *Bíos: Biopolitics and Philosophy*, Esposito develops the notion of "affirmative biopolitics" in a brilliant chapter on Nietzsche's philosophy. Like Timothy Campbell, who doesn't quite arrive at articulating this dimension of Agamben's work in his book *Improper Life: Technology and Biopolitics from Heidegger to Agamben*, I see a connection between such an affirmative biopolitics, or power of life, and Michel Foucault's late work on the aesthetico-ethical techniques of the self – on the so-called care of the self. As I argue in Chapter 5, I consider Foucault to have developed his thoughts on the care of the self in direct response to his critique of biopolitics (see also Boever, *Narrative Care: Biopolitics and the Novel*). In the volume from his history of sexuality titled *The Care of the Self*, Foucault theorizes a technique of the self, a biotechnics or technique *of* life (a "techne tou biou"), *against* the power *over* life that he criticized in an earlier stage of his work. If it has taken us many years to see this connection, it is now time to also consider how this connection can inform our reading of Agamben's

work. Agamben's recent book *The Highest Poverty: Monastic Rules and Form-Of-Life*, confirms the validity of such a project.

28 Alex Murray is one of the only Agamben scholars to have commented on it. See Murray, *Giorgio Agamben*, 74–5.

29 I have not yet seen her argument on biopolitics in print; Malabou has been presenting it in recent public lectures, some of which I'll rely on for this book.

30 Jodi Dean's recent account of Agamben's politics in *Blog Theory* confirms this suggestion.

31 In Chapter 2, I will expand this discussion by considering a chapter from his book *Stanzas*, titled "Oedipus and the Sphinx."

32 See Agamben, *MWC*. Agamben calls there for a "destruction of aesthetics" (ibid., 6).

33 Murray notes that in Agamben's theory of language, there is a "general aesthetic" at work to which "Agamben often gives the name 'poetics'" (Murray, *Giorgio Agamben*, 78). I am trying to distinguish aesthetics and poetics in my approach to Agamben's thought because a separation of these terms will enable me to more precisely assess its different political moments.

34 I use the word "distribution" here in loose reference to the work of Jacques Rancière, and his oft-used phrase "the distribution of the sensible." I will return to the difference between Rancière's and Agamben's work at the end of this chapter, as well as in several of the other chapters in this book.

35 That the political issue is ultimately one of communication, of reading and interpretation, and possibly also of translation (as I will discuss in Chapter 3), is in a way already clear because of the centrality that Agamben accords to tattooing in his text in *Le Monde*. The tattoo evokes a story that is central to Agamben's oeuvre, and that many scholars have discussed in relation to it, namely Franz Kafka's "In the Penal Colony." In this story, a condemned man is set to have his sentence – which he does not know or understand – tattooed on his body by an extraordinary machine ("a remarkable piece of apparatus") that is designed to administer justice. There is no need for the condemned person to be able to read his sentence; instead, "he'll learn it on his body." Through the punishment of the torture, the condemned man's life comes to gradually coincide with the law that is being tattooed onto it; it becomes identical to the sentence that it is supposed to live by, there no longer is any difference between life and the law. The problem is, of course, that this moment of identification of life and law is also the moment of death: the condemned man will die once his sentence has been

accomplished. The story can be read as an allegory for biopower's attempt to turn life into communication – at which point biopolitics turns into thanatopolitics. Agamben's project, insofar as it involves the body, aims for precisely the opposite: he aspires to a world in which bodies would be their own signs, and would mean nothing other than what they are – just bodies. When we are making this point about the body, we obviously already find ourselves in the realm of biopolitics; but given that the problem is one of communication, it will be necessary to articulate this point in the realm of language, and of reading and interpretation, as well.

36 Agamben, *IH*, 3.

37 Ibid., 4.

38 Ibid.

39 Ibid.

40 Ibid.

41 In his excursus on the politics of dance in *Power of Life*, Kishik summarizes this position with Spinoza's insistence on "what the body can do" (Spinoza qtd. Kishik, *Power of Life*, 32).

42 One could argue that being valued politically for the simple fact of being alive would not resolve this issue, since "life" itself could be considered as a symbolic value that is added to the body, dead *or* alive. Indeed, it is very clear from the opening pages of *Homo Sacer* that Agamben starts with life; but ultimately, as Benjamin already suggested in his "Theses on the Philosophy of History," it may be that we need to be valued *as dead* first in order for the politics that Agamben criticizes to be dismantled. It is, perhaps, from this perspective that the veneration of the dead can be understood not as a sacralization but precisely as a critique of the politics of sacrality that Agamben criticizes. As we know well, today not even the dead are safe.

43 See Cooper, *Life as Surplus*.

44 And it is important to point out here that just being is not necessarily "being alive," which risks adding another symbolic identity ("alive") to mere being. In the perspective that I am developing here, "being dead" is on the same plane as "being alive," with "dead" being merely a symbolic identity added to just being. Agamben's discussion of nudity, to which I turn in Chapter 3, needs to be understood in this context.

45 As Alex Murray has explained, "gesture" in Agamben's work functions as a third term next to both a unity of gestures, and Agamben's argument that the unity of gestures has gone lost. Thus, it takes up a position similar to infancy, which functions as a third term next to speech (unity of gestures)

and silence (loss of unity). This is why Murray can conclude that "gesture is the process of making a means visible as such" (Murray, *Giorgio Agamben*, 87), in the same way that "infancy" makes language as such visible, in its mediation.

46 Bringing together the linguistic and political stakes in a single term, Connal Parsley has helpfully characterized this position as "post-representational" (Parsley, "'A Particular Fetishism,'" 43).

47 In spite of what the English title suggests, the pamphlet was written in Dutch (Flemish) and to my knowledge it has not been translated into English. As Dirk Pülltau in his short introduction to Vande Veire's follow-up text explains, the version that was published in *De Morgen* in August 2003 was a shorter version of the full text that had appeared several months earlier in two other journals (*HTV* and *Yang*) and was published again in October 2003 in the journal *Kunstbeeld*. The original pamphlet is available at: <http://www.network54.com/Forum/113844/thread/1054633068/last-1061224920/I+Love+Art---+Een+pamflet+over+de+kunstwereld>. For the follow-up text, see <http://www.dewitteraaf.be/artikel/detail/nl/2725>. All quotations are taken from these sources; all translations are mine.

48 This ideology of wakefulness characterizes the history of capitalism as well. See Reiss, "Sleep's Hidden Histories."

49 Adorno, *Prisms*, 34.

50 Adorno, "Commitment," 188.

51 Ibid.

52 Freud, "The 'Uncanny.'"

53 The term needs to be used with some caution, as I pointed out earlier.

54 Agamben, *MWC*, 2.

55 Ibid.

56 Ibid.

57 Ibid., 3–4.

58 Ibid., 4.

59 With Sophocles' description of the human being's technical capacity – her or his uncanny ability to bring something from nonbeing into being – we are decidedly within the dynamic of what Jacques Derrida has called the "pharmakon," a cure that can also be poisoning.

60 In a recent text on aesthetics, Bernard Stiegler has argued something similar with respect to our aesthetic judgments (he discusses Kant's *Critique of Judgment* in this context – his take on it is much more positive than Nietzsche's or Agamben's) which, as he sees it, are reduced to the "merely

interesting." My translation of Stiegler's text is available at: <http://www.lanaturnerjournal.com/essays/prolsensestiegler.html>.

61 Agamben, *MWC*, 5.

62 Ibid., 7.

63 See Agamben, *S*, xv–xix.

64 Sontag, *Against Interpretation*, 3–14. Others have also noted Agamben's critical relation to interpretation: Murray, *Giorgio Agamben*, 113.

65 Sontag, *Against Interpretation*, 5.

66 Ibid., 6.

67 Ibid., 7.

68 Ibid.

69 Ibid., 9.

70 Ibid.

71 Ibid., 10.

72 Ibid.

73 Of course, what is being mobilized in this paragraph as "interpretation" is only one "interpretation" of the term. It would need to be distinguished, for example, from the interpretation of interpretation that is put forward in Santiago Zabala's work on hermeneutics, where interpretation is theorized precisely at a distance from metaphysical truth, as one interpretation among many that must nevertheless be risked. See Zabala and Vattimo, *Hermeneutic Communism*. I ultimately think of Zabala's project with interpretation as being quite similar to my own project with sovereignty: in both instances, there is an attempt to "unwork" the theologico-political dimensions of these notions in order to put forward a plural, plastic understanding of the two as form-giving, -receiving, and -exploding.

74 Connal Parsley has commented on the role of "eros" in Agamben's work and linked it to infancy and the experience of "language itself" (Parsley, "'A Particular Fetishism,'" 33). The main philosophical problem with Sontag is that her text, which sets out as a deconstruction of the form/content distinction, ultimately comes down on the side of form *at the cost of* content (she praises abstract painting in the essay for being "without content"). Interpretation, and the sovereign mastery that it brings, thus goes out the window entirely, but paradoxically through a reproduction of the very logic of representational sovereignty. To plastically deconstruct the ontological distinction between form/matter (which is mirrored by the linguistic form/content distinction), however, would mean to think form as matter – to think form as content (in Sontag's terms), post-representationally. Such form-as-content is not necessarily entirely without

interpretation, in the same way that (I argue in this book) form-as-matter is not necessarily entirely without sovereignty. Indeed, there are very good reasons to hold on to some degree of interpretation/sovereignty – but practiced otherwise. I would therefore argue that Sontag is giving up too much in her criticism of interpretation, in the same way that Agamben – and others working in his tracks – risks giving up too much in his criticism of sovereignty. Interestingly, Agamben does not give up on interpretation; in fact, his work promotes interpretation – a certain kind of interpreta-tion – as a form of writing theory today. Analogously, I ask in this book whether the same project is possible with sovereignty.

75 Indeed, there is arguably a shift in Agamben's work from what one could call an "apocalyptic" concern with "ends" – for example, the end of art in the modern era in *The Man Without Content* – to a concern with "remains" in later works such as *Remnants of Auschwitz* and *The Time That Remains*. Although the notion of the remnant recalls, of course, Friedrich Hölderlin's line, quoted by Agamben, that "what remains, the poets establish," there is thus also an emphatically political dimension to Agamben's interest in the remains.

76 It would not take too much of an effort to connect many of modern times' psychopathologies – depression, to name just one – to this logic.

77 Rockhill, "Janus-Face," 49.

78 See Berardi, *Precarious Rhapsody*.

2

The Divine Violence of Storytelling

Setting the Scene

In his essay "The Work of Art in the Age of Mechanical Reproduction," Walter Benjamin famously reflects on how technological developments have affected the work of art and our understanding of it. Recalling Paul Valéry's prophetic statement that "*[w]e must expect great innovations to transform the entire technique of the arts, thereby affecting artistic invention itself and perhaps even bringing about an amazing change in our very notion of art,*"[1] Benjamin begins by describing the historical era that was opened up by the development of lithography, which led to the illustrated newspaper, and photography, which foreshadowed the birth of sound film. Although one senses Benjamin's excitement about these developments, he is also quick to note that "[e]ven the most perfect reproduction of a work of art is lacking in one element":[2] uniqueness, originality, authenticity. "One might subsume the eliminated element in the term 'aura,'" he writes a little later: "that which withers in the age of mechanical reproduction is the aura of the work of art."[3] As many of Benjamin's texts, the "Work of Art" essay thus oscillates between excitement and nostalgia in its analysis of the developments of modern times.

77

Benjamin's essay has been criticized by artists and theorists alike. One artist whose work is often discussed in this context is the Canadian photographer Jeff Wall. As a photographer who mounts his large-scale photographs as transparencies in light-boxes, Wall appears to participate in *both* the modern history of reproducibility that Benjamin analyzes *and* the history of the auratic work of art that Benjamin opposes to it, thus drawing Benjamin's opposition of the two into question.

The "Work of Art" essay is by no means the only one of Benjamin's essays that resonates with Wall's work. Wall also has a photograph titled "The Storyteller" that recalls Benjamin's essay "The Storyteller: Observations on the Works of Nikolai Leskov." In "The Storyteller" as in the "Work of Art" essay, Benjamin begins with a brief characterization of modern times, in this case the period after the First World War. Here too, it appears that something has gone lost:

> Less and less frequently do we encounter people with the *ability* to tell a tale properly. More and more often there is embarrassment all around when the wish to hear a story is expressed. It is as if something that seemed inalienable to us, the securest among our possessions, were taken from us: the *ability* to exchange experiences. [emphases mine][4]

Like the aura, storytelling has "withered" in modern times, and although the essay reveals some genuine excitement about modern developments such as the newspaper and the novel, there is also plenty of nostalgia here for the premodern times of the story.

As I mentioned in the previous chapter, Agamben takes Benjamin's observation about the modern destruction of experience as the starting point for his book *Infancy and History*.

His argument (laid out in the preface to that book) about experimenting with language ultimately leads here, to this understanding of storytelling as the exchange of experiences. However, by "the exchange of experiences," Agamben is clearly not referring to a "report" on or even an actual "story" about things that may have happened to us. Instead, he has in mind the experience of what he calls the *thing* of language: "not something ineffable but something superlatively sayable,"[5] our very capacity for speaking itself (our potentiality not-to-speak). His reference to "The Storyteller" suggests that he considers the story to be capable of passing on this particular experience, and Benjamin's focus on the "ability" to tell a story rather than on the story or even storytelling itself indeed seems to lead in this direction. In the previous chapter, I proposed to theorize this particular issue as an aesthetic issue that takes precedence over the story and storytelling, which properly speaking belong in the realm of poetics.

But how can the story pass on such an experience? And how might such an understanding of the story relate to Agamben's political work? If the story is generally understood as a poetic phenomenon, what might it mean to theorize it as an aesthetic, and ultimately an aesthetico-political phenomenon? These are the questions I propose to address in this chapter, starting from Benjamin's at first sight un-political essay.

When Wall states that his work "The Storyteller" expresses "the historical crisis of the Native peoples of Canada, whose traditions of oral history have been eroded by modern life,"[6] Benjamin's essay resonates in this statement. As with the "Work of Art" essay, however, Wall's relation to "The Storyteller" is ambiguous: photography is obviously part and parcel of the modern developments that are responsible for the erosion of oral history. Wall's photograph may be said to reflect on this through its silent representation of a scene of storytelling that is presumably vocal: although the photograph seeks to make the storyteller speak, it simultaneously silences the storyteller through its medium.

However, it seems that yet another reading is possible. In between the options of either an image that silences, or an image that captures the ability to tell a story – a potentiality on the brink of actualization, of speech – Wall's image could arguably also capture neither a loss of potentiality (storytelling is no longer possible; negative) nor a potentiality that would automatically flip over into actuality (storytelling is still possible; positive), but a potentiality (neither negative nor positive) not-to tell a story. A pure potentiality of storytelling, a pure ability – without an actual story to come with it. What if Benjamin, in his essay on storytelling, was not interested in either the negative or the positive possibilities of storytelling, but in this pure potentiality of storytelling and its communication – in the exchange of this particular ability, and the particular kind of silence that it would require one to speak? The reading of Wall's image as expressing the erosion of the storytelling traditions of the Native peoples of Canada (and the call for restoring these traditions to speech) is one kind of politics that one may find in his photograph; but what about this other, aesthetic politics of pure potentiality that the image arguably also carries within it?

In what follows, I pursue this project by reading Benjamin's "The Storyteller" next to one of his more explicitly political texts, "Critique of Violence," a foundational text for Agamben's thought. Although these two texts at first sight have very little in common, I will expose their intimate connections in order to sketch out Benjamin's aesthetico-political conception of storytelling. Though Benjamin's and Agamben's conceptions of the story will also turn out to be different, it is by way of Benjamin that I approach Agamben's aesthetico-political theory of the story, as one that is in line with his theory of language. Along the way, I will take into consideration a number of other interlocutors who will further enable me to sketch out the politics of aesthetics that is linked to the plastic sovereignty I theorize in this book.

Divine Violence and Storytelling

Benjamin's essay "Critique of Violence" is a foundational text for Agamben's study of sovereign power because it lays bare the link between violence and law that is so important for Agamben's critical project. As Agamben observes, Benjamin understands this link as a dialectical oscillation between the violence that posits the law (the violence associated with a foundational figure) and the violence that preserves it (the violence of the police, for example). The aim of Benjamin's essay is to propose a third figure that would break the circularity of this dialectic: divine violence or pure violence. Agamben finds Benjamin's essay problematic, however, in that it leaves this figure largely undefined, suggesting even that it can't be recognized in the concrete case. Benjamin concentrates instead on the bearer of the link between violence and the law, bare life.[7] All the more surprising, then, that Agamben's own work also largely leaves it unclear as to what form the divine violence that constitutes an alternative to the problems of modern sovereignty should take. What would be an example of an act of divine violence? How should one understand divine violence to break the circular dialectic between law-founding and law-preserving violence? And what remains of sovereignty and law after this break has been achieved? I argue that Benjamin's and Agamben's theories of storytelling provide a surprising way into this problematic.

"What is certain [about divine violence]," Agamben writes in *Homo Sacer: Sovereign Power and Bare Life*, "is only that it neither posits or preserves law, but rather 'de-poses' (*entsetzt*) it."[8] The break between law-positing and law-preserving violence that divine violence achieves, creates a zone of indistinction between the two and introduces a politics liberated from the law. The importance of this theoretical insight can be better appreciated when it is considered in the context of the debate between Benjamin and Carl Schmitt. As Agamben explains in *State of Exception*, whereas Benjamin in "Critique of Violence" is interested in an anomic type of violence that breaks the dialectic between law-positing and law-preserving violence, Schmitt could not tolerate the possibility of such a politics outside the law.[9] In *Political Theology*, he uses the device of the state of exception to bring divine violence within the legal order, defining the sovereign as "he who decides on the state of exception." Following Samuel Weber, Agamben reads Benjamin's *Origin of German Tragic Drama* to be a literary critical response to Schmitt's conservative move.[10] Benjamin restates there his theory of divine violence and proposes a theory of sovereign power as the impossibility to decide.

Whereas Schmitt's sovereignty – the power to decide on the state of exception – *confirms* the difference between law-positing and law-preserving violence by creating a zone of indistinction between them (namely the state of exception), Benjamin's divine violence creates a "real" state of exception that *does not* leave the difference between these two kinds of violence intact.

Schmitt's sovereignty confirms the dialectic between violence and the law; Benjamin's divine violence *breaks* with it. For his theory of sovereign power, Agamben is indebted to Schmitt. But when it comes to formulating political responses to the problems of modern sovereignty, he turns to Benjamin. *State of Exception* shows him trying to theorize an anomic violence that would end the "lasting eclipse" that politics has suffered through its (Schmittian) contamination by the law. By calling for a break between law-positing and law-preserving violence, Agamben wants to end the ways in which politics has been "seeing itself, at best, as constituent power … , when it is not merely the power to negotiate with the law." "The only truly political action," he continues, "is that which severs the nexus between violence and law."[11] Divine violence is able to achieve this.

At this point, although I will have to come back to this in detail in the final part of this book, it seems that Agamben wants to liberate politics from the law by dismantling the device of the state of exception through which Schmitt brought politics within the legal order (paradoxically, as the power to suspend it). However, a number of important matters still remain unclear. What would constitute an act of divine violence? In what sense would such an act be divine? In what sense would it be violent? How does divine violence break with the dialectic between violence and the law? Agamben observes that it "de-poses" it. Does that mean that it destroys it? What remains of sovereignty and law after divine violence has passed through town? These questions go to the heart of the debates about sovereignty that I opened up in my Prologue.

Benjamin's interest in Schmitt is always judged as scandalous. In *State of Exception*, Agamben turns the scandal around, and argues that Schmitt's *Political Theology* was written in response to "Critique of Violence." He also shows that "the decisive document in the Benjamin–Schmitt dossier is certainly the eighth thesis on the concept of history, composed by Benjamin a few months before his death."[12] (The eighth thesis is the one where Benjamin speaks of a "real" state of exception that would break the dialectic of law-positing and law-preserving violence, as opposed to Schmitt's state of exception, which only confirms it.) In other words: both Benjamin's early writings – the texts written during the 1920s – and very last ones – those written only a few months before his death – can be read as documents in the Benjamin–Schmitt debate.

What interests Agamben is how this debate and the position Benjamin took up in it were anticipated in Benjamin's work before 1921 and elaborated in the texts he wrote between 1921 and 1940.[13] I do not mean to reduce all of Benjamin's thought to his disagreement with Schmitt; but rather than stating that Schmitt suddenly reappears in Benjamin's thought in 1940, my premise would be that he is latently present in the work that was done between 1921 and 1940, and that reading Benjamin's work of this period through this lens can give us an insight into the aesthetic dimensions of divine violence.

Rather than looking at the essays on language as such or translation that would easily lend themselves to such a reading because of the closeness of the concept of pure language that they propose to what Benjamin calls divine violence or pure violence, I will focus on a less likely candidate, Benjamin's essay "The Storyteller." I want to propose, quite simply, that Benjamin's theory of the story and of storytelling can be read as an elaboration of the figure of divine violence. Considering that Benjamin formulated his response to Schmitt's *Political Theology* in a book of literary criticism, it is not all that strange to assume that there would be a legal and political dimension to this literary-critical essay. Apart from the fact that law and politics cannot have been too far from Benjamin's mind when he was writing the essay – "The Storyteller" was written in the 1930s, while Nazism was on the rise in Germany – Benjamin's "The Work of Art in the Age of Mechanical Reproduction" also reveals that Benjamin was thinking about the connection between art, law, and politics around the time when he was writing "The Storyteller."

But the presence of law and politics in "The Storyteller" exceeds the circumstantial. As commentators have pointed out, the essay begins by tracing back a loss of community – of the ability to share experiences through storytelling – to the events of the First World War.[14] This inscription of "The Storyteller" in the world war sets the tone for the essay. In order to understand the precise tone of the essay, one needs to turn to the German original, where it becomes clear that throughout the essay, Benjamin associates what he calls the story and storytelling with the words "recht" (law, justice, right) and "Freiheit" (freedom). These words add an emphatic legal and political dimension to the text. On the first page of the essay, for example, when Benjamin writes that "one meets fewer and fewer people who know how to tell a tale properly," the German word for "properly" is "*recht*schaffen [emphasis mine, as in the following]."[15] A couple of pages later, he writes:

> It is half the art of storytelling to keep a story free [*freizuhalten*] from explanation as one recounts it. … [In a story,] the most extraordinary things, marvelous things, are related with the greatest accuracy, but the psychological events are not forced on the reader. It is left up to him to interpret things the way he understands them.[16]

In the German, this last sentence reads: "Es ist ihm *frei*gestellt sich die Sache zu*recht*zulegen."[17] Sentences like this can be found throughout the text, whenever Benjamin is trying to define what he means by the story and storytelling. The legal and political dimension to the story and storytelling, even if not stated in the text directly, nevertheless becomes visible in the very fabric of its writing (in its *text*, from the Latin "texere," to weave).

The essay's obsession with law and politics becomes perhaps most explicit in a passage in which Benjamin tries to capture the difference between the fairy tale, which he offers as a prime example of what he means by the story, and myth, which in the essay he associates with law:

> In the figure of the fool it [the fairy tale] shows how mankind "acts dumb" toward myth; in the figure of the youngest brother, it shows how one's chances increase as the mythical primordial time is left behind; in the figure of the youth who sets out to learn what fear is, it shows us that the things we are afraid of can be seen through; in the figure of the wiseacre, it shows us that the questions posed by myth are simple-minded, like the riddle of the Sphinx; in the shape of the animals which come to the aid of the child in the fairy tale, it shows that nature not only is subservient to myth, but much prefers to be aligned with man. The wisest thing – so the fairy tale taught mankind in olden times and teaches children to this day – is to meet the forces of the mythical world with cunning and with high spirits.[18]

Benjamin's theorization of the story and storytelling takes on a revolutionary dimension as Benjamin lists the ways in which the fairy tale liberates mankind from myth. Considering the world-historical events that Benjamin is witnessing around the time when he is writing, it is difficult not to read this passage as a political passage. But if Benjamin associates myth with law and is trying to describe the story's political work on mythical law, how are we to understand this work exactly? What does the story do to law? What remains of law in the story? These questions seem crucial, given the law's difficult place in the state of exception. To address them, I now turn to "Critique of Violence."

That there is a relation between the politics of "The Storyteller" and "Critique of Violence" becomes clear when one begins to compare the conceptual framework of the two essays. "The Storyteller" begins by opposing the story to the novel, which is associated with modern, secular times. The opposition revolves around the terms "voice" (as opposed to "book"), "counsel" (unlike the story, the novel is devoid of counsel), and "explanation" (the story is free from explanation).[19] Later in the essay, Benjamin introduces a third form of textual production that is also opposed to the story: information. This time, the opposition revolves around the term "verifiability." Information is incompatible with storytelling because it "must absolutely sound plausible." The story, on the other hand, is "intelligence that came from afar."[20] What interests me is that the particularity of the story and of storytelling only really gets articulated through the story's opposition to myth, associated by Benjamin with primitive times. It is here that the essay's association of the story with "recht" and "Freiheit" becomes most explicit. Benjamin speaks of the "liberating magic" of the story and argues that the story "tells us of the earliest arrangements that mankind made to shake off the nightmare which myth had placed upon its chest."[21] In another section of the essay, he refers to the characters in a story as "righteous" figures that are "magically escaped."[22]

"Critique of Violence" also begins with a set of oppositions: in the first instance, between means and ends, natural law and positive law, sanctioned and unsanctioned violence; then, more importantly, between violence's law-positing and law-preserving function.[23] All of this leads – via Benjamin's discussion of two different kinds of strike – into the final opposition to which all of these previous oppositions amount, namely that between mythical violence and divine violence. Although myth is first introduced in the essay as a violence that would escape the oppositions that "Critique of Violence" sets up, it eventually turns out to be "closely related, indeed identical, to lawmaking violence."[24] "Far from inaugurating a purer sphere, the mythic manifestation of immediate violence shows itself fundamentally identical with all legal violence."[25] This is why the essay ends by proposing a "real" third figure that would break the dialectic between law-positing and law-preserving violence (or, as we can now also say, the dialectic of myth): divine violence. It is with divine violence that Benjamin is able at last to make the leap that myth in the essay was introduced to make but ultimately could not.

In both essays, Benjamin's opponent is myth. In opposition to myth, which is Benjamin's name for the various dialectics between the opposite terms that the essays list, each essay proposes a third figure that would break with these dialectics, by creating a "real" state of exception in which the difference between these oppositions would no longer exist. In "The Storyteller," this figure is the story or storytelling. In "Critique of Violence," it is divine violence. This reveals that Benjamin is ultimately not interested in "The Storyteller" in tracing out the differences between the story, the novel, and information. The essay is an attempt, instead, to theorize a mode of speaking/ writing that would exist beyond these differences and break the complicity of the story, the novel, or information with myth; in this sense, Benjamin's project here is very close to Agamben's work on infancy. It also reveals that with divine violence, Benjamin is interested in a non-violent violence, something like the violence of the story or storytelling, and its effects on myth. He is interested in a kind of "intelligence," as he puts it, a kind of "spirit" that would supersede the mythical dialectic of law-making. In the final sentence of "Critique of Violence," he characterizes divine violence as "die waltende" – mistranslated, as Agamben's reading of the essay would lead one to conclude,[26] as the "sovereign" violence.[27] "Mistranslated": unless Benjamin is rethinking the concept of sovereignty here without fully giving up on it.

Whereas a certain "sovereign" violence that Benjamin criticizes would reconfirm the mythical link that unites violence and law, the divine violence (sovereign, but otherwise?) that Benjamin calls for breaks with this dialectic in order to create a "real" state of exception in which the difference between law-positing and law-preserving violence would no longer exist. This break should not be conceived as destructive, but as the "waltende" violence that is afflicted by the non-violent violence of the story or storytelling. As I see it, this is a debate that takes place on the inside of sovereignty, rather than in the more comfortable zone of its outside.

The Riddle of the Sphinx

What is the relation of this understanding of the story and storytelling to community? Let me try to approach what is at stake in these questions again somewhat circuitously, through a comparative discussion of two types of literary communities proposed by, on the one hand, the German philosopher Peter

Sloterdijk, and (on the other) the French artist Sophie Calle. I am thinking specifically of Sloterdijk's reflection on literature and community in "*Rules for the Human Zoo*: A Response to the *Letter on Humanism*." "Books," Sloterdijk begins, "are thick letters to friends. With this phrase, [the poet Jean Paul] aptly articulated the quintessential nature and function of humanism: It is telecommunication in the medium of print to underwrite friendship."[28] Humanism – a highly suspect notion for Agamben – is a consequence of literacy. As a literary genre, philosophy has done nothing but produce letters to friends, letters that have been "reinscribed like a chain letter through the generations," ultimately producing community – or what the translator of Sloterdijk's essay calls, at the end of the first paragraph of the text, a "brotherhood."[29]

Implicitly echoing Benedict Anderson's work on this count,[30] Sloterdijk draws out literature's importance for nation-building. "At the heart of humanism so understood, we discover a cult or club fantasy: the dream of the portentous solidarity of those who have been chosen to be allowed to read."[31] This dream is transformed from the late eighteenth, throughout the nineteenth and into the twentieth (and twenty-first) centuries into a literary humanism of the nation-state: "Thus, the nation-state itself was to some extent a literary and postal product: the fiction of a fateful friendship with distant peoples and sympathetically united readers of bewitching common (or individual) authors."[32]

What happens to this community of the nation-state, Sloterdijk asks, in an age when humanism has come to an end "because the art of writing love-inspiring letters to a nation of friends, however professionally it is practiced, is no longer sufficient to form a telecommunicative bond between members of a modern mass society"?[33] What happens to this community in contemporary societies that are "clearly postliterary, post-epistolary, and thus posthumanistic"?[34] His questions echo not only Benjamin's discussion of the story, but also Agamben's discussion of language. Sloterdijk states his thesis as follows:

> modern societies can produce their political and cultural synthesis only marginally through literary, letter-writing, humanistic media.... New means of political-cultural telecom-munication have come into prominence ... The period when modern humanism was the model for schooling and education has passed, because it is no longer possible to retain the illusion that political and economic structures could be organized on the amiable model of literary societies.[35]

When Sloterdijk describes this situation as a "disillusionment,"[36] one wonders whether this word also reveals his own feelings about the situation.

Although there is clearly excitement in his essay about the development of new means of "political-cultural telecom-munication," Sloterdijk also sounds worried about the loss of community that they have brought. His essay thus recalls the essays by Benjamin I discussed earlier on. Indeed, when Sloterdijk closes with the image of letters that used to be mailed as "missives for possible friends" now turning into "archived things," and when he expresses the hope that "perhaps" some archivist "in the dead cellars of culture" will catch sight of "the long-ignored texts [that] begin to glimmer, as if a distant light flickers over them," one senses a desire on the author's part to return to an older, lost sense of community.[37]

Consider, as a point counter-point, another experiment of letter-writing that arguably incorporates some of these criticisms: the French artist Sophie Calle's work *Take Care of Yourself*. When Calle received a break-up letter that ended with the words "Take care of yourself," she started wondering what that imperative might mean. And so she sent the letter to over one hundred women, asking them to interpret it according to their professional activities. The responses she received were collected in the work *Take Care of Yourself*. In the case of Calle's work, we are also dealing with a literary community, a community that is constituted through the practice of letter-writing. Calle does not only write to women who were already her friends; she also contacts women whom she did not know before, thus forging relations with these unfamiliar women through letter-writing. One should note that whereas Sloterdijk talks about letters to friends, letters that are written out of love, and that invite loving, Calle is dealing with a break-up letter. It is a letter that does not *establish* a love relationship, but *ends* one. Sloterdijk might write positively about a letter that wants to establish a friendship; here, on the other hand, the letter asks Calle to be "just friends" (that dreaded formula!) – thus instituting a friendship that is decidedly less positive than the one that Sloterdijk has in mind. This means, importantly, that the community that Calle's work creates is established not so much around a positive content, but around an interruption. It breaks with the mythical conception of community that still circulates in Sloterdijk's writing.[38]

My argument here is that Agamben's understanding of the story, and of the communities it can found, is much closer to the understanding of community that can be found in Calle, than to the mythical understanding of community that still circulates in Sloterdijk. Nevertheless, Sloterdijk's work will still prove useful when, in a final movement, I try to tie a specific politics to these different positions.

To lay out this argument, let me return once more to Benjamin's "The Storyteller," and the fine difference between

Benjamin's and Agamben's theories of the story. As I noted earlier, Agamben finds it problematic that "Critique of Violence" leaves divine violence largely undefined. "The Storyteller" does make an attempt if not to define, then at least to capture the spirit of the story and storytelling. This is a risky undertaking – indeed, the essay is generally considered not to be Benjamin's strongest – and I would argue that this risk is also the risk of the politics of "recht" and "Freiheit" that Benjamin in his theorization of the story and storytelling is exploring. On the one hand, the story emerges in the essay as something homely, supportive, emancipating, nurturing, and illuminating (it brings counsel, for example). On the other, and at the same time, it is something much more unhomely, enigmatic, disturbing, subversive, and opaque (it is free from explanation). This tension is certainly not an unpolitical one, in the sense that it reflects a basic problem of the relation between "recht" and "Freiheit" that Benjamin is also writing about, with "recht" providing the (legal) home that the subject is looking for, and "Freiheit" marking the much more unhomely (political) quality that "recht" is supposed to realize.[39]

"The Storyteller" can be read as an attempt to negotiate this tension, as an essay in which Benjamin is constantly torn not just between the story and myth, but also between home and the unhomely, and between "recht" and "Freiheit." There is a certain point in the essay at which this negotiation fails, and Benjamin allows myth to slip back into his defense of the story and storytelling. This occurs in the political passage that I quoted above, where Benjamin characterizes the story and storytelling as what "shows us that the questions posed by myth are simple-minded, like the riddle of the Sphinx." The story and storytelling are aligned here with the mythical Oedipus, who in Sophocles' tragedy *King Oedipus* solves the riddle that plunges the Sphinx into the abyss. Because of the ways in which it inaugurates the incest–taboo, the tragedy is considered foundational for Western civilization. But in his book *Stanzas*, Agamben offers another reading of why the tragedy is foundational, and one that can be considered as an implicit critique of Benjamin's essay.

"The son of Laius resolves in the simplest way 'the enigma proposed by the ferocious jaws of the virgin,'" Agamben writes,

> showing the hidden meaning behind the enigmatic signifier, and, with this act alone, plunges the half-human, half-feral monster into the abyss. The liberating teaching of Oedipus is that what is uncanny and frightening in the enigma disappears as soon as its utterance is reduced to the transparency of the relation between the signified and its form, which the signified only apparently succeeds in escaping.[40]

For Benjamin, this is an example of the story and storytelling. For Agamben, it is an example of (what Benjamin calls) myth.[41] "The sin of Oedipus is not so much incest," he writes, "as it is hubris toward the power of the symbolic in general."[42] Oedipus is a civilizational hero – but an ambiguous one, as will be clear – because he makes us forget the original fracture between the signifier and the signified, the "/" that bars the signifier from the signified and turns language into something symbolic rather than diabolic. For Agamben, this bar marks a fracturing presence that is eclipsed by the "togetherness" of the sym-bolic. "From the point of view of signification," he writes, "metaphysics is nothing but the forgetting of the originary difference between signifier and signified."[43]

Agamben's reading of Oedipus and the Sphinx turns into an implicit critique of Benjamin when he develops his preference of the enigmatic Sphinx over and against the transparency that Oedipus brings, into a reflection on the story:

What the Sphinx proposed was not simply something whose signified is hidden and veiled under an "enigmatic" signifier, but a mode of speech in which the original fracture of presence was alluded to in the paradox of a word that approaches its object while keeping it indefinitely at a distance. The *ainos* (story, fable) of the *ainigma* is not only obscurity, but a more original mode of speaking. Like the labyrinth, like the Gorgon, and like the Sphinx that utters it, the enigma belongs to the sphere of the apotropaic, that is, to a protective power that repels the uncanny by attracting it and assuming it within itself. The dancing path of the labyrinth, which leads into the heart of that which is held at a distance, is the model of this relation with the uncanny that is expressed in the enigma.[44]

In this passage, which returns us to my discussion of the uncanny in the previous chapter, Agamben offers a theorization of a mode of speaking that would repel the uncanny by assuming it within its law. The question is no longer whether one's speech should exclude the uncanny or destroy it, but how one can achieve a mode of speaking that would carry within itself the uncanny's subversive power. Although Agamben is mostly interested in the question of a transformed "speech," which is ultimately the question of how language is not merely communication but the communication of communicability, the passage I quoted also reveals that the theory of speech he develops comes with an implicit theorization of the story that, because of the ways in which it presents itself as a reading of the story of the Sphinx, can very well be read as a critique of Benjamin, and as a theorization of a "Freiheit" that would not be opposed to "recht" but be assumed within it, as its deactivation or inactivity.

The story is a form of the transformed mode of speaking that Agamben is interested in. It represents a kind of pure speech that, contrary to what Benjamin suggests, lies with the Sphinx rather than with Oedipus. As such, I would argue that the story actually figures in Agamben's text as an example of the divine violence that he will much later call for in response to his theory of sovereignty. The examples of divine violence that he gives in the closing essay of *Infancy and History* are in fact similar, in the sense that they all involve language: philology, poetry, and criticism. It is through these linguistic acts that a break with the dialectic of law-positing and law-preserving violence can be achieved. These linguistic acts achieve the overcoming of myth that Benjamin in both "The Storyteller" and "Critique of Violence" is after. Philology, for example, is defined in the essay as "critical mythology." It is an "Aufhebung" of mythology.[45] Part of Agamben's aim is to restore these linguistic acts to "[their] status and [their] violence"[46] so that their connection with politics is laid bare.

Strike, Messianism, and the Idea of Peace

At this point, a number of the questions that I raised at the beginning of this chapter have been addressed. It is still unclear, however, what a politics would look like that would remain true to its original cohesion with linguistics. Agamben's writings do not offer much to work with in this respect, maybe because he does not consider it to be his task to answer the question of "what needs to be done." (He is interested, rather, in what comes before any doing, namely the meaning of the political act in itself, or the conditions under which an act qualifies as political.) However, Benjamin does provide an example of such a political act in "Critique of Violence," when he discusses the strike as an instance of non-violent – or, I would also say, divinely violent – political resolution. Having a closer look at this example will enable me to answer a question that I have left unaddressed, namely what remains of sovereignty and law after divine violence?

Making reference to Georges Sorel,[47] Benjamin distinguishes between two kinds of strike: the political strike and the proletarian general strike. He observes that they are "antithetical in their relation to violence."[48] Quoting Sorel, he writes: "The political general strike demonstrates how the state will lose none of its strength, how power is transferred from the privileged to the privileged, how the mass of producers will change their masters."[49] The proletarian general strike, in contrast, "sets itself the sole task [Aufgabe] of destroying [Vernichtung] state power."[50] And, quoting Sorel again: "This general strike clearly announces its indifference toward material gain through conquest by declaring its intention to abolish [aufheben] the state."[51] The way in which Benjamin rephrases the distinction between two kinds of strike is counter-intuitive: he considers political strike to be violent, "since it causes only an external modification of labor conditions."[52] The proletarian strike, however, he calls non-violent since it does not take place "in readiness to resume work following external concessions" but "in the determination to resume only a wholly transformed work [eine gänzlich veränderte Arbeit], no longer enforced by the state [eine nicht staatlich erzwungene]."[53] It is for these reasons that he characterizes the former as law-making and the latter as anarchistic.

The distinction between the violent political strike and the non-violent proletarian strike makes perfect sense in the context of Agamben's reading of the Benjamin–Schmitt debate. Because the political strike leaves intact the link uniting violence and the law, or the dialectic between law-positing violence and law-preserving violence, Benjamin considers it to be violent. It functions in the essay as an example of a violence that would cause only an external change of labor conditions but that wouldn't change anything on the inside. (It is an example of a violence that remains within the logic of sovereignty and does not create a "real" state of exception.) The proletarian strike, however, Benjamin calls non-violent because it severs the nexus between violence and law and creates a "real" state of exception by suspending the difference between law-positing violence and law-preserving violence. The non-violent proletarian strike thus becomes an example of the divine violence that "Critique of Violence" proposes: it destroys mythical law-making but – and this is important to emphasize – *this does not mean that it destroys the law*. The verb that Benjamin chooses to describe the work of divine violence is not "destroy" ("vernichten," as one might expect) or even "abolish" (as the English translation has it) but "aufheben."[54] The Hegelian term "Aufhebung" captures perfectly the suspension or fulfillment of the law that Benjamin envisions the end of mythical law-making will achieve. Thus, the proletarian general strike does not lead to the destruction of work, but to resuming "a wholly transformed work" in the same way that divine violence does not lead to the end of law but to another use of it. Benjamin is not calling for the end of law but for the end of the link between violence and law. It is in this way that Benjamin's insistence on "de-posing" ("entsetzen") the law needs to be understood.

Although Agamben rarely discusses examples of political action in his work, one can see how Benjamin's example and specifically the language in which it is expressed pervade the idea of politics that it contains. If *Homo Sacer* is the book that contains Agamben's theory of sovereign power, the philological study of *The Time That Remains*, his book on Saint Paul, provides his divinely violent answer to the problems of sovereignty that *Homo Sacer* exposes. In response to, for example, the problematic political economy of the sovereign nation-state, in which there is no place for something like "the human as such," Agamben uses philology to show how Paul in his "Letter to the Romans" offers a theory of human life beyond all categories of identification, as a kind of rest that would remain in-between identitarian categories. Through the division of flesh and spirit, Paul divides the division between Jews and Greeks, arguing that one can be a Jew in spirit but not according to the flesh (that is: un-circumcised), and that one can be a Jew according to the flesh (that is: circumcised) but not in spirit. This messianic rest within identitarian categories poses a radical challenge to the political economy of the sovereign nation-state and announces the coming of a political community of whatever being, a community that would not be indifferent to difference but in which identitarian categories would not constitute differences that would limit and condition the community. Such a political community would also mark the end of the political theology of sovereignty by dismantling the device of the state of exception through which politics was brought within the law. As such, the messianic rest that Paul's letter theorizes actually functions as a critique of theology; it is in this secular (or maybe better post-secular) sense that it can be called divine.[55]

Philology's divinely violent acts of deposition lead to what Agamben calls a messianic fulfillment of the law, or a time in which the law would not be destroyed but deactivated and rendered inoperative – that is: used in a different way. Although one can already begin to see the relation between what Agamben is proposing and Benjamin's discussion of the strike, the connection can also be made philologically. *The Time That Remains* reveals that there is a historical-etymological relation between the word "inoperativity" that is central to Nancy's work and that Agamben uses to describe the messianic fulfillment of the law, and Hegel's term "Aufhebung." This puts Agamben's theorization of divine violence in direct relation with Benjamin's characterization of the divinely violent work of the strike as an "Aufhebung."[56] That there is also a relation between the messianic fulfillment of the law and Agamben's theorization of the "ainos," the story or fable, becomes clear in at least one of the concrete cases of messianism that his work proposes, namely the enigmatic – from the Greek word "ainigma," related to "ainos" – law-copyist from Herman Melville's story "Bartleby, the Scrivener."[57] Recalling his statement in the closing essay of *Infancy and History* that poetry is an example of divine violence, *The Time That Remains* also offers a poem as a concrete case of the messianic fulfillment of the law.[58] At first sight, it may seem odd that Agamben would find in the play with rhyme that this poem develops a vision of a political future that would supersede the mythical violence of sovereignty. But I hope this chapter, even if it does not provide answers to the question "what needs to be done," at least reveals the philosophy from which such a vision emerges: a philosophy of language that insists on the disjunction of language and meaning and draws attention instead to language's communication of communicability.

Superhumanism

In contrast with the conceptualization of politics as "war continued by other means" that can be found in Schmitt's work, but also on the far side of depoliticized liberalism, Agamben's message is radically democratic and related to what in one of his earlier books he theorizes as "the idea of peace." In a passage that resonates both with the discussion of his "Oedipus and the Sphinx" and Benjamin's remarks about the difference between the political and the proletarian general strike that I have offered here, and that anticipates wonderfully well the critique of identity politics that is contained in his book on Saint Paul, Agamben writes:

> The truth is, however, that there is not, nor can there be, a sign of peace, since true peace would only be there where all the signs were fulfilled and exhausted. Every struggle among men is in fact a struggle for recognition and the peace that follows such a struggle is only a convention instituting the signs and conditions of mutual, precarious recognition. Such a peace is only and always a peace amongst states and of the law, a fiction of the recognition of an identity in language, which comes from war and will end in war.
>
> Not the appeal to guaranteed signs, or images, but the fact that we cannot recognize ourselves in any sign or image: that is peace – or, if you like, that is the bliss more ancient than peace which a marvelous parable of St. Francis's defines as sojourn: nocturnal, patient, homeless – in non-recognition. Peace is the perfectly empty sky of humanity; it is the display of non-appearance as the only homeland of man.[59]

The question that some will no doubt continue to ask is whether such a "display of non-appearance" can really constitute a politics?

Although there are many problems with Sloterdijk's essay, the reflection on humanism that it ultimately develops is extremely powerful. In the opening pages of the essay, Sloterdijk characterizes our "postliterary" and "postepistolary" age as a "posthumanistic" age. He does so in the context of his earlier assertion of the connection between literacy and humanism. The word "posthumanistic" becomes meaningful in his essay, however, in the context of a discussion of post–Second World War humanism: a humanism that was committed "to save men from barbarism."[60]

> Anyone who is asking today about the future of humanity and about the methods of humanization wants to know if there is any hope of mastering the contemporary tendency towards the bestialization of humanity. … The latent message of humanism, then, is the taming of men. And its hidden thesis is: reading the right books calms the inner beast.[61]

In the essay, Sloterdijk is clearly critical of this development. His critique is provocative, given that the post–Second World War humanism emerged in part in response to the "bestializing" experience of the camps.[62]

Sloterdijk's position on humanism is clarified towards the end of the essay. Having discussed what he calls the social history of taming – the profound connection between human beings, pets, and the house that, as Sloterdijk points out, Elizabeth de Fontenay and Thomas Macho have also considered – he challenges this history of domestication, which is also the history of theorization.[63] This is the history of what Friedrich Nietzsche calls "the last man." In response to this history, Sloterdijk urges his readers to rediscover Nietzsche's superhuman – another provocative statement in post–Second World War Germany. Almost impossibly so, Sloterdijk embraces certain practices of breeding, a certain breeding-politics or biopolitics: not, of course, the one to which we were passively exposed in the history of humanism and the history of the camps – not the one that aims to domesticate and tame us. Instead, he advocates *a superhumanism of self-shepherding* and he argues that we should all become anthropotechnologists. In the age of biotechnology, in which our bodies are being shaped by power in unprecedented ways, we need to grab hold of the means of biopolitical production, and become the subjects of our own biopolitical production (to use an expression from Hardt and Negri's *Commonwealth*).[64]

Today, we are already more and more slipping into the role of such subjects – but because the topic that these developments raise is taboo, any real reflection on "a codex of anthropo-technology"[65] is lacking. As a result, we do not actively confront the fact that we are biopolitical agents. "Such a codex will retroactively alter the meaning of the old humanism, for it will be made explicit, and codified, that humanity is not just the friendship of man with man, but that man has become the higher power for man."[66] In other words: it will make explicit that we have become our own gods. The move that Immanuel Kant already advocated in his essay on the Enlightenment – dare to know! become major! – is accomplished today in the realm of biopolitics: man has become a "force majeure,"[67] as Sloterdijk puts it, and because we are too politically correct when it comes to this fact, we are incapable of thinking it through and of using this newly discovered power for our own good.[68]

"For the next period of time," Sloterdijk writes, "species politics will be decisive."

That is, when it will be learned whether humanity (or at least its culturally decisive faction) will be able to achieve effective means of self-taming. A titanic battle is being waged in our contemporary culture between the civilizing and bestializing impulses and their associated media. Certainly, any great success in taming would be surprising in the face of an unparalleled wave of social developments that seems to be irresistibly eroding inhibitions. But whether this process will also eventuate in a genetic reform of the characteristics of the species; whether the present anthropotechnology portends an explicit future determination of traits; whether human beings as a species can transform birth fatalities into optimal births and prenatal selection – these are questions with which the evolutionary horizon, as always vague and risky, begins to glimmer.[69]

This passage has triggered a scandal, providing evidence of Sloterdijk's supposed proximity to "eugenics" and "Nazism."

But there is also something else that is worth considering here – something that escapes the limitations of such a reading. The question of our time, according to Sloterdijk, is to turn the politics of shepherding and breeding into a politics of self-shepherding and self-breeding – we need to "dare to know!" *in this domain as well*. Politics today is about the maintenance of the human zoo, and about who will write its rules, its codex.

> If there is one virtue of human beings which deserves to be spoken about in a philosophical way, it is above all this: that people are not forced into political theme parks but, rather, put themselves there. Humans are self-fencing, self-shepherding creatures. Wherever they live they create parks around themselves. In city-parks, national parks, provincial or state parks, eco-parks – everywhere people must create for themselves rules according to which their comportment is to be governed.[70]

This is where Sloterdijk and Calle become unlikely bedfellows, for Sloterdijk is – like Calle – urging all of us to take care of ourselves. *Dare to open up a debate about these issues. Dare to confront these issues head on. Become superhumanists*. It is also here that his argument links up with the Foucaultian thematic that I launched in the previous chapter: species politics is about becoming the subject of one's own biopolitical production. One could argue that this imperative comes very close to Foucault's late work on the care of the self: on aesthetico-ethical practices of self-production, a *"cura sui"* or "techne tou biou" – an "art of the self," or even a *biotechnic*.[71] The paradigm that opens up here is that of human beings as bioartists: as those who, through the application of sophisticated techniques, come to shape their own species lives and thus rediscover a form of sovereignty.

The question is whether such shaping is not always inevitably caught up in the biopolitical logic of the surplus, in the sense that it adds a "more" to a biological life that, by itself, is never enough. One could consider here, as an example, Eduardo Kac's genetically manipulated bunny Alba, which becomes a work of bioart only after the artist's intervention in the bunny's genetic material (even though a bunny is arguably already a work of bioart by itself, before this intervention – in that sense, its mere being is already enough). The answer to this question is likely not to stop "shaping" but to begin to shape otherwise: not at the expense of just or mere being, beyond the destruction of its experience that so troubled Agamben. It is at this point that another kind of bioart – an art of the simple, incommunicable fact of biological life – and thus another kind of storytelling – the story of infancy – becomes possible.

Notes

1   Benjamin, *Illuminations*, 217.
2   Ibid., 220.
3   Ibid., 221.

4 Ibid., 83.

5 Agamben, *IH*, 4.

6 See <http://www.tate.org.uk/modern/exhibitions/jeffwall/infocus/section2/img1.shtm>.

7 Agamben, *HS*, 63–6.

8 Ibid., 64.

9 Agamben, *SE*, 52–64.

10 See Weber, "Taking Exception."

11 Agamben, *SE*, 88. I will come back to the issue that is raised here in the third part of this book.

12 Ibid., 57.

13 Consider, for example, how he urges his readers to extend the Benjamin–Schmitt dossier to much more than just those documents that are strictly speaking a part of it (ibid., 52–3).

14 Benjamin, "Storyteller." For the German original, see Benjamin, "Erzähler."

15 Benjamin, "Storyteller," 143 / "Erzähler," 229.

16 Benjamin, "Storyteller," 148.

17 Benjamin, "Erzähler," 236.

18 Benjamin, "Storyteller," 157.

19 Ibid., 143–6.

20 Ibid., 147–8.

21 Ibid., 157.

22 Ibid., 158.

23 Benjamin, "Critique." For the German original, see Benjamin, "Kritik."

24 Benjamin, "Critique," 248.

25 Ibid.

26 My own position will be different, as will become clear. By the term "waltende," Benjamin captures precisely the plastic sovereignty that I theorize in this book. So whereas the translation of "waltende" as "sovereign" at first sight appears to miss the point, I argue that to characterize it as a mistranslation fails to do justice to the history of sovereignty's transformations.

27 Benjamin, "Critique," 252 / "Kritik," 203.

28 Sloterdijk, "*Rules*," 12.

29 Ibid.

30 See Anderson, *Imagined Communities*.

31 Sloterdijk, "*Rules*," 13.

32 Ibid., 14.

33 Ibid.
34 Ibid.
35 Ibid.
36 Ibid.
37 Ibid., 27.
38 The fact that Calle asks the women to interpret the letter according to their professional activity – through the lens of their *work* – appears to underline even more, through its point–counterpoint, the *in*-operative or work-*less* nature of the community that Calle is constituting around the *interruption* of the letter. Of course, one can also read the insistence on working women otherwise: for her artwork on care – a notion that is usually associated with women who do not pursue a career in order to take care of their partner and children – Calle turns to *working women*, to women who did choose to pursue a career. Other understandings of care might emerge from this particular test group. The category to consider here would be that of *affective labor*.
39 But as Michel Foucault in a discussion with Noam Chomsky observed, freedom *is* freedom. It will never be realized by legal means, it can only be practiced politically. Interview available on YouTube at: <https://www.youtube.com/watch?v=3wfNl2L0Gf8>.
40 Agamben, *S*, 137–8.
41 Although Agamben's own understanding of myth is, in essays such as "Project for a Review," very close if not identical to Benjamin's, there is at least one indication that it may also be different and that he is also trying to rethink myth. See Agamben, *IH*, 168.
42 Agamben, *S*, 138.
43 Ibid., 137.
44 Ibid., 138.
45 Agamben, *IH*, 163.
46 Ibid., 164.
47 For a detailed analysis of Benjamin's relation to Sorel on the issue of power, violence, and myth, see Ruda and Voelker, "Necessary Critique." Ruda and Voelker's analysis shares many elements with my own, which was initially published in 2008. See Boever, "Politics and Poetics."
48 Benjamin, "Critique," 245.
49 Ibid., 246.
50 Benjamin, "Critique," 246 / "Kritik," 194.
51 Benjamin, "Critique," 246 / "Kritik," 194.
52 Benjamin, "Critique," 246.

53 Benjamin, "Critique," 246 / "Kritik," 194.

54 When he uses the word "Vernichtung" it is in combination with the word "Aufgabe," which as commentators on Benjamin's translation essay have tirelessly pointed out, contains both the semantic components of a "task" and a "letting go." One shouldn't conclude too quickly that "destruction" is the "task" that Benjamin sets before the reader but rather "let go" of such easy readings (and politics). "Aufhebung" is closer to what Benjamin has in mind.

55 Agamben, *TR*, 44–58.

56 Ibid., 88–112.

57 Agamben, *P*, 243–71.

58 Agamben, *TR*, 78–87.

59 Agamben, *IP*, 81–2.

60 Sloterdijk, "*Rules*," 15.

61 Ibid.

62 A few points that Sloterdijk's essay enables one to make: it is not at all clear that what happened in the camps can be described as *bestializing*. To the best of my knowledge, no animals have ever killed their own kind in the same systematic way that human beings did during the Second World War. Given that the camps could never have happened without the support of modern technology, it may be that what happened to human beings in the camps can more accurately be described as *hypermodernization*. In the camps, human beings were turned into technological objects rather than into beasts; they behaved like robots rather than like human beings. (And even here, one would have to ask to what extent life in camps actually resembles machine life.) When Agamben argues that the camp prisoner is a figure of bare life, a zone of indeterminacy between human and animal life, one wonders whether the particular form of life that the camp opens up should not be reconceived as a life between human and technological life. This shifts the ethical issues involved in the camp from a concern with the animal towards a concern with technology.

63 Sloterdijk can make this case because of the fact that theory is considered as a type of leisure: as sitting at home and looking out at the world through the window. Theory's etymological link to the Greek word "theoria," "a looking at, viewing, beholding," appears to justify such a reading.

64 See Hardt and Negri, *Commonwealth*.

65 Sloterdijk, "*Rules*," 24.

66 Ibid.

67 Ibid.

68 In response to the question "Was ist Aufklärung?," Kant famously gives the answer: "Dare to know!" Having the courage to use one's own reason is characterized, in Kant's essay, as a "becoming major" – as an emancipation from a childhood where one is not yet able to walk on one's own. Sloterdijk's essay is (like Foucault's essay on the Enlightenment, Agamben's essay "What is an Apparatus?," and Catherine Malabou's book on the brain) one of those texts that were written "after" Kant and need to be considered within this lineage. I consider Kant's essay in more detail in Chapter 5.

69 Sloterdijk, "*Rules*," 24.

70 Ibid., 25.

71 See Foucault, *Care*.

3

From Translatability to Politics

To my fellow translators.

Aesthetic Education

In an interview titled "The Janus-Face of Politicized Art," Jacques Rancière offers a description of his methodology that resonates with Agamben's work on language (as I have presented it in previous chapters) as well as its politics:

> I always try to think in terms of horizontal distributions, combinations between systems of possibilities, not in terms of surface and substratum. Where one searches for the hidden beneath the apparent, a position of mastery is established. I have tried to conceive of a topography that does not presuppose this position of mastery.[1]

The aim is to construct "little by little, an egalitarian or anarchist theoretical position that does not presuppose this vertical relationship of top to bottom."[2] Such a redistribution of the sensible has something to do with what Rancière calls the politics of aesthetics. Rancière's work explores the consequences of this not just for visual art, but also for theatre, and even for education.[3]

The relation between Rancière and Agamben has not always been easy. Agamben is heavily criticized in Rancière's essay "Who is the Subject of the Rights of Man?";[4] Agamben distances himself from Rancière's theory of politics in *The Time That Remains*.[5] Clearly, they do not see eye to eye, at least politically. Nevertheless, I want to briefly tease out some connections between Rancière's aesthetic politics and Agamben's work on language as a way into my discussion of one other, under-recognized political practice of language in Agamben's work: translation.

Indeed, in addition to poetry, philology, and criticism – all of which are discussed in the final section of *Infancy and History* as practices that maintain the original cohesion between poetry and politics – storytelling and translation are arguably linguistic activities where the experiment with language, the experience of the *thing* of language, can take place. In the previous chapter, I have shown how this is the case for storytelling; here, I turn to translation, more precisely *translatability*, to do the same. Once again, I will be moving by way of Walter Benjamin (specifically, his classic essay "The Task of the Translator") in order to draw out the close connection between translatability and politics. Given the centrality of the practice of translation in Agamben's philological work, this chapter thus provides an insight into one of Agamben's most powerful linguistic tools, one that will be revealed to have a profound political significance as well. In addition, this chapter will continue my concern with aesthetic education, which already received some airplay in the Prologue to this book where I mentioned Walter Benjamin's notion of "educative violence."

First, a word about "translatability" as what I consider to be the plastic dimension of translation. I am not the only one to have noted the relation between plasticity and translation. Indeed, one of Catherine Malabou's translators, Carolyn Shread, has explored this relation on at least two occasions: in her preface to her translation of Malabou's *Ontology of the Accident: An Essay on Destructive Plasticity* and in her essay "The Horror of Translation," published in a special issue of *theory@buffalo* on Malabou's work. In "The Horror of Translation," Shread notes that "Malabou has never written directly on translation," and that the connection of her work to translation is not evident.[6] Nevertheless, Shread notes that when reading about how neuroscience for Malabou "offered a concrete manifestation of her concept of plasticity," she recognized that she "had a similar experience when I began to translate her work":

> [I]t became increasingly clear to me that in many ways the plasticity Malabou described corresponded exactly to what her text was undergoing in translation, and, moreover, that translation offered a concrete manifestation of her philosophical concept, that translation itself offered "la traduction d'un concept dans les choses mêmes."[7]

Translation as a concrete manifestation of plasticity, then, as "the translation of plasticity into the things themselves" ("la traduction d'un concept dans les choses mêmes"). Keeping in mind what are arguably the two most familiar components of plasticity – receiving form and giving form – this claim is hardly controversial: translation is plastic, in the way clay is plastic, for example (it can receive form); the translator is like a plastic surgeon in the sense that she or he gives form to translation. In translation, however, there is also something that resists: for the translation is not infinitely moldable. It is not flexible, but plastic. It can explode.

And yet, one must ask oneself here, as I will in this chapter, whether it is really the translation that is plastic – that receives form or gives form. I will want to push Shread a little bit on this count through my reading of Benjamin's essay on translation, to suggest that it is *translatability* that marks the properly plastic component of translation – and not translation itself.

This becomes remarkably clear, I think, in Shread's preface to *Ontology of the Accident*, where she ties translation to what Malabou calls "destructive plasticity" (theorized at length in Malabou's marvelous book on Freud). Here, Shread makes the case for what she labels a "translational ontology" that would "[assume] also destructive plasticity," "explosive plasticity."[8] Such an ontology – of the accident – could make us see "that translating has something to offer beyond a means to an end":

> An embracing of translation as a practice that goes beyond pragmatics could alter the voice of translators as mediators of change. Translation might then assume its ontology as a valid mode of being in the world – a mode of being that is becoming.[9]

One wonders why Shread still holds on to the term ontology, both in the phrase "translational ontology" and in the passage I just quoted (one reason may be, of course, that Malabou does, too, in the title of her book). For Shread is clearly talking about a translational ontogenesis here – *not* an ontology.[10] She is interested in translation insofar as it denotes the process of translating and the translatability with which it is associated.

Furthermore, when Shread writes, earlier on, that the translational ontology she has in mind "evokes fear and is used to justify security measures and normative structures that seek to delimit the field of translation,"[11] she is not only taking on translation studies. She is targeting the *sovereignty* of translation studies, more specifically the sovereignty that it wants to project into the practice of translation. This particular sovereignty – of security measures and normative structures – is *not* plastic, and it is important to see that Shread is mobilizing the plasticity of translation against such a sovereignty. That is, in short, what I propose to do in this chapter as well: it is the way in which I propose to enlist translation and more specifically translatability for my project to think another kind of sovereignty.

This is Not a Pipe

But let me start with another element that I said would have a central role in this chapter: education. Education is par excellence a practice that gives form (it shapes us), receives form (we shape it – education is always a two-way process, it is changed by those who are educated), and explodes it (Socrates, as the one who claims he knows only that he does not know, is probably the most obvious figure of this explosion – though Rancière would prefer Joseph Jacotot over Socrates as a figure of this explosion[12]). If the Platonic dialogues, at the origin of Western philosophy, are essentially projects of education that are driven by the question "what is?" ("ti esti"), it is worth noting that in the dialogues, this question rarely gets answered. This has led philosopher Bernard Stiegler to translate the Platonic "ti esti" using what Roland Barthes in a text on Raymond Queneau's "Zazie dans le métro" calls Zazie's "clausule," her "formula": "mon cul," "my ass." Indeed, Zazie's "assification" of the bourgeois values into which she is being educated comes to mark, for Stiegler, the spirit of education as such, the *thing* of education: a hole that invites filling, it can nevertheless never be filled – it resists being filled. This is education's properly explosive, plastic component that will, with translation, be central to this chapter.[13]

114

"Education" is present as a concern as soon as one considers Rancière's characterization of his methodology with which I opened this chapter. One of the figures associated in Rancière's work with the methodology that establishes a position of mastery by "[attempting] to unveil the truth hidden behind the obscure surface of appearances" is Sigmund Freud. Freud, who begins his text on "The Moses of Michelangelo" by stating that he is "no connoisseur in art" – he is mostly interested in the work's content and not in its "formal and technical qualities" – can indeed easily be read as a representative of the "vertical relationship of top to bottom" that Rancière in the quote with which I began this chapter rejects.[14] In the Michelangelo essay, Freud confesses that he cannot obtain any pleasure from artworks that he cannot understand: music, for example, resists his attempts at explanation, and as a consequence frustrates him immensely. Although Freud recognizes that some of the greatest artworks remain, until his day, "unsolved riddles to his understanding,"[15] his entire text is driven by the desire to solve these riddles. Like that hero from Greek tragedy who figures prominently in some of his other writings – Sophocles' Oedipus, whom we encountered in the previous chapter – Freud simply cannot let the riddle be.

Confronted with the riddle of the Sphinx, Oedipus feels the need to solve it, and critics have tended to praise him for this. But what reward does Oedipus get for solving the riddle? He gets to sleep with his mother … Even more so, and going back to the beginning of Sophocles' play, it is because Oedipus tries to solve the riddle of the oracle earlier on that he leaves behind his adoptive parents, and ends up killing his biological father. Clearly, solving the riddle has disastrous consequences for our protagonist. If both these scenes – confronting the oracle and confronting the Sphinx – are also educational scenes, it appears that another type of education is called for: one that would not be characterized by the symptomatology of the vertical, but by the logic of lateral, egalitarian and anarchistic distributions that Rancière espouses. In the previous chapter, I have begun to show that Agamben's theory of language, and by extension his politics, are *in part* designed against the symptomatology of the vertical that Rancière also criticizes. In this chapter, translation will reveal itself to be a powerful ally in this struggle.

The methodological distinction that Rancière sets up can be characterized as a distinction between the logic of *presentation* on the one hand (the logic of "horizontal distributions, combinations between systems of possibilities"), and the logic of *re-presentation* on the other (the logic of "unveiling the truth hidden behind the obscure surface of appearances"; "a vertical relation of top to bottom"). According to the logic of *representation*, something always represents something else, a truth that surface appearance leaves to be discovered. I would characterize this, somewhat counter-intuitively, as the logic of *identity*, in which it is never about *you* but about something else – a *who* – that you are. In the logic of representation, *you* are valued not simply as *you* but as the *who* that you are. This leads to *a hierarchy of whos* in which *one who* is more valuable than *another*; it leads to a *market* of identities. (This is the logic of the surplus that I analyzed in Chapter 1.)

The logic of *presentation*, by contrast, does not assume that a truth needs to be uncovered behind the surface of appearances: the vertical relation of representation is instead collapsed into presentation's horizontality. Surface appearance coincides with truth, thus doing away with this distinction altogether. This is *not* the logic of identity. In the logic of presentation, it is no longer about a *who* that *you* are, and for which you are valued. Instead, *you* become part of an anarchist, horizontal distribution of *yous* that are all *equal*, though *not the same*. (This is the logic of just being that I also discussed in Chapter 1.) Whereas the logic of presentation preserves difference, the logic of representation artificially recreates it as exchange value. In a horizontal distribution, there is no hierarchy; there can be no market. The value of each *you* is the same (even though that does not mean that everyone is the same).

Traditionally, sovereignty has been thought according to the vertical logic of representation – that is, as I explained in Chapter 1, the sovereignty that Agamben criticizes. What I propose in this book is to partly rethink it according to the horizontal logic of presentation. It is an impossible, flat – or at least, flat*ter* – sovereignty that may characterize new movements of self-determination emerging today – even if, as will become clear toward the end of this chapter, sovereignty's vertical dimension does (and should, in my view) not entirely disappear.

This distinction – between presentation and re-presentation – is hardly new. Michel Foucault also rehearses it, though not exactly in these terms, in *This is Not a Pipe*.[16] As the title illustrates, this book revolves around René Magritte's painting *Ceci n'est pas une pipe* (1926). "But," as Foucault reminds one throughout the book, "there is more." The painting that is in fact central to Foucault's analysis is not so much *Ceci n'est pas une pipe*, but a work that Magritte painted many years later, and that repeats the earlier work: *Les deux mystères*, from 1966. Part of the reason why Foucault is interested in that painting is because it engages the relation between art and education. As Foucault notes, *Ceci n'est pas une pipe* is reproduced in *Les deux mystères*, but the repetition also and inevitably generates difference:

117

"everything" about its representation "suggests a blackboard in a classroom."[17] This will lead Foucault to imagine the painting, a little later in the book, as "a pedagogic space."[18]

At this point, Foucault imagines a teacher standing in front of a blackboard, pointing at the drawing of a pipe, "articulating very clearly, 'This is a pipe.'"[19] But "scarcely has he stated, 'This is a pipe,' before he must correct himself and stutter, 'This is not a pipe, but a drawing of a pipe.'"[20] The teacher's voice thus becomes "confused and choked"; "The baffled master lowers his extended pointer, turns his back to the board, regards the uproarious students"[21] – and then the miracle, the mystery of *Les deux mystères* happens. For there are not one, but two pipes: the teacher "does not realize that they [the students] laugh so loudly because above the blackboard and his stammered denials, a vapor has just risen, little by little taking shape and now creating, precisely and without a doubt, a pipe."[22] "'A pipe, a pipe,' cry the students, stamping away while the teacher, his voice sinking ever lower, murmurs always with the same obstinacy though no one is listening, 'And yet it is not a pipe.'"[23] And Foucault notes that the teacher is right: for even the second pipe that has emerged behind his back, above the blackboard, is not a pipe.

And thus, in this utter lack of a common ground between the teacher and the students, in this remarkable scene of aesthetic education, "the easel has but to tilt, the frame to loosen, the painting to tumble down."[24] *A pipe my ass! It's just painting.*

Heterotopias

In his introduction to the book, the translator of Foucault's text associates this scene of aesthetic education – this loss of a common ground, a "lieu commun" – with the birth of what Foucault in *The Order of Things* (*Les mots et les choses* – a book that took its title from a show by Magritte) and other texts calls "heterotopias." With this term, Foucault does not merely refer to the disorder of "the *incongruous*, the linking together of things that are inappropriate."[25] Instead, he is thinking of

the disorder in which a large number of possible orders glitter separately, in the lawless and uncharted dimension of the *heteroclite* … it is impossible to find a common place beneath them all…. *Heterotopias* are disturbing, probably because they secretly undermine language, because they make it impossible to name this *and* that, because they shatter or tangle common names, because they destroy syntax in advance, and not only the syntax with which we construct sentences but also that less apparent syntax which causes words and things … to "hang together"…. Heterotopias dessicate speech, stop words in their tracks, contest the very possibility of language at its source; they dissolve our myths and sterilize the lyricism of our sentences.[26]

In short: "A pipe, a pipe!" *and* "This is not a pipe" – an impossible combination.

The interesting thing, in view of the distinction between presentation and representation that I set up earlier on, is that this scene of aesthetic education, which marks the birth of a heterotopia, is associated with the difference between resemblance and similitude in Foucault – a difference that can without much difficulty be matched onto the distinction between presentation and representation. Here is Foucault's translator again:

Foucault accounts for the simultaneously familiar and non-representational quality of Magritte's images by drawing a distinction between resemblance and similitude. Resemblance, says Foucault, "presumes a primary reference that prescribes and classes" copies on the basis of the rigor of their mimetic relation to itself. Resemblance serves and is dominated by representation. With similitude, on the other hand, the reference "anchor" is gone. Things are cast adrift, more or less like one another without any of them being able to claim the privileged status of "model" for the rest. Hierarchy gives way to a series of exclusively lateral relations: "Similitude circulates the simulacrum as the indefinite and reversible relation of the similar to the similar". Painting becomes an endless series of repetitions, variations set free from a theme.[27]

In short: representation (Foucault's term; associated with "resemblance") versus presentation (what Foucault calls "similitude"). Note also how this passage resonates with Rancière's characterization of his methodology as operating according to an anti-hierarchical logic of horizontal distributions that that does not presuppose the position of mastery. This is confirmed in the fifth chapter of Foucault's book.

Our Music

One of the ways in which this tension between resemblance and similitude – hierarchy and anarchistic lateral relations – is played out in Magritte's *Ceci n'est pas une pipe*, is in the relation between the image (a pipe) and the text ("Ceci n'est pas une pipe"). In Magritte's painting, Foucault argues, these "two systems can neither merge nor intersect. In one way or another, subordination is required. Either the text is ruled by the image ... or else the image is ruled by the text."[28] Either way, "[an] order always hierarchizes them, running from the figure to discourse or from discourse to the figure."[29] As Foucault presents it, Paul

Klee abolished this principle; Magritte, however, goes further than Klee through the ways in which he brings similitude into play against resemblance, something that, for reasons of focus, I will not go into here. Such a project would involve tracing the *dynamic* relation of presentation to representation, which is at work in every work of art and scene of aesthetic education.

With all of this in mind, however, I want to turn to a scene of aesthetic education from Jean-Luc Godard's film *Notre Musique* (2004), because it involves the practice of translation, which is caught up in all of this. In the film, Godard has traveled to Sarajevo to give a talk about the relation between text and image, precisely what is at stake, for Foucault, in Magritte's painting. The scene that I am interested in is about five minutes long and represents Godard's lecture.[30] Perhaps because this is an educational scene, and perhaps because Godard himself plays the teacher, I tend to approach this scene according to the logic of representation, in other words by trying to understand, along the vertical axis that orients it, what the "master" is saying. So, what is Godard *saying*? Godard's lecture is about the shot reverse shot film technique. He starts out by criticizing Howard Hawks for doing a shot reverse shot of a man and a woman that is not really a shot *reverse* shot: instead, the man and the woman are represented in exactly the same way, and Godard seems to value negatively Hawks's incapacity of seeing the difference between a man and a woman. There is no *contre* in Hawks's *contre*champ.

The situation is worse, Godard continues, when two images are alike: for example, in the case of two images representing the same moment in history. At this point in Godard's lecture, something very peculiar happens: the film shows the viewer *not two, but three* images; moreover, they clearly do *not* represent the same moment in history (the first image says "Kosovo";

the second says "Egypt"; the third image is not identified). The images, in other words, *do* not *illustrate the teacher's lesson* – instead, they appear to lead somewhere else. The images that *do* illustrate the teacher's lesson come later, when Godard returns to his discussion of shot reverse shot and talks about Israel–Palestine: "For example in 1948," he lectures, "the Israelites walked in the water to reach the Holy Land … the Palestinians walk in the water to drown. Shot and reverse shot. Shot and reverse shot. The Jews become the stuff of fiction … the Palestinians of documentary." How can one not see the difference between the Jews and the Palestinians in this situation? This seems to be where Godard's critique of Hawks's shot reverse shot – which could initially be read as a feminist critique – reaches its full political swing: with a problem of sovereignty and self-determination (autonomy).

Godard blames our incapacity to see the difference between a man and a woman, and between the Israelites and the Palestinians, on how the field of vision (which operates, as Godard sees it, according to the logic of presentation; "ce n'est pas une image juste, c'est juste une image," as the famous quote from *Vent d'Est* goes) has been taken over by a field of text (representation). And he associates the logic of representation with the calculus of the accountants, who keep the books … Here again, the resonances with the logic of surplus versus the logic of mere being that I discussed in Chapter 1 are strong.

Much more can obviously be said about this scene. But given Godard's point, I would now like to approach this scene following the logic of presentation, by asking "What do we see?" rather than: "What is Godard saying?" So, what do we *see*? First of all, the scene is set up along a vertical axis, with the viewer joining the students at the bottom of the image and Godard, as the teacher, seated at the top. This vertical axis enters into tension with the dynamic of showing the two shots from Hawks's film: while Godard is talking, the shots are first super-imposed, but then they enter into a horizontal dynamic – they are placed next to each other. The vertical dynamic of the scene thus appears to give way to a horizontal one that leads, at least in part, *away from Godard* who is seated at the top of the vertical axis. When Godard is talking about the accountants keeping the books, he is walking from left to right before his audience, *along a horizontal rather than a vertical axis.* (His voice seems very agitated at this moment.)

This experience, this *pull into horizontality*, which of course does not come at the cost of a total destruction of verticality, is reinforced by two other aspects of the scene. The first is the fact that this is a scene of translation. Throughout this scene, Godard's lecture is being translated. As a result, the viewer is constantly drawn *sideways, away from Godard* as the sole source of what she or he is hearing. Secondly, music plays a very important role in this scene: during the lecture, one can hear a door open to an adjacent room on the left-hand side, and from this room music is playing. There is, clearly, a world *outside* this pedagogical space.

Music enters into the scene and is abruptly broken off at various moments throughout the scene, creating an experience of horizontality that interrupts the generally vertical dynamic of this – and other, similar – scenes of aesthetic education. Music thus appears to undermine the vertical authority of the teacher in this scene. The scene culminates in a reversal of the top-to-bottom dynamic: with a student asking a question, and the translator translating the student. Godard's answer never arrives … He stays silent.

It is no coincidence that music ultimately achieves this silence, especially since Godard appears to present music in this scene as the program of cinema: "the principle of cinema," the voice-over goes, "to go toward the light and shine it on our night. Our music." Music is also what gives Freud such a hard time, because it forces him towards the logic of presentation, which he is incapable of following. How are we going to listen to it? What sovereignty does it sing?

Translation

In Godard's scene of aesthetic education, music is thus aligned with translation as what guides the viewer away from what Godard is saying, into an experience of the *thing* of film, into proper "viewing." The scene is not so much about listening to what Godard has to say. Instead, music subversively works its way into our ears, and leads us away from that vertical dynamic, into a visual experience of horizontality. Something happens here to language, music, image, and mastery – and it happens through translation.

Given the explicitly political context in which this scene is set (post-war Sarajevo, which takes us back to my discussion of Susan Sontag in Chapter 1; Sontag has written extensively on Godard), and the explicitly political content that the scene discusses – moving from gender politics in Howard Hawks to the Israeli–Palestinian conflict which traverses Godard's entire oeuvre – one is left wondering about the politics of music, as well as translation, in this scene. I have framed my understanding of the politics of music by aligning music, and the experience that it produces, with what Agamben theorizes as the experience of language.[31] But what about the practice of translation? As linguistic practice, how does it link up with Agamben's theory of language? What are its politics in the era of a progressive actualization of the human being's life?

As many commentators of Benjamin's essay "The Task of the Translator" have noted, Benjamin theorizes translation in "The Task of the Translator" as something unrelated to either a reader or an author. "Translation is a form," he writes. "To understand it as such, one has to return to the original. Because it is in the latter that the law of translation lies hidden, as in the original's translatability."[32] Benjamin is thus not so much interested in translation, but in translatability: a potentiality that precedes any actual translation and operates as such as the translation's law, a law that lies occluded in the original.[33] Benjamin's essay is an attempt to inquire into this law that governs translation. This means that the project of "The Task of the Translator" is not at all anthropocentric. Indeed, Benjamin emphasizes that "certain relational concepts [and translation, for Benjamin, is one of those concepts] retain their proper, perhaps even their most proper, sense when they are not in advance exclusively related to the human being [wenn sie nicht von vorne herein ausschliesslich auf den Menschen bezogen werden]."[34] Benjamin concludes from this that "one would need to risk the translatability of certain linguistic constructions even if they were untranslatable for human beings [auch dann ... wenn diese für den Menschen unübersetzbar wären]."[35] "And, according to a strict understanding of translation, should they not be precisely that, to a certain extent [i.e. untranslatable]?"[36] Translation should thus strictly speaking always include a degree of untranslatability – otherwise a slackness is introduced into the concept. "In such a liberation of the notion of translation," Benjamin goes on, "one must ask whether the translation of certain linguistic constructions is desirable. Because the following appears to be true:

if translation is a form, then translatability must be an essential feature of certain works."[37]

Harry Zohn's translation of this passage misses the specifics of the German original. For Benjamin, first of all, translation is not a mode (as Zohn's translation has it) but a form – it is a *form of translatability*. Translation is thus defined as the symbolic *actualization* of material *translatability*, with the latter being a potentiality that lies occluded in the original and is different from both the original and the translation. In the original, translatability is present as a promise; in the translation, it resides as a memory (hence, Benjamin's insistence on the translation's afterlife or more-than-life). Both the original and the translation are symbolic forms in which translatability manifests itself; but translatability is a material, third term *that cannot be reduced to either*.

From the retranslated passages above, it is clear that Benjamin is not interested in translation but in translatability: that feature of both the original and the translation that is neither, but is instead a potentiality that the task of translation puts one in touch with. Translation puts one in touch with this effective mode of potentiality's existence, a mode of being that does not necessarily topple over into actuality. If translatability is to have its own reality, and not simply disappear into the actuality of a translation, then it is necessary that translatability be safeguarded from passing over into actuality, that it is constitutively the "potentiality not-to do or be." This is not to say, of course, that translation is any less necessary. It is to ask, instead, how translation can be turned back upon itself, so as to liberate its potentiality.

Whereas Zohn translates that "certain correlative concepts retain their meaning, and possibly their foremost significance if they are referred exclusively to man,"[38] Benjamin instead insists on translation's importance *outside* of the human sphere ("*nicht auf den Menschen bezogen*"; "für den Menschen *unübersetz-bar*"). As a relational concept, translation should not only be considered in relation to the human agents of reader and author, but also in relation to the notions of the original, and the notion of translatability (which is the third term that Benjamin insists on). If translation is considered exclusively within the human sphere, as Zohn's translation of Benjamin's text suggests it should be, the notion of translatability would appear to be absolutely meaningless: indeed, in practical, human terms, neither the reader nor the author are helped by *translatability*; what *they* are interested in is *translation*. Benjamin is trying to show, however, that translation's value – its philosophical significance – does not reside in these practical, human concerns but in the notion of translatability that in such a reductive understanding of translation risks falling by the wayside.

By reading Benjamin's essay next to Agamben's *The Coming Community*, as I will do in the next section of this chapter, it will become possible to see however that Benjamin is not merely moving *away* from practical, human concerns. In addition, his essay could also be read as an attempt to rethink, by way of this distance, something that is also of value *for* human beings but may challenge the value of the "human" along the way. Indeed – this is what the comparison with Agamben will reveal – the notion of translatability and the potentiality that it names might ultimately be much more valuable for "human" beings than an actual translation.

When Zohn translates that, "[g]iven a strict concept of translation," the linguistic constructions that Benjamin refers to would "*be translatable to some degree*,"[39] one understands that the English misses the point: what Benjamin insists on is, precisely, a remainder of translatability in the translation, that is: a degree to which every translation is *untranslatable*, and thus retains a remnant of its translatability. Benjamin's argument is about a potentiality that is *not* fully exhausted within a given actuality – a translatability that is *not* fully actualized in a translation. Instead, the translation is haunted by translatability; any strict understanding of translation would have to do justice to this translatability, for otherwise it would miss an essential feature of the original, and be incapable of theorizing translation as a form. This means that even if certain linguistic constructions would prove untranslatable for human beings, their translation should nevertheless still be risked, because for Benjamin's philosophy of translation it ultimately does not matter whether a translation is "possible" (that is: actualizable) or not. Instead, what matters is translatability, that is: the potentiality not-to of translation (which resists its actualization). Translation's infancy.

This is why Benjamin in his text theorizes the task of the translator as an emancipatory task. To translate means to liberate – but to liberate what? Not the *translation*, as my retranslation and discussion of the above passages has made clear, but *translatability* – that law of translation that lies occluded within the original, and of which translation is a form. It is this potentiality that precedes (and unworks, if we want to move away from the temporal, sequential logic) the actuality of any translation that the translator sets free. Importantly, such an insistence on translatability is not followed in Benjamin by a giving up on translation. Benjamin insists, in fact, that one *must* translate; translation must be *risked*. However, the very fact that translation is risky draws out the limits of untranslatability. The key feature of Benjamin's essay, however, is that this is not merely a negative limit – a narrow *un*translatability – but that this limit also names the broader *translatability*, the potentiality not-to be translated. This is the being of translation that Benjamin's essay sets free: the translatability that joins the original and the translation as the third term in Benjamin's philosophical reflection, and that does not simply have the negative properties of untranslatability.

From the perspective of Benjamin's theorization of translatability, it appears that translatability is doomed to always exist at odds with a particular text, whether it is the original (in which it lies occluded) or the translation (which, in its actuality, is one step removed from translatability). Towards the end of Benjamin's essay, it becomes clear however that there is one text in which translatability is able to appear as such – that there is one text that is, in Benjamin's terms, "unconditionally translatable."[40] That text is "the Holy writ."[41] In the Holy Writ, a text and its translatability are one – they are "contracted" into one (to recall the language I used in my Prologue). There, the original coincides with its translatability; it "is" its translatability. Therefore, it is translatable as such, without any of the modifications that translations otherwise require. Benjamin writes that one must have such confidence in the Holy Writ that its translation can simply take the form of an interlinear version and notes that to a certain extent, this is the case for all great writings. Thus, Benjamin extends the "theological" translatability of the Holy Writ to all great writing – either bringing all great writing closer to God, or secularizing the Holy Writ's translatability. On the far side of the relational pair original–translation lies the mere writing of translatability.

Before such a writing of translatability is criticized as "theological," it's worth recalling a letter by Pierre Klossowski, in which Klossowski reports about his attempts to translate Benjamin's famous essay on the work of art with Benjamin himself. The letter reveals that Benjamin may have considered his own writing to be this mere writing of translatability: apparently he wanted his German to be copied exactly into French and accepted none of Klossowski's more idiomatic adaptations. Klossowski remarks that it made the translation "illegible," which fits perfectly Benjamin's non-anthropocentric argument about translatability.[42]

Potentiality and Politics

What is the connection between the translatability I uncovered in Benjamin's essay and Agamben's work? In an essay entitled "On Potentiality," Agamben writes that "I could state the subject of my work as an attempt to understand the meaning of the verb "can" [potere]. What do I mean when I say: 'I can, I cannot'?"[43] As Agamben goes on to explain, he is interested in what Aristotle calls a "hexis," a "'having', on the basis of which [one] can also not bring [one's] knowledge into actuality (*me energein*) by not making a work, for example."[44] "Thus, the architect is potential insofar as he has the potential to not-build, the poet the potential to not-write poems."[45] "Here we already discern what, for Aristotle, will be the key figure of potentiality," the next section of the chapter begins: "the mode of its existence as potentiality. It is a potentiality that is not simply the potential to do this or that thing but potential to not-do, potential not to pass into actuality."[46]

This idea is perhaps developed most memorably in a later essay in the same collection in which "On Potentiality" was published, namely the essay with which the book closes, titled "Bartleby, or On Contingency." In this essay, Agamben turns to

Herman Melville's famous scrivener Bartleby in order to situate Bartleby in a "philosophical constellation"[47] that is shaped by Aristotle's "potentiality not to." For Agamben, Bartleby, a law-copyist who on the third day of his employment on Wall Street refuses copying and ultimately gives up writing altogether, becomes the figure of a "complete or perfect potentiality that belongs to the scribe who is in full possession of the art of writing in the moment in which he does not write."[48] One is reminded of those ancient statues of Greek athletes, captured in the moment just before they will throw the disk – in that moment of extreme tension just before the spring of the throw is released; and if this image is perhaps still too closely linked to actuality, think instead of the disk lying around, no longer in use, and the athletes just lazing about.

Agamben argues that,

> [i]n its deepest intention, philosophy is a firm assertion of potentiality, the construction of an experience of the possible as such. Not thought but the potential to think, not writing but the white sheet is what philosophy refuses at all costs to forget.[49]

The argument is a polemical one that implicitly chastises philosophers for forgetting about the potentiality that this essay, and Agamben's work as a whole, uncovers. Indeed, if my discussion of Benjamin's essay on translation in the previous section has revealed anything, it is its translator's – and by consequence, its commentators' – refusal to acknowledge the "potentiality not-to" around which the essay revolves. As I discussed above, Benjamin is interested in his essay in neither the reader nor the author, neither the original nor the translation, but in translatability: that particular feature that lies occluded in the original and governs the translation as its forgotten law. Translatability

is something like the translation's *arche*, its unforgettable that –
analogously to the Freudian trauma – continues to shape the
translation.[50] Like Agamben, Benjamin was to a certain extent
uninterested in actual translations – even if he was a translator
himself. Instead, he considered it to be the philosophical task
of the translator to liberate translatability: that feature of the
translation that lies occluded in the original, namely its potentiality not to be translated. It is here that the connections between
Agamben's thought and Benjamin's notion of translatability are
revealed – connections that the English translation of Benjamin's
essay unfortunately – and ironically – obscures.

As I have observed above, translation appears in Agamben's
work as a method, and as such it wields the divine type of
violence or force capable of dismantling the state of exception
that Agamben in his work is interested in (it undermines the
link between law and violence that Agamben associated with
sovereign power). But from the comparative reading of Benjamin's
essay and Agamben's work that I am developing, it appears that
there also exist connections between translation and Agamben's
work at another, theoretical level. As is well known, Agamben's
insistence on potentiality is not simply philosophical but also
ethical and, ultimately, political. What Benjamin uncovers with
the notion of translatability, Agamben uncovers with his theory
of language; and, as recent discussions of Agamben's work have
argued, it is upon this theory of language that Agamben's notion
of community is built.

In the chapter "The Pure Potentiality of Representation,"
which deals with Agamben's *Idea of Prose*, in his book *Giorgio
Agamben: A Critical Introduction*, Leland de la Durantaye connects Agamben's theory of language to two essays with which it
had until then not yet been associated, namely Benjamin's essay

on translation, and Paul de Man's essay on Benjamin's essay.[51] First, de la Durantaye reveals de Man's interest in "a tremendous expropriative force in language":[52] the ways in which de Man understands Benjamin's notion of "pure language," associated in Benjamin's essay with "translatability," to refer to a *language which would be pure signifier, which would be completely devoid of any semantic function whatsoever.*"[53] De la Durantaye notes, however, that for de Man, this materiality of language is not messianic but "blocks access to judgments of all sorts and prevents the certain and stable enunciation of presuppositions, propositions, and postulates that would form the bases for aesthetic and ethical precepts."[54]

Then, de la Durantaye moves on to Agamben's *Idea of Prose*, showing that whereas Agamben's interest in language to a certain extent matches de Man's discussion of materiality, for Agamben it is language's communicability – the faculty of language, as Agamben puts it – rather than its communication that "offers the foundation of an ethics and an aesthetics transforming the *aporia* that the 'matter of language' formed for de Man into an *euporia*"[55] – in plain English: transforming it from something bad into something good.

De la Durantaye's reading not only nails the difference between Agamben and de Man – potentiality not-to versus de Man's materiality; it also captures the point, I would argue, where de Man in his essay moves away from Benjamin in order to develop a position of his own. For Benjamin's notion of the "materiality" of language, specifically of the unconditional translatability of the Holy Writ, might not have had the "negative" connotations that de Man associates with it; indeed, it may even open up another understanding of materiality altogether. The tie that Benjamin establishes in his essay between unconditional translatability and the Holy Writ appears to suggest, rather, the opposite – *euporia* rather than *aporia*, as de la Durantaye puts it. If by translatability, language's potentiality not-to rather than language in its meaning-making function, Benjamin meant a potentiality not-to be said, a potentiality that would hold back from meaning-making in order to state itself as such, it is Agamben who has articulated the ethical and political implications of such a thought, specifically the ways in which it can function as the foundation of community.

Indeed, the being in which Agamben roots his idea of community is nothing but the being of what Benjamin calls unconditional translatability, a saying that would simply say itself rather than be part of a meaning-making process – the being of a potentiality not-to, in other words. "The coming being," Agamben writes in the opening entry of *The Coming Community*, "is whatever being [quodlibet ens].... *Quodlibet ens* is not 'being, it does not matter which', but rather 'being such that it always matters.'"[56] "The Whatever in question here relates to singularity not in its indifference with respect to a common property (to a concept, for example: being red, being French, being Muslim), but only in its being *such as it is*."[57] In the closing entry of the book, titled "Tiananmen," Agamben raises what is forcefully stated in the book's opening pages as a question:

> What could be the politics of whatever singularity, that is, of a being whose community is mediated not by any condition of belonging (being red, being Italian, being Communist) nor by the simple absence of conditions (a negative community, such as that recently proposed in France by Maurice Blanchot), but by belonging itself?[58]

Agamben's answer, which I will let stand for now but which I will revisit in Parts II and III of this book, is that this is a politics of whatever being versus the state:

The novelty of the coming politics is that it will no longer be a struggle for the conquest or control of the state, but a struggle between the State and the non-State (humanity), an insurmountable disjunction between whatever singularity and the State organization.[59]

The challenge that *The Coming Community* poses is to connect Agamben's insistence in this passage on "being such as it is" with his interest in language such as it is – the *thing* of language, which though it is material is *no object*. In addition, however, it needs to be connected with Benjamin's notion of translatability – more precisely, with the unconditional translatability of the Holy Writ and of certain great writings (possibly including Benjamin's own), which are the only concrete instantiations of what Benjamin calls translatability. As a potentiality, which exists at a difference from both the original (in which it lies occluded like a promise) and the translation (in which it resides as a memory), translatability marks precisely the whatever being that Agamben in *The Coming Community* theorizes. Indeed, in the same way that whatever being marks the being such as it is of any human being (whether red, Italian, Communist, French, Muslim, et cetera), translatability marks a text's tense being-held within the potentiality of its translation, within its potentiality not-to be translated. This metastable state rich in potentials is characteristic of both the original and the translation – but it needs to be uncovered by the translator. That is what we can now understand to be the translator's political task.[60]

In *The Coming Community*, Agamben thus arguably completes the task of the translator but with respect to human beings: with respect to the original – the empty universal of the human – and the translation – the actualized particular of the identitarian categories in which it is caught (and the human itself may count as such a category, as Agamben's work indicates) – Agamben's work liberates instead a potentiality that exists at a distance from both. A being that is not indifferent to the particular, but whose particulars do not upset the community that the empty universal of the human promises. It is a plastic component that can receive form and give form and upon which any attempt to include mere being in the logic of surplus is shipwrecked.

Cindy Sherman's *Untitled Film Stills* (Epilogue)

As I suggested in the first part of this chapter, my argument is that with the notion of "translatability," so closely linked to the notion of a "potentiality not-to" that lies at the origin of Agamben's reconceptualization of community, we encounter something like a "plastic" moment of a theory of translation. Indeed, translatability marks a capacity to receive form (the capacity to be translated); however, the genius of Benjamin's text is that it also theorizes translatability in relation to the capacity to give form (it resists being subsumed into translation, it remains as a subversive potential within a translation). To place oneself within translatability in fact means to confront translation's explosive core, its "matter" where not just the distinction between original and translation is established but where the very passage from the one to the other takes place – a passage that mimics, as will by now be clear, the passage from language (form) to its referent (matter), and from the logic of mere being (the contract of matter and form) to the logic of the surplus, of a symbolic life added to mere being (the logic of a certain kind of sovereignty). To theorize translatability thus means, in Agamben's terms, to experiment with language, to experience the thing of language, the material faculty of language. In the first part of this chapter, this experience was associated with music: for it was music that, in Godard's film, led the viewer from "what is Godard saying?" to "what are we seeing?" I suggested that this regime change enabled the viewer to experience the thing of film. Indeed, Agamben's experiment with language arguably mimics Godard's experiment with film: "ce n'est pas une image juste, c'est juste une image" resonates with Agamben's insistence on "just being," on a being that would, by itself, be enough.

I now want to turn to another work of art – related to film but nevertheless different from it – that mobilizes these concerns and will enable me to put a few finer points on what has already been said. Created between 1977 and 1980, Cindy Sherman's *Untitled Film Stills* is a series of black-and-white photographs that "is widely seen as one of the most original and influential achievements in recent art."[61] I am interested in a detail that appears in a number of the stills and that has captured the critics' attention (like many, I only noticed it after a few viewings): the camera's shutter release mechanism. In 1976, the year before Sherman started working on the film stills, the shutter had already appeared – and very obviously – in her work *The Play of Selves*. During the years to follow, it reappears in more subtle ways in several of the film stills (but not in all of them). In picture #33, for example, the character-photographer is holding the shutter in her right hand, hiding it behind her thigh. Picture #62, a photograph that Sherman added to the series only after it had already been "completed," offers the series' most explicit engagement with its status as a work of art.

I initially became interested in the detail of the shutter release mechanism because of the questions it raises about the genre of Sherman's work. Whereas the (non-)title of the series invites one to look at the photographs as film stills – the fact that the series has no title focuses one's attention on the question of genre – the visibility of the shutter recalls that one is in fact looking at original photographs, and that the larger film from which these pictures are supposedly excerpted exists only as a suggestion. Whereas the still could be described as an image to which an entire film or an important aspect of it is reduced, or in which it is *contained*, Sherman's photographs are images out of which – or perhaps better: inside of which – an entire film or an important aspect of it *expands*. Normally, the film of course precedes the still; with Sherman's photographs, the still seems to either come after a film that was never made, or precede a film that will never be. To recall my discussion of Agamben's *"Experimentum Linguae"* in Chapter 1, they are pro-logues or epi-logues without anything after or before. Whereas the film still's normal gesture is thus one of containment, I would argue that the gesture of Sherman's photographs achieves an entropic liberation: her photographs expand, and – quite extraordinarily, considering the cramped spaces in which many of the stills are set – they expand in all directions; and they *can* expand in all directions since there is not an actual film that would pose a limit to the viewer's imagination. The stills are simultaneously permeated by a sense of infinite possibility ("entropic liberation") and by a sense of irreparable loss ("a film that was never made," "a film that will never be"). They capture, as I see it, the supremely ineffable, translatable *thing* of the image – film's infancy.

One encounters this idea in Agamben's text "Image and Silence," where he suggests that "[p]ainting silences language because it interrupts the signifying relation between name and thing, returning, if only for an instant, the thing to itself, to its namelessness." However, this anonymity of the thing is not one where something is lacking, it is not a distressing impossibility of saying. It is, instead, the presentation of the thing in its pure sayability. Separating name from thing, painting … allows [the thing] to appear in its luminous, beatific sayability.[62]

He mentions, at the end of the essay, two genres that accomplish this particularly well: the still life; and the portrait. Sherman's *Untitled Film Stills* could arguably be housed under either; they most obviously reveal an early interest in the portrait that Sherman will continue later on in her *History Portraits*.

"Silence," meaning here, I think, "infancy": isn't this what translatability accomplishes as well, interrupting the relation between the original and the translation as a potentiality that does not so much mark their impossibility but instead reveals the thing of language in both? For that is a revelation that Agamben, oddly, does not mention in the passage that I have just quoted: focusing on the separation between the name and the thing that reveals the thing in its sayability, he does not state that this separation also – and perhaps even more enigmatically – makes the name appear in its sayability, thus effectively revealing the thing of the name. But it is, perhaps, in painters like Magritte, whose experiment with text and image I discussed above, that this revelation is more obvious.

A Tale that Does Not Count

It is in this sense that the *Untitled Film Stills* are political. If their aesthetic, their exposure of the thing of the image, the image as such, already recalls Agamben's theory of language, then the politics that Sherman associates with the stills couldn't be closer to Agamben's politics of whatever being. In "The Making of *Untitled*," Sherman mentions two films – but no photographs – that inspired her to make the *Untitled Film Stills*. The first is Chris Marker's *La Jetée*, a film that consists entirely of still images, except for one of the final scenes, which moves. The second is Alfred Hitchcock's *Rear Window*. About *Rear Window*, she writes: "I loved all those vignettes Jimmy Stewart watches in the windows around him – you don't know much about any of those characters so you try to fill in the pieces of their lives."[63] The ignorance that *Rear Window* introduces to the viewer is also crucial to the project of the film stills. About her 1976 cutouts, Sherman observes that she thought they were "too feminine."[64] After visiting David Salle's studio and seeing the "quasi-soft porn, cheesecakey things" he was working on, "something clicked."[65] Sherman loves the fact that "it was hard to figure out what was going on in any of [Salle's images], they were totally ambiguous."[66] "This kind of imagery would solve my problem," she writes, "of trying to imply a story without involving other people, just suggesting them outside the frame."[67]

Interestingly, it is when she confronts the ambiguity of Salle's work, that "something clicked": at the moment when the story escapes, that is when Sherman's camera clicks, that is when she captures her image, that is when the shutter release mechanism closes – at the moment when it sees its own opening. Sherman will use the ambiguity of Salle's images for her portrayal of women. She is not interested for example in strong emotions, but aims for an almost expressionless face. "In European film stills," she finds "women who were more neutral ... harder to figure out ... more mysterious."[68] Although focused on women, the stills are about looking androgynous.[69] Some tell the story of a solitary woman. Others allude to another person outside the frame. But the film stills are really a "whole jumble of ambiguity."[70] Sherman's point, in other words, is not to allude to something that is going on outside of the frame; it is to unwork that which is framed, specifically the femininity of the women who are being framed. Thus, she introduces her viewers to whatever being.

It is not surprising, in this context, that this aesthetics – which is evidently also political – would center on the face, and specifically on the face that is almost expressionless. In the final section of his text "In Praise of Profanation," Agamben discusses Walter Benjamin's concept of "exhibition-value."[71] Benjamin uses this concept "to characterize the transformation that the work of art undergoes in the era of its technological reproducibility."[72] According to Agamben, it characterizes better than any other concept "the new condition of objects and even of the human body in the era of fulfilled capitalism."[73] As an example of what he understands by exhibition-value, Agamben turns to the human face:

> It is a common experience that the face of a woman who feels she is being looked at becomes inexpressive. That is, the awareness of being exposed to the gaze creates a vacuum in consciousness and powerfully disrupts the expressive processes that usually animate the face.[74]

In a more recent text titled "Nudity," Agamben character-izes the attitude expressed here as the "nihilism of beauty":[75] "common to many beautiful women," this attitude

> consists in reducing one's own beauty to pure appearance and then exhibiting this appearance with a sort of remote sadness, stubbornly denying the idea that beauty can signify something other than itself.... This disenchantment of beauty, this special

nihilism, reaches its extreme stage with the mannequins or the fashion models, who learn before all else to erase all expression from their faces. In so doing, their faces become pure exhibition value and, as a result, acquire a particular allure.[76]

In the profanation essay, Agamben turns to the art porn star Chloë des Lysses to develop his point. She is cited as an example of someone who "has recently pushed this procedure to the extreme":[77]

> She has herself photographed in the act of performing or submitting to the most obscene acts, but always so that her face is fully visible in the foreground. But instead of simulating pleasure, as dictated by the conventions of the genre, she affects and displays – like fashion models – the most absolute indifference, the most stoic ataraxy.... Her impassive face breaks every connection between lived experience and the expressive sphere; it no longer expresses anything but shows itself as a place without a hint of expression, as pure means.[78]

Agamben characterizes the face's capacity to show itself as pure means as a "profanatory potential."[79] As such, "[n]either the brazen-faced gesture of the porn star nor the impassive face of the fashion model is … to be blamed."[80] What he condemns, instead, is pornography's attempt to neutralize this potential; the fashion show's attempt to divert the fashion model from the use of this potential. In *Nudities*, the conclusion that Agamben draws from his discussion of exhibition value is clear:

> The only thing that the beautiful face can say, exhibiting its nudity with a smile, is, "You wanted to see my secret? You wanted to clarify my envelopment? Then look right at it, if you can. Look at this absolute, unforgivable absence of secrets!" The matheme of nudity is, in this sense, simply this: *haecce*! there is nothing other than this.[81]

Presumably, this *haecce* also leads beyond Agamben's focus on the face of *beautiful women* – into the faces of women as such, whether they are beautiful or not, as well as into the faces of men.

"A beautiful face," he writes in the already mentioned "Image and Silence," "is perhaps the only place where true silence is to be found"[82] – "true silence" referring here not to "the impossibility of saying," as he notes, but to "the presentation of the thing in its pure sayability."[83] Or, as he puts it at the very end of his even earlier text "The Face": "Be only your face. Go to the threshold. Do not remain the subjects of your properties or faculties, do not stay beneath them; rather, go with them, in them, beyond them."[84] It's in this way that the infancy of the face can be discovered. Though Sherman would likely also question Agamben's peculiar focus on "beautiful women," couldn't these powerful imperatives from *Means Without End* not also be used to sum up the politics of Sherman's images?[85]

Notes

1 Rockhill, "Janus-Face," 49.

2 Ibid.

3 See Rancière, *Future*; Rancière, *Ignorant Schoolmaster*.

4 See Rancière, "Who is the Subject?"

5 Agamben, *TR*, 57–8.

6 Shread, "Horror."

7 Ibid., 81.

8 Shread, "Translator's Preface," vii.

9 Ibid., ix.

10 I am repeating a point I made about my approach to sovereignty in my Prologue: I am not interested in sovereignty's ontology but in its ontogenesis. I have developed the point about a translational ontogenesis in a conference presentation I gave about translation in the work of Gilbert Simondon: see Boever, "La traduction."

11 Shread, "Translator's Preface," vii–viii.

12 Rancière, *Ignorant Schoolmaster*, 29.

13 I first heard Stiegler develop this idea in response to a question I asked after a talk he gave at the University of California, Irvine, in the spring of 2011. Of his many books, *Taking Care of Youth and the Generations* most closely addresses the concerns I focus on here. For Barthes's essay, see Barthes, "Zazie."

14 Freud, "Moses," 122.

15 Ibid., 123.

16 Note the echo of the Platonic "What is" in this title.

17 Foucault, *This is Not a Pipe*, 16.

18 Ibid., 29.

19 Ibid., 30.

20 Ibid.

21 Ibid.

22 Ibid.

23 Ibid.

24 Ibid., 31.

25 Ibid., 4.

26 Ibid.

27 Ibid., 10.

28 Ibid., 33.

29 Ibid.

30 An edited version of the clip is available at: <http://www.youtube.com/watch?v=PN3uTy8NI78>.

31 François Noudelmann's book *The Philosopher's Touch*, and in particular his chapter on Roland Barthes, is very helpful in this context.

32 Benjamin, *Gesammelte Schriften, Vol. 4.1*, 9. Until I begin to discuss Harry Zohn's translation of the essay, all translations are mine. For the English translation, see Benjamin, "The Task of the Translator."

33 The only texts I know that pay serious attention to this otherwise ignored notion of translatability are Samuel Weber's *Benjamin's -Abilities* and Antoine Berman's *The Experience of the Foreign: Culture and Translation in Romantic Germany*. I would like to thank Farah Khelil and Bernard Stiegler for recommending Berman's book to me.

34 Benjamin, "Aufgabe," 10.

35 Ibid.

36 Ibid.

37 Ibid.

38 Benjamin, "Task," 70.
39 Ibid.
40 Ibid., 82.
41 Ibid.
42 See Klossowski, *Tableaux Vivants*, 81–7.
43 Agamben, *P*, 177.
44 Ibid., 179. See also Boever, "Bio-Paulitics."
45 Agamben, *P*, 179.
46 Ibid., 179–80.
47 Ibid., 243.
48 Ibid., 246–7.
49 Ibid., 249.
50 See Agamben, *SR*, in particular the volume's opening essay.
51 See Man, "'Conclusions.'"
52 Durantaye, *Giorgio Agamben*, 131.
53 De Man qtd. Durantaye, *Giorgio Agamben*, 130.
54 Durantaye, *Giorgio Agamben*, 132.
55 Ibid., 133–4.
56 Agamben, *CC*, 1.
57 Ibid.
58 Ibid., 85.
59 Ibid., 86.
60 I am expressing this task here in terms borrowed from Gilbert Simondon, to whose work I will turn in Chapter 6.
61 Sherman, *Complete*, cover jacket.
62 Agamben, *IS*, 96.
63 Sherman, "Making," 4.
64 Ibid., 6.
65 Ibid.
66 Ibid.
67 Ibid.
68 Ibid., 8.
69 Ibid., 8–9.
70 Ibid., 9.
71 Agamben, *PR*, 90.
72 Ibid.
73 Ibid.
74 Ibid.
75 Agamben, *N*, 88.

76 Ibid.
77 Agamben, *PR*, 90.
78 Ibid., 91.
79 Ibid.
80 Ibid.
81 Agamben, *N*, 90.
82 Agamben, *IS*, 97.
83 Ibid., 96.
84 Agamben, *MWE*, 100.
85 I have explored the problematic of the face in relation to Agamben's work in more detail in my article "Losing Face: Francis Bacon's *25th Hour*."

Part II: Economy

<h1 style="text-align:center">4</h1>

The Proletariat's Bare Life

The Biopolitical Mode of Production

After the September 11 terror attacks, Judith Butler wrote a collection of essays in which she addressed the psychic (ethical) and political consequences of this event. The book, which was published as *Precarious Life: The Powers of Mourning and Violence*, took its title from the French philosopher of ethics Emmanuel Levinas. Central to Levinas's philosophy of ethics is what he calls "the face of the other." The face, Butler explains, "is" Levinas's name for precarious life (she also notes that Levinas avoids saying what the face "is" since its otherness defies such definition). Strangely, precarious life *both* excites *and* forbids the temptation to kill. Butler reconfigures Levinas's theory for a global age in which human lives are increasingly interdependent, to an extent that no degree of self-fortification is able to match. In such a context, she argues, the investigation of precarious life can begin to take on new meaning, one she finds particularly pressing in the post-9/11 era of sovereign excesses in which the US shied away from reinvestigating its role in international politics.

As her book's title reveals, one of the things that Butler is interested in is how the post-9/11 era can be linked to what

149

could be called, bringing two divergent bodies of theory together, "a mode of biopolitical production." The mode of production language I take from Karl Marx; the term biopolitics I borrow from Michel Foucault. In the post-9/11 era, Butler's title suggests, life is rendered precarious. Today, "precariousness" is the "dominant" (if it can still make sense to use the adjective in this context) form of life, marking life's violent exposure to a political power that claims the sovereign privilege to act outside of the law, paradoxically in order to protect it. Clearly, there is a link – and Butler acknowledges this – between Butler's notion of precarious life and Giorgio Agamben's notion of bare life. Situated in a zone of indistinction between human and animal life, "bare life" names a thoroughly politicized "zoe" which is marked either by "too much law" (as in the case of the over-comatose Terri Schiavo, for example) or "not enough law" (as with the detainees at Guantánamo Bay). As Eric Santner has suggested in a text that was written on the occasion of the publication of his book *On Creaturely Life*, both situations mark a state of exception in which the relation between life and law is unbalanced, and life is brutally confronted with power.[1]

However, Butler's choice for and development of the term "precarious life" invites one to consider a few dimensions of bare life that both Agamben and Santner leave largely unexplored. One such dimension is the theory of international relations, which Agamben addresses briefly in his essay "Beyond Human Rights," but never develops in any sustained way. Butler notes the importance of a theory of precarious life for international relations theory (and practice) in her introduction to *Precarious Life*. I will be interested, however, in how Butler's understanding of the post-9/11 era as what I call a "mode of biopolitical production" opens up new insights into Agamben's *economic* thought and in the economic state of exception that followed the "war on terror" era that the 9/11 terror attacks opened up.

This focus on biopolitics is, of course, not new; it has been present throughout the previous chapters and will continue to resonate in what follows. However, the Marxist, "mode of production" language may come as somewhat of a surprise for readers of Agamben. Indeed, Marx does not take up a prominent place in Agamben's work, and Agamben has at least on one occasion said that Marx's work would need to undergo an extreme make-over in order to become relevant again in our time. Today's issues, he argues, are decidedly different from what they were at the time when Marx was writing.[2] Still, it should be noted that for Foucault, on whom Agamben is relying for his use of the term biopolitics, the problematic of biopolitics was certainly not separate from that of the modern economy.[3] Indeed, when Foucault presents his investigations on biopolitics, he spends much of his time talking about liberalism and the rise of neoliberalism. So even if Agamben may not explicitly connect his investigation into biopolitics to problems of the modern economy, it seems an obvious connection to pursue — and indeed, some of his most perceptive readers have been doing so in their discussions of his work.[4]

Now, Butler's use of the term "precarious" of course cannot but draw us into the Marxist tradition. Although she does not emphasize this (at least not here — it does come up in her book *Notes Toward a Performative Theory of Assembly*), "precarity" has long been used to refer to the conditions of labor and laborers under capitalism. Given these "economic" resonances, it is uncanny to look back at Butler's book now, more than a decade after it was published, as a prophetic text that in the choice of its central concept anticipated what turned out to be the real significance of the 9/11 event. As we now know, the collapse of the World Trade Center was ominous not only because it opened up the era of the war on terror (of which we are yet to see the end) but also because it pre-figured, years in advance, the crisis and crash of the economic system that began in 2008, and is ongoing.[5] If both Butler and Agamben arguably study biopolitical modes of production – states in which certain forms of life are produced – Butler's choice of words – *precarious* life – arguably already accounted for this economic crisis that was only to arrive many years later, at a time when the war on terror had become the order of the day.

All of this is not to say that economy is not a major component of Agamben's work: indeed, he has dedicated an entire installment of the *Homo Sacer* project to it, titled *The Kingdom and the Glory: For a Theological Genealogy of Economy and Government.* However, the economy that is discussed in that book is not the same as the one that is discussed in Marx. Although Agamben's economy is political, one could hardly characterize *The Kingdom and the Glory* as a treatise on political economy in the tradition of David Ricardo, Adam Smith, or Marx, even if such a tradition were to include more contemporary and unorthodox "political economists" such as Naomi Klein or David Graeber. By economy, Agamben refers to the trinity, in other words: the way in which God, who is thought to be One, governs on earth as three. This divided mode of government, which nevertheless does not contradict God's unity, is called "economy" in theological treatises and Agamben argues that it underlies all of our modern political structures. It is here that the word economy's etymological origins are exposed (the Ancient Greek word "oikonomia" refers to the law of the house, the rule or government of the house). Theological economy was nothing more than a name for the ways in which God managed his house, namely through the dispositif or apparatus of the trinity. It is only later that the modern sense of economy comes into being, and that the managerial dimension of "oikonomia" migrates into politics.

But this leaves us with (at least) one major question: how does Agamben's work relate to the *modern* sense of economy – to notions such as "the proletariat"; to the technological developments that were central in the transition from Ancient to Modern times; to "labor," "work," and "action" (to recall Hannah Arendt's political thought of human doings)? Although Agamben has circuitously addressed these questions, his work does not contain a sustained investigation into these notions, and part of what I propose to do in what follows is to pursue the connection between Agamben's work and "Marxism" in a little more detail so as to get a better sense of this particular "economic" dimension of Agamben's project.

I will begin, in this chapter, by investigating the connection between Agamben's notion of bare life and the Marxist proletariat. In Chapter 5, I will assess Agamben's evaluation of technology in light of his already discussed reference in *The Man Without Content* to the human being's *techne*: its uncanny – and politically risky – capacity to bring something from nonbeing into being; and in relation to the ontology and politics he proposes in his work. I will end Part II of this book with an investigation of the question of work, which Agamben has explicitly addressed in at least one text – and implicitly, through a discussion of the notion of "worklessness," in numerous other places. In view of this interest in worklessness, my discussion will focus on the politics of retirement, a topic that Agamben has never explicitly raised but that will reveal itself to be a productive pathway into the question of worklessness in his philosophy.

To pursue the connection between Agamben and "Marx" (if I can put it in this way, using a proper name to capture the general interest in modern economy from where the following chapters emerge) means to pair the plastic sovereignty that I have been theorizing in this book to the term with which sovereignty forms a couple in Agamben's writings: bare life. I theorize bare life in this chapter as life's explosive, limit-form – as the threshold beyond which life risks no longer being alive. Within such a configuration, *zoe* and *bios* can be considered the two other plastic dimensions of life: *zoe* is the simple fact of living, the life that can receive form; *bios* refers to ethical and political life, the ethical and political sculpting of life, the ways in which it can be shaped into individual and collective ways of living. Although Agamben might not see things this way, and although his writing might not on every count support this claim, I would argue that with the triangle of *zoe–bios*–bare life, he was able to name life's plasticity (receive–give–explode), which has become absolutely central not only to the life sciences, but also for example to the work of philosophers such as Catherine Malabou. It is in relation to this constellation, as I will show, that the terms "form-of-life" and "whatever being," the most promising names of a "positive" politics in his work, must be considered.

★

As is well known, Foucault started using the term biopower in his lectures at the Collège de France in Paris in the mid-1970s. He used it to refer to a kind of power that is "focused on the species body, the body imbued with the mechanics of life and serving as the basis of biological processes: propagation, births and mortality, the level of health, life expectancy and longevity."[6]

154

Bio-power was a key term in Foucault's analysis of what he called governmentality, or the ways in which power regulates the life of the population, for example through marriage laws, by regulating commerce, changing people's moral and religious values, et cetera. Unlike disciplinary power, which is "centered on the body as machine: its disciplining, the optimization of its capabilities, the extortion of its forces, the parallel increase of its usefulness and docility, its integration into systems of efficient and economic controls,"[7] and sovereignty, which is concerned with territory and imposes laws on people to protect the government against both civil war and external enemies, governmentality aspires to security. A government is secure when the population, through the ways in which its life is organized, guarantees the continuation of power. As Foucault explains, security does not aim to control in a disciplinary or sovereign way, but operates through *laissez-faire*. It does not force power onto the people, but aims to make the people live in such a way that the organization of their lives contributes to the consolidation of power.[8]

Both in the lectures and elsewhere, Foucault maintains an analytical separation – stricter in some texts than in others – between the different concepts he defines, for example between discipline and security, or between governmentality and sovereignty. Whereas discipline is centripetal and aims for final control, security is centrifugal and operates through *laissez-faire*. Whereas sovereignty imposes laws on people, governmentality disposes things, specifically people in their relation to things such as natural resources, riches, et cetera. The idea here is not so much that these different modes of power are actually separate, or would chronologically supersede each other, but that they operate at the same time. In order to understand the dynamics of power, one needs to take recourse to these analytical distinctions, even though actual power relations can never be reduced to one mode of power that would be fully separate from another. When in the lectures, Foucault argues that capitalism is biopolitical, he thus implies that as a power relation, it should be understood as a *predominantly* governmental relation.[9] Although such an argument has revealed much about capitalism that would otherwise have remained in the dark, it also partly risks forgetting the ways in which sovereignty is implicated in capitalism. Sovereignty is, in fact, an essential part of the prehistory of capital as Marx tells it in the section in *Capital* entitled "So-Called Primitive Accumulation." The capitalist relation demands an analysis of power that would integrate the different concepts and kinds of power that Foucault defines.[10]

In this chapter, I reconsider Marx's prehistory of capital through the lens of Agamben's work. In the wake of Foucault, Agamben has proposed a biopolitical theory of sovereign power in order to draw attention to the ways in which governmentality and sovereignty operate together. Although Agamben mentions Marx only once in his study of sovereign power,[11] I argue that his study nevertheless contributes to our understanding of the capitalist relation as not only a governmental but also a sovereign power relation. My aim is not just to highlight the presence of sovereignty in Marx's prehistory of capital, or to draw attention to the Marxist dimension of Agamben's work, but also to explore a mode of power analysis that would integrate the concepts and kinds of power that Foucault defines. As Judith Butler has argued, such integrated modes of analysis are of crucial importance today, when we are witnessing a return of sovereignty within the field of governmentality, as the power to suspend national and international law in the name of national security or a national emergency.[12]

In the first part of the chapter, I show that the proletariat in Marx is a figure of what Agamben in his study of sovereign power calls bare life. I do so not by considering bare life through the lens of Marx's theory of value (which could be another interesting track to pursue – in a way, my discussion of the logic of the surplus in Chapter 1 has already done this with reference to both language and the body), but through a philological commentary on the adjective that Marx uses again and again to characterize the proletariat and that partly goes lost in the English translation of his text, namely the word "vogelfrei" or "free, rightless, without protection, outlawed."

This sovereign dimension of the capitalist relation is also substantiated, as I show in the second part of the chapter, by Marx's analysis of the logic of the capitalist relation as that of the exception. After Carl Schmitt, who wrote that "sovereign is who decides on the state of exception,"[13] Agamben has argued that the logic of the exception is the logic of sovereign power. Reconsidered through the lens of Agamben's argument, Marx's account of the prehistory of capital reveals that there is a sovereign logic of the exception at work in the capitalist relation. It is this logic that produces the proletariat as a figure of bare life.

In the final part of the chapter, I start from Agamben's single reference to Marx in his study of sovereign power to discuss the importance of these conclusions for Agamben's political message, specifically for the acts of divine violence that he is calling for in response to the problems of sovereign power that he analyzes. If the answer to some of these problems is an economic politics of "the highest poverty" as Agamben theorizes it in a later volume in the *Homo Sacer* series, then what is the relation of this poverty and the form–of–life that it names to the exceptionalist sovereignty that Agamben criticizes?

The Sacred Proletariat

Taking his cue from Foucault's work on biopolitics, and deconstructing the separation between governmentality and sovereignty that Foucault sets up, Agamben proposes a biopolitical theory of sovereign power. Following Schmitt, he defines sovereign power as the power to decide on the state of exception; sovereign power is the power to suspend national and international law in the name of a national emergency or national security. In modern sovereign nation-states, the possibility that is contained within the law to suspend the law in exceptional circumstances has become the rule. All human life that is related to the legal and political order of the sovereign nation-state is related to it through the logic of exception. Whereas a citizen of a sovereign nation-state may think she or he is living under the protection of sovereign power, she or he is in fact internally excluded within the legal and political community that sovereign power founds. One of the examples Agamben discusses that make this clear is human rights. The very fact that they exist illustrates that there is no place within the legal and political community of the sovereign nation-state for something like "the human as such." Instead, this "human as such" is internally excluded within it. If a human being does not want to assimilate to the identity the sovereign community believes to share, and if she or he refuses to be repatriated as well, she or he will be held indefinitely in a camp at the borders of the sovereign territory. Thus, as far as we are all instances of "the human as such," we all live in a virtual state of internal exclusion within the sovereign nation-states to which we belong or to which we relate. The camp is the biopolitical matrix of the modern sovereign nation-state.

The life that is produced in the camps at the borders of the sovereign territory Agamben calls bare life. He uses this term to refer to a life stripped of all its qualities except for the mere fact of being alive. Bare life is the ultimate biopolitical substance: it is life that is produced by sovereign power. Although this ultimately risks erasing the concrete differences between a citizen and a refugee, Agamben will polemically assert that all human life (both that of a citizen and of a refugee) relates to sovereign power as bare life. His work is filled with figures of bare life. The most important one, which he also uses as the title of his book on sovereign power, he takes from Roman law: *homo sacer* or the holy person.[14] Contrary to what one may expect, the holy person was a person who was in-between human law and divine law and could be killed but not sacrificed. What interests Agamben about this figure is that she or he could be killed with impunity, without the killing being considered a crime. As an outlaw figure, the holy person belonged to the legal and political order of the Roman Empire by being excluded from it. Although Agamben does not discuss this, I want to argue that the proletariat in Marx is a figure of what Agamben calls bare life. Excavating this relationship can contribute much to our understanding of the capitalist relation as a power relation.

The relation between the holy person and the proletariat becomes visible in the first volume of Marx's *Capital I* in a section entitled "So-Called Primitive Accumulation." In this section, Marx describes the historical process through which the producers (the workers) were divorced from the means of production. As he points out, this process produced a kind of freedom around which two sorts of commodity owners arose: on the one hand, "the owners of money, means of production, and means of subsistence"; and, on the other, the "free workers, sellers of their own labor-power, and therefore the sellers of labor."[15] As Marx tells the story, what was produced during this prehistory of capital was a kind of life: whereas human life used to be a part of the means of production, it is now split from the means of production, a split through which it enters into a freedom that Marx understands to be the absence of a protection that was guaranteed by the structures of feudalism. All the guarantees of the old feudal relations suddenly fell away and what remained was an extremely vulnerable kind of life that existed in-between the dying feudalist and the emerging capitalist orders.

It is not difficult to see how what Marx is describing can be read as an example of what Foucault called governmentality, and specifically of biopolitics.[16] The prehistory of capital tells the story of how people's lives are being reorganized in such a way that they contribute to the consolidation of the new capitalist order. This reorganization pertains to the biological life of the people, the life of the population, which is produced as biopolitical substance by the emerging capitalist order. This reorganization is not forced on the people but actually operates through *laissez-faire*, by creating the desire for freedom that then leads to the people's expropriation. But to limit one's analysis of capitalism as a power relation to governmentality and biopolitics, that is: to forget about the role that sovereignty plays within these developments, would mean to overlook an important dimension of the prehistory that Marx narrates.

Consider, for example, how Marx describes the group of people – the "class that does not form a class" – that capitalism's biopolitics (or, more precisely, that the biopolitics of the *prehistory* of capitalism) produces, the proletariat. Of the forty instances of the word "proletariat" or "proletarian" in the first volume of *Capital*, nineteen occur in the section on so-called primitive accumulation; in seven of those nineteen instances the word is accompanied by the adjective "vogelfrei." Ben Fowkes variously translates "vogelfrei" as "free," "rightless," "unattached," or "unprotected." Although the word is highly idiomatic and poses some difficulties for the translator, Fowkes does not comment on it until the beginning of the chapter on bloody legislation, where he adds the note: "Here, as elsewhere, Marx uses the word 'vogelfrei', literally 'free as a bird', i.e. free but outside of the human community and therefore entirely unprotected and without legal rights."[17] Although Fowkes's translations of "vogelfrei" are of course correct, it also needs to be noted that the dictionary translation of the word is "outlawed," a word that in combination with the other translations that Fowkes offers begins to reveal the connection between the proletariat and the holy person.

This connection can be made more substantive by adding a few historical etymological remarks about the word "vogelfrei." According to most dictionaries, it means both "frei von Herrschaftsdiensten, frei wie ein Vogel in der Luft" ("free from [feudalist] servitude, free as a bird in the sky"; end of the fifteenth century) and also "rechtlos, ohne gesetzlichen Schutz, geächtet" ("rightless, without legal protection, outlawed"; sixteenth century).[18] From the sixteenth century onwards, this second semantic component becomes dominant, which means that by the time that Marx is writing (1867), even though he is of course also interested in the word's meaning "free from servitude," its primary meaning is actually that of "outlawed" or "free, rightless, unprotected." It thus seems that for Marx, the proletariat is a figure of a legal and political abandonment that Agamben is also interested in.

The literal meaning of the word "vogelfrei" underlines the biopolitical dimension of this abandonment. It literally means "den Vögeln (zum Frasse) freigegeben, da dem Körper eines Geächteten das Grab versagt wurde" ("free for the birds to eat, since the body of an outlawed person could not be buried").[19] The relation between the proletariat and the holy person becomes most explicit in Jacob and Wilhelm Grimm's explanation of the word: "exlex ... verbannet ... expositus ad necem" ("outside the law ... banned ... exposed to death"); "dem körper eines geächteten wird das grab versagt mit der sich mehr und mehr vordrängenden vorstellung dasz der geächtete der tötung ausgesetzt ist und nicht behaust werden darf" ("the body of an outlawed person cannot be buried, with the more and more foregrounded idea that the outlawed person can be killed and cannot be put up in one's house").[20] This last semantic component actually works well with another figure of bare life that I mentioned earlier on, the refugee.

These philological notes reveal that the proletariat is related to the holy person. They show that the life of the proletariat is considered by Marx to be a kind of life that can be killed with impunity, without the killing being considered a crime. This is the situation that is evoked by the adjective "vogelfrei."

On the basis of Agamben's study of bare life, which argues this kind of life to be inextricably related to sovereignty, one can thus begin to see that there is something sovereign about the capitalist relation as a power relation. This is not only because the proletariat is a figure of bare life, but also because capitalism acts in the ways that sovereignty does, that is: through the logic of exception – something that Naomi Klein has powerfully demonstrated in her book *The Shock Doctrine*, one of the most important works of political economy of our time.

A Tale of Exception

"Sovereign is who decides on the state of exception," Schmitt famously writes at the beginning of *Political Theology*.[21] Agamben starts from there in order to formulate the paradox of sovereign power: in order to declare that there is nothing outside the law, the sovereign needs to take up a position outside the law, that is: she or he needs to except her- or himself from the law in order to take up a place from where the legal order can be founded and suspended. According to Schmitt, the logic of the exception is that of theology. The sovereign relates to the law from a transcendental position of exception. That the law contains the sovereign possibility of its own suspension also means that human life relates to sovereign power through the exception. Its position in relation to the law is not a transcendental one, however, but a biopolitical position of subjection. Agamben's aim is to dismantle the device of the state of exception through which life has been brought within the law, and through which politics has been eclipsed by biopolitics.

Marx's use of the word "vogelfrei" reveals his interest in the relation of the proletariat to the law. But he also discusses the relation of the capitalist to the law. What he describes in the prehistory of capital is, basically, how capitalism came into being through a series of exceptional measures that are situated at the limit of the legal order. The prehistory of capital was carried out by legal means, he writes, but "without any legal formality."[22] It happened "without the slightest observance of legal etiquette."[23] In the end, *the law itself* became "the instrument by which the people's land is stolen";[24] in other words, the law became a capitalist law, a mere tactic in an economic game of power. As Marx sees it, the capitalists acted like little sovereigns in order to put through their reorganization of the lives of the people. They were side-stepping the legal and political order that was guaranteed by the sovereign in a successful attempt to continue the relation of servitude that existed under feudalism.

Although this means there is a complicity between sovereignty and capitalism through the ways in which they both operate according to the logic of exception, it also reveals there is a difference between the two because the capitalists are actually side-stepping a legal order that is guaranteed by the sovereign. This side-stepping move may be a move that is familiar to sovereignty; but it does not come with sovereignty's important ethical and political implications – and this is one of the reasons, as I indicated in my Prologue, why I refuse to give up on sovereignty in this book (there are others who have insisted on this, that is: that we must distinguish between sovereignty and abusive sovereignty). It may thus be that the prehistory of capital as Marx tells it actually opens up new possibilities for sovereignty in the resistance against capitalism, that is: it gestures to a kind of power that would be greater than economic power, and would be able to limit and condition the claims of capitalism. Politics also emerges here – with some goodwill on the part of the reader, goodwill that is hard to come by, of course, in the era of post-sovereignty – as what could keep economics in check. The problem is, however, that both sovereignty and capitalism suffer from the logic of exception, which is responsible for political and economic abuses of power. As Marx's discussion anticipates, the mere granting of rights – associated with capitalism – does not necessarily overcome this problem, since in the pre-history of capital, it is ultimately *the law itself* that becomes the instrument of exploitation. Marx's account thus raises the need not simply for law, but for what I will call, for the moment, for lack of a better expression, its *other uses*.

Reconsidered through the lens of Agamben's biopolitical theory of sovereign power, Marx's prehistory of capital thus shows not only that the capitalist relation as a power relation is biopolitical, and that the transition of feudalism to capitalism is an example of what Foucault called governmentality, but also that sovereignty plays a crucial role in this development. It shows the capitalists to be acting like little sovereigns, according to the logic of exception. Their actions produce a figure of bare life, namely the proletariat. In order to understand the capitalist relation as a power relation, we need to integrate the different kinds of power that Foucault outlines in his lectures at the Collège de France, governmentality and sovereignty.

This insight is particularly important today, when we try to understand, for example, a phenomenon like the Guantánamo Bay detention center. In this "prison" (in Agamben's language, one would call it a "camp"), human beings suspected of terrorist activities are being held indefinitely, on the basis of no or very little evidence, and without the possibility of a civil trial. Guantánamo is not only an example of disciplinary power; in order to understand its existence, we need to understand the exceptional, sovereign measures taken in the name of national security that make indefinite detention possible and that produce human life as bare life – a life stripped of all its qualities, lived in suspense, at the borders of the legal and political order of the sovereign nation-state. In this last sense, Guantánamo is an example of a biopolitical state of exception. Guantánamo Bay necessitates, in other words, a much more integrated analysis of power than the one that could be all too easily derived from the analytical framework Foucault sets up in his lectures. As I have tried to emphasize above, this does not mean such an integrated analysis should erase the differences between discipline, security, sovereignty, biopolitics, et cetera. Sovereignty is not capitalism; capitalism does not have sovereignty's important ethical and political implications; there is a more dynamic relation between both that opens up possibilities for other uses of both politics and economy. It is from this insight, I would argue, that we can begin to get a better sense of Agamben's politics, and of the plastic sovercignty that I theorize in this book.

Sovereignty and Capitalism after Divine Violence

At first sight, Marx and Agamben seem to be thinkers who are interested in fundamentally different issues. Whereas Marx is interested in the question of economic exploitation, Agamben is interested in the relation of sovereign power to bare life. These interests are similar though in the sense that they both concern questions of political economy. Marx is interested in the political economy of capitalism; Agamben in the political economy of sovereign power. Agamben's argument, for example, that within the legal and political order of the modern sovereign nation-state, there is no place for something like "the human as such" is nothing but a critique of the political economy of the sovereign nation-state, the ways in which its methods of "counting" internally exclude human life and produce it as biopolitical substance. It is within the field of political economy that the connections between Marx and Agamben, and the complicities between capitalism and sovereign power, are revealed. This shows that there is a relation between the economic exploitation that Marx was interested in and the relation between sovereign power and totalitarianism that Agamben addresses.

Although Agamben has written about Marx in his aesthetic works and in his philological commentary on Saint Paul's "Letter to the Romans,"[25] he mentions him only once in his study of sovereign power and bare life, *Homo Sacer*. In the final chapter of this book, in a meditation about the notion of "the people," Agamben suggests we understand the Marxian "class conflict" as

> nothing other than the civil war that divides every people and that will come to an end only when, in the classless society or the messianic kingdom, People and people will coincide and there will no longer be, strictly speaking, any people.[26]

Class conflict would thus become an instance of the civil war that Agamben considers to divide every people, in other words, of the practices of internal exclusion through which sovereign power biopolitically separates the People from the people (for example, the practices through which power within the legal and political order of the sovereign nation-state separates citizens from second-class citizens).

As he will explain in his later *The Time That Remains*, it is only through the division of this biopolitical separation – by dividing the division itself – that we will enter into a classless society and that something like the community of "the human as such" will arrive. Because of the ways in which Saint Paul in his "Letter to the Romans" divides the division between Jews and Greeks through the division between flesh and spirit, arguing that one can be a Jew in spirit but not according to the flesh (that is: there can be such a thing as an uncircumcised Jew), Paul's thought achieves something that puts us on the way to the "classless society or the messianic kingdom" that Agamben is talking about when he refers to Marx in *Homo Sacer*. It is in this way that the proletariat becomes interesting for Agamben, as a name for the group of people – or more precisely, as a name for the group that would come into being through the dissolution of the people – that is created by Paul's division of the division. Like Marx, who both diagnoses the class situation of the proletariat and finds in the proletariat the potential for a revolutionary overthrow of class society, Agamben considers the proletariat to be both a figure of bare life and the site from where the coming community emerges.

Although Marx is largely absent from the bleak diagnosis of sovereign power's biopolitics that *Homo Sacer* offers, he neverthe-less appears in the book's closing chapter, in one of those frequent passages where Agamben is trying to gesture beyond mere diagnosis toward a vision of the legal and political community that would remain after sovereign power's biopolitics has been dismantled. This presence of Marx in Agamben's vision of a coming community begs the question that I have tried to address above, namely of the relation of Marx's work – specifically, the biopolitical theory of capitalism that Foucault uncovered in it – to Agamben's theory of sovereign power. If there is a relation between Marx's work and Agamben's vision of a coming community, then what is the place of Marx in the critique of sovereign power from which this vision emerges? Although Agamben so far has not explicitly addressed this question, he does reveal in interviews that the questions Marx raises are important for him, and for our time. They have not become obsolete, but they need to be thought anew, within the paradigm of modern power, which is that of the sovereign nation-state's biopolitics.

Agamben acknowledges this is a difficult task, and I have merely offered a few philological notes and reflections that go in the direction of such a rethinking. Interestingly, however, philology and criticism are directly implicated in the realization of the coming community that Agamben is calling for. How will the classless society or messianic kingdom that is announced in the closing chapter of *Homo Sacer* be achieved? Agamben argues this will come about through acts of what he calls "divine violence." As I have discussed in Chapter 2, he takes this figure from Benjamin's essay "Critique of Violence." In "Critique of Violence," Benjamin calls for a human agency outside the law, more specifically one that would break with the mythical dialectic of law-making and law-preserving violence that is character-istic of sovereign power (this should be clear from what I wrote above about the sovereign logic of the exception). In response to Benjamin's essay, the conservative juror Carl Schmitt – who could not tolerate Benjamin's call for a human agency outside the law – brought divine violence within the law through the device of the state of exception. Thus, his concept of sover-eignty, defined as the power to decide on the state of exception, was born. For his analysis of sovereign power, Agamben is with Schmitt. When he is proposing solutions to the problems that he analyses, however, he is with Benjamin. Throughout his work, Agamben is calling for non-violent acts of divine violence that would dismantle the state of exception, mark the end of sover-eign violence, and liberate politics from its "lasting eclipse."[27] This has to do with severing the nexus between life and law through which human life has become biopoliticized.

But what are the acts of divine violence that Agamben is calling for? Perhaps surprisingly, and maybe frustratingly so, they are all in some sense "poetic," and in an ultimate sense "aes-thetic," as I have argued – related to language, art, storytelling, translation, and the distribution that informs these terms. The examples of acts of divine violence that he gives in the closing text of *Infancy and History: On the Destruction of Experience* are: philology, poetry, and criticism. These acts of divine violence are intensely political according to Agamben because they achieve an "*Aufhebung* of the mythology"[28] that he (following Benjamin) considers to characterize sovereign power. What Agamben is concerned with, however, is not so much the politics of these acts, but whether there can be a politics that would remain true to its cohesion with philology, poetry, and criticism. He is arguing for a kind of linguistic activity that would reclaim its place within the political, in such a way that a politics true to its cohesion with the linguistic would become possible.

What would such a politics look like, and what would be its effect on sovereignty and the law? This is one of the questions about Agamben's work that is most difficult to answer, and that divides his critics into those who think he advocates the destruction of sovereignty and law and those who think otherwise. In certain places, Agamben seems to argue for the former, that is: critics have cited passages in *Homo Sacer* or Agamben's notes on politics entitled *Means Without End*, that explicitly advocate a non-statist, sovereignty-less community. But there are other places where Agamben writes that he is not interested in the destruction of sovereign power and law, but in another use of them. This suggests that a reading of Agamben's work as advocating a blind destruction of sovereign power and law is too easy and does not take seriously enough the difficult task it sets before humanity. The acts of divine violence that Agamben is interested in lead to a messianic fulfillment of the law, or a time in which the law would not be destroyed but deactivated and rendered inoperative – that is, be used in a different way, as Agamben explains.[29] As such, divine violence does not violently destroy the law, but in a non-violent way introduces a difference into it through which the device of the state of exception is dismantled, and sovereign power and law are not abandoned but wholly transformed.[30]

When Agamben proposes that the notion of "right" be replaced by that of "refuge" so as to dismantle the logic of exception that characterizes the political economy of the sovereign nation-state, one begins to get a sense of what such a transformation would look like; also helpful in this respect is his discussion of the problem of Jerusalem, which he develops into a new model for international relations that would liberate the transnational constellation of Europe from the sovereign nation-state's logic of exception.[31] In this book, I am proposing a theory of plastic sovereignty to capture the transformation of sovereignty that Agamben is proposing.

The question that remains, at this point, is what this entails for capitalism. Is a similar "other use" of capitalism possible? Maybe one should broaden the question here and ask about uses of the economic order that would be other than capitalist. It makes no sense, obviously, to take up a position that is against all political economies; the question is, rather: what kind of political economy do we want? How can the political economies that we have and in which we live be improved on? (And what does "improve" mean? Improve for whom?) As I suggested above, it may be that the alternative uses of sovereign power and law that will emerge from acts of divine violence will inspire alternative uses of political economy also.

Agamben has come closest to these questions in his book *The Highest Poverty: Monastic Rules and Form-Of-Life*, a book that, while it does not explicitly deal with the problem of economy, has been presented (by its translator) in this way; in addition, the title appears to invite an economic reading of the book. With *The Highest Poverty*, Agamben's work seems to have taken a different, "positive" turn after the grim diagnostic of the earlier volumes in the *Homo Sacer* series.

Let me quickly recall: *Homo Sacer*, and the theory of sovereign power and bare life it develops, famously starts with what Agamben presents to be a distinction, made by the Ancient Greeks, between *zoe* (the simple fact of living) and *bios* (individual and collective forms of living). It is from the dynamic relation between these two words for life that "bare life" emerges. While few readers have acknowledged this, bare life is thus a third – and, as I have suggested earlier, plastic – kind of life that exists in addition to *zoe* and *bios*, and comes into being through the fact that when a distinction between the simple fact of living and forms of living is maintained, the former always risks being stripped from the latter, and be produced as bare life – as life brutally exposed to power, as the simple fact of living without the protection that an added symbolic identity would give to it (this is the logic of surplus that I have discussed in the first part of this book). Bare life is the explosive dimension of life's plasticity. When Agamben, in a text titled "Nudity," takes on the opposition between nudity and clothing, or what he also calls nature and culture, stating that his aim "is not to tap into an original state prior to [their] separation but to comprehend and neutralize the apparatus that produced this separation,"[32] one understands that he is targeting the separation between *zoe* and *bios* that is at the center of all of his work (with *zoe* coming down on the side of nudity/nature and *bios* on the side of clothing/culture).

As I have already mentioned, Eric Santner's discussion of the Terri Schiavo cases through the lens of Agamben's work has shown that brutal exposure to power can be generated in two ways, not just by stripping *bios* away but also by enforcing it, with the result that *zoe* comes to coincide fully with *bios*. Not enough law or too much law are the two types of excess that risk generating bare life in the vicious dynamic between *zoe* and *bios*.

The generation of bare life is the typical activity of sovereignty, Agamben argues. This was realized in a most extreme way in the twentieth-century concentration camp (though some would doubt that this can be analyzed as an example of sovereignty; they would argue, rather, that is an example of a sovereignty that has failed, a sovereignty that is no longer sovereign). Much of Agamben's work seeks to expose the ways in which these operations of sovereignty are still ongoing today, sometimes through the very legalo-political institutions that we hold most dearly – for example, human rights. Agamben's project has been to dismantle the biopolitical machine of Western power that incessantly generates bare life.

In the later volumes of the *Homo Sacer* series, this project has begun to receive a positive articulation, developing the negative diagnostic of bare life toward the theorization of what Agamben calls, in *The Highest Poverty* and elsewhere, form-of-life. In *Means Without End*, Agamben had already proposed the syntagma "form-of-life" – with hyphens, to distinguish it from mere *bios*, which also names forms of life – "in which it is never possible to isolate something like naked life,"[33] as a response to the problem of bare life that he diagnoses. The phrase appears on the final page of *Homo Sacer* as well, but remains undeveloped there.

So: what is form-of-life, and how does it respond to the problem of bare life? Given bare life's close relation to sovereignty with which it forms a couple, what is form-of-life's relation to sovereignty? Does form-of-life leave sovereignty entirely behind? If form-of-life is intimately associated with "the highest poverty," what is its economy? How does it challenge the exceptionalist economy of capitalism with which exceptionalist sovereignty is complicit?

"The object of this study," *The Highest Poverty* begins, "is to construct a form-of-life, that is to say, a life that is linked so closely to its form that it proves to be inseparable from it."[34] The book's main focus will be on the relation between "rule" and "life," specifically the "rule" according to which monks live, and live together. It is important to realize, from the get-go, that as such, the relation between rule and life will not be the *same* as form-of-life; rather, Agamben begins from the relation between rule and life in order to arrive at his construction of form-of-life. That said, the relation between rule and life will already be an important step on the way toward form-of-life, because it already marks a complex step beyond the relation between life and law that is at the heart of the problems of sovereignty that Agamben diagnoses.

At the end of his book *State of Exception*, in which (as I will discuss in the final part of this book) the question "What does it mean to act politically?" is central, Agamben makes a plea for a politics that would exist in life's non-relation to law. The problem of life and politics today, he argues, is that life has become so thoroughly saturated with law that no room for properly political action remains. In this way, the law has eclipsed politics, an eclipse that is marked by the hyphen that splices law and politics together in the term "legalo-political." He argues instead that the law needs to be separated from life so that politics can be restored to its proper place outside of the law. It is only from such a separation that we will be able to answer the question about what it means to act *politically* – and not *legalo*-politically. This problem of life's saturation by law, of life's total coincision with law to the extent that the two become nearly indistinguishable, is central to *The Highest Poverty*. Agamben's theorization of form-of-life needs to be understood as a response to this problem.

Why is the relation between rule and life of interest to Agamben, and how does it differ from the tortured relation between life and law that he criticizes elsewhere? The relation between rule and life will be a step for Agamben to think a form-of-life that is "entirely removed from the grasp of the law"; this will involve – and this is where we link up with the economic concerns of this part of my book – "a use of bodies and of the world that would never be substantiated into an appropria-tion." The project is, instead, "to think life as that which is never given as property but only as common use." It is this "common use" that the title of the book, "the highest poverty," refers to. "The highest poverty" marks, in other words, not just a highly specific kind of poverty (the wealth of common use – it is well known that the monks, while their rule may prescribe common use, were not necessarily poor), but also a specific relation – or rather, non-relation – to law.

Agamben states elsewhere that "the highest poverty" names an "extraneousness to the law."[35] This statement arrives in the section of the book titled "Form-of-Life" that deals specifically with the Franciscan order. Here, the problematic of the state of exception that is central to Agamben's critique of sovereignty returns. Agamben explains that the monks, through the rule by which they live (or rather: the rule *that* they live, for their life perfectly coincides with the rule), retire or withdraw from law and rights. In other words, they choose "a human existence beyond the law."[36] When all is normal, they live in something that can arguably be compared to a state of exception. As

Agamben explains, it is only in an exceptional situation, that is: when there is a situation of emergency or crisis, that they take recourse to the law – thus effectively transforming the logic of the state of exception as it operates in Western democratic politics. Normally, in a state of exception, the law is suspended in the name of a national emergency or security situation; it is precisely in such situations that the monks take recourse to the law. In all other, normal situations, they withdraw from the law and from every right. As Agamben points out, this practice at the same time "reverses" and "absolutizes" the state of exception, because it turns its logic inside out and takes the exceptional situation in which the law is suspended as its "rule." However, it is as such that it becomes the starting point for Agamben to think a form-of-life, where life would be its own form beyond the law.

As Agamben discusses, there is a power struggle that developed around the monks' choice to live outside the grip of the law. The Church was quick to try to appropriate this practice within its law, and thus to turn this into a situation in which life would absolutely coincide with law. This is, in fact, the risk of the rule: the ways in which monasticism can be appropriated by the Church for its own purposes. It is this development that has contributed to the absolute coincision of life and law that Agamben criticizes. The monastic rule, however, is different from this, since it defines itself precisely through its distance from the law – a potentiality or "can" that precisely cannot be fully absorbed by the law. It is therefore the monks' practice, their rule of life, that separates them from life's relation to law and puts Agamben on the track of form-of-life. Thus, the life of the rule, and form-of-life, begin to function as counterparts to bare life and the stripping away of law or excessive coincision of life and law that it marks. They are the messianic counterparts to the dark, destructive plasticity of bare life.

As far as the rule and form-of-life's relation to sovereignty go, it is not entirely clear that this form-of-life would mark the end of sovereignty. Indeed, in the first part of *The Highest Poverty* – a title that, by its very taking recourse to "the highest," appears to mark a certain kind of sovereignty – Agamben writes about the "superior power" or "sovereignty" of the abbot, distinguishing it from the kind of sovereignty that can be found in Hobbes or Rousseau. Whereas the latter knows no limits, Agamben points out that the former is obliged "to govern with justice and equity."[37] So it appears that, at least when we are talking about the rule, a sense of sovereignty is still maintained: one that would be quite different from the sovereignty that Agamben criticizes. As I have already pointed out, this other sovereignty also maintains a relation to the state of exception, even if it reverses and absolutizes it. It is not clear, at least to this reader, whether form-of-life (which appears to go one step beyond the rule) would maintain this relation to sovereignty and the state of exception.

Indeed, this proximity of the rule to the state of exception can be confusing in Agamben's work, as for example at the end of *Homo Sacer*, where he offers an extreme if not arbitrary list of what appear to be figures of bare life. However, the first of these figures, the so-called *Flamen Diale*, may ultimately be closer to the monks whose lives Agamben is analyzing in *The Highest Poverty*. Agamben explains that the life of the *Flamen Diale*, "one of the greatest priests of classical Rome," was

> remarkable in that it is at every moment indistinguishable from the cultic functions that the *Flamen* fulfills. This is why the Romans said that the *Flamen Diale* is *quotidie feriatus* and *assiduus sacerdos*, that is, in an act of uninterrupted celebration at every

instant. Accordingly, there is no gesture or detail of his life, the way he dresses or the way he walks, that does not have a precise meaning and is not caught up in a series of functions and meticulously studied effects.[38]

When Agamben writes, in the conclusion of the section, that in the life of this priest, it is no longer possible to isolate something like bare life, we can read this as an echo of the discussion of form-of-life in *Means Without End*, where Agamben defines form-of-life's accomplishment to be that in this kind of life, it would no longer be possible to isolate something like naked life. The *Flamen*, then, may be a "positive," albeit extreme, example of a development toward form-of-life that Agamben will later become interested in.

However, I have elsewhere taken a different approach to this figure, presenting it as a negative example of how our lives are being written today.[39] This specific, literary-political concern is not extraneous to Agamben's project. In the second part of *The Highest Poverty*, he is interested precisely in the writing of life, the coincision of life and text: "The text of the rule," he notes,

> is thus not only a text in which the distinction between writing and reading tends to become blurred, but also one in which writing and life, being and living become properly indiscernible in the form of a total liturgicization of life and a vivification of liturgy that is just as entire.[40]

It is, however, as this liturgicization that the Church's power hold on the rule begins. Hence, the rule is not entirely positive but pharmacological, and the example of the *Flamen* can be developed in both a positive and a negative direction.

The confusion can be summed up by Agamben's definition of form-of-life on the final page of *Homo Sacer* as "this being that is only its own bare existence."[41] How is such a being – bare existence – different, one cannot but ask, from the bare life that Agamben has so sharply criticized? When, at the end of his text "Nudity," Agamben embraces Benjamin's claim "that beauty can exist as essence only where the duality of nudity and clothing no longer exists: in art and the phenomena of naked nature [blossen Natur],"[42] one cannot but wonder here as well what the difference is, exactly, between this "naked nature" and the "naked life" that both Benjamin and Agamben criticize elsewhere.

In short: while the rule already marks a significant step away from the problematic relation of life and law that Agamben criticizes – with the life of the monk being opposed to the life of *homo sacer* – one also gets the sense in *The Highest Poverty* that with the rule, one has not reached the final point of Agamben's investigations yet. And indeed, *The Highest Poverty* announces a final volume in the *Homo Sacer* series dedicated to the question of use. It is most likely there that Agamben's critical investigation of economy – with its implications for the modern economy that he spends so little time talking about – will come to fruition, given that the highest poverty names a common use that marks the end of the property-relation that lies at the origin of capitalism.

Notes

1   See <http://www.press.uchicago.edu/Misc/Chicago/05april_santner. html>. I will return to these two types of exceptional excess in the final part of this book.
2   See <http://www.vacarme.org/article255.html>.
3   Foucault's relation to Marx and Marxism is a complicated one that I do not have time to discuss here.

4 See, for example, Kotsko, "Saint Paul"; see also Whyte, "'The king.'"
5 I hope to be able to return to this point in a book on finance and the contemporary US novel, tentatively titled *Finance Fictions*.
6 Foucault, *History*, 139.
7 Ibid.
8 See Foucault, *Security*.
9 See Foucault, *Birth*.
10 One of the most interesting things about the lectures is that they show Foucault trying to analytically separate between different concepts and kinds of power, a separation that he is then partly forced to undo when he turns to the particular historical examples he analyzes.
11 It is perhaps for this reason that the relation between Agamben's work, Marx, and Marxism remains relatively unexplored. Antonio Negri has emphasized the importance of Marx and Marxism for Agamben's thought (Negri, "Giorgio Agamben").
12 See Butler, "Indefinite Detention."
13 Schmitt, *Political Theology*, 5. Translation slightly modified.
14 See Agamben, *HS*.
15 Marx, *Capital*, 874.
16 Again, much could be said here about Foucault's relation to Marx and Marxism, but doing so would lead me too far away from the immediate concerns of this chapter.
17 Marx, *Capital*, 896.
18 *Etymologisches Wörterbuch*, 1916.
19 Ibid.
20 *Deutsches Wörterbuch*, 408–9.
21 Schmitt, *Political Theology*, 5. Translation slightly modified.
22 Marx, *Capital*, 883.
23 Ibid., 884.
24 Ibid., 885.
25 See Agamben, *TR*.
26 Agamben, *HS*, 178.
27 Agamben, *SE*, 88.
28 Agamben, *IH*, 163.
29 Agamben, *SE*, 64; Agamben, *TR*, 97–8.
30 Tom Frost makes this point in his discussion of Agamben's relation to "tradition": Frost, "Agamben."
31 See Agamben, *MWE*.
32 Agamben, *N*, 66.

33 Agamben, *MWE*, 8–9.
34 Agamben, *HP*, xi.
35 Ibid., 122.
36 Ibid., 110.
37 Ibid., 52.
38 Agamben, *HS*, 182–3.
39 Boever, *Narrative Care*, 71.
40 Agamben, *HP*, 82.
41 Agamben, *HS*, 188.
42 Agamben, *N*, 85.

5

Technology, Ontology, Politics

Technology's Plasticity

Although the birth of the proletariat is linked first of all to the processes of expropriation from land that Marx describes in the chapter from *Capital I* titled "So-Called Primitive Accumulation" that I discussed in the previous chapter, it is impossible to think the proletariat as separate from the heavy industrial machinery crowding the nineteenth-century factories in the cities to which this new form of life was banned. Today, in the sweatshop and branding era, our pristine, high-tech apparatuses may very well have been designed in white-out offices in the US, with their aesthetic of transparency that has become quasi-identified with the high-tech era; they are generally still made in factories in China, under conditions that are much worse than those that would be tolerated at home. In that sense the world that Marx describes is still very much with us, even if the place of technology within it has changed.

Technology holds a contested place in Agamben's philosophy, and it is intimately related there to the "economic" horizon of Agamben's thought.[1] Whereas in his book on aesthetics, *The Man Without Content*, Agamben still appears to praise what he calls the human being's *"techne"* as its uncanny capacity to bring something from nonbeing into being, as a capacity that is potentially politically subversive, by the time *Homo Sacer* is published, "technology" – not the same as *techne*, of course, but nevertheless etymologically related – becomes associated with the *nomos* of political modernity, namely the camp. This association is further played out in texts such as "No to Bio-Political Tattooing," with which I began this book, and "What is an Apparatus?," an essay that I discuss in more detail in this chapter. In both texts, technology does not play a positive role, to say the least. Indeed, in "What is an Apparatus?," it is only the practice of profanation that appears to present a way out of technology's suspicious subjectivation of life. Only a child's play – or a monk's life – can liberate or "retire" (literally, to "re-draw," to "with-draw") apparatuses from their traditional uses for good.

It thus appears that in Agamben's work, "technology" in the broadest sense of the term – tied to aesthetics, economy, and politics – is an essential element in the analysis of sovereignty, and in particular of sovereignty's contemporary, capitalist and biopolitical articulation. As Agamben in "What is an Apparatus?" makes clear, the *techne* of language is part of this picture. As an ancient apparatus in which primates at some point in time became caught up – thinking, perhaps, that it would present their liberation (their becoming subject-of) whereas in fact it presented the beginning of their subjectivation (their becoming subject-to) – language belongs in the history of technology that Agamben presents. As I have already shown, language in fact takes up a privileged position in this history: Agamben's answer to the situation he diagnoses – the positive politics that his work also contains – focuses on language, this most ancient of apparatuses, in order to see where, in the danger that language thus presents, a saving grace can also grow. And indeed, my discussion of the experiment of language at the beginning of this book shows that Agamben finds such a saving grace in what he calls "the thing of language," human beings' faculty of language, more precisely their potentiality not-to speak (infancy).

One wonders, however, what a similar experience would look like with other technological objects such as, for example, the cell phone, which takes on a particularly negative role in "What is an Apparatus?" Does the cell phone, like language, also hold such a saving grace?[2] How? As I have already said, the key element here would the practice of profanation, which is developed in Agamben's work as a question of "use": a child's play that could liberate – retire – such technological objects from their traditional use for good.[3] Even though Agamben's work contains this suggestion (with a promise, stated in *The Highest Poverty*, of its being worked out in more detail in the concluding volume of the *Homo Sacer* series), his philosophy does not offer a sustained engagement with technology in the same way that it develops an engagement with language. If language is part of the apparatuses that Agamben criticizes, the reader comes away from his writing thinking that language, unlike other apparatuses, holds *more* of a promise when it comes to thinking a positive politics. There appears to be an implicit hierarchy that underlies Agamben's long list of apparatuses that I will quote below.

One thing that thus appears to be lacking in Agamben's oeuvre so far is a thorough investigation of technology – one that would do for technology what Agamben's work has done for language. An investigation that would introduce technology – again, etymologically related to the uncanny *techne* that Agamben still praises in his book on aesthetics – into the politics of aesthetics that I have uncovered here through my engagement with Agamben's work.

If sovereignty is the central concern of this book, then it could be argued, in fact, that the history of sovereignty is a technical and ultimately technological history as marked, for example, by Thomas Hobbes's figuration of the state in 1651 as nothing but "an artificial man."[4] Today more than ever, our lives are saturated with technologies. In the West, the heavy industries that ruled the day when Marx was writing have been transformed into the ethereal, "high" tech apparatuses of the contemporary era – technologies that are so transparent that they have become quasi-invisible, quasi-naturalized components of our lives[5] – even if "low" tech continues its existence in other corners of the globe. It no longer makes much sense to speak, as Agamben does, of two great classes of beings: living beings, on the one hand, and apparatuses on the other. Today, apparatuses have begun to merge with living beings to such an extent that a scholarly consensus about posthumanism seems to have opened up. Once-revolutionary manifestoes such as Donna Haraway's text about cyborgs have become "the norm" for students confronting our life-world today.[6]

This has triggered something like what Friedrich Nietzsche calls "the will to power": everywhere, new apparatuses are being formed. Everywhere, various interests are trying to give form to new technologies that seek to govern our contemporary existence. Technology, intimately related (as Agamben points out) to the human being's uncanny capacity to create, is obviously defined by such plastic processes.[7] And yet, there appear to be ways in which technology is not infinitely flexible: there appears to be something within the technology that resists, that opens up a resistance against these interests and against the governance they try to implement. *Enough is sometimes enough*: the company that uses a social media network to advertise becomes the target of a campaign against it that is largely run through that same social network. Of course, technology itself does not organize this campaign; but couldn't one say that it invites it, that there is something within technology (in the technological object itself) that addresses us, that incites us into these practices? Not simply a deconstruction, but a deconstruction that opens up the technological object to other uses, other forms and formations? The same technological infrastructure that enables human beings to get organized (to create new forms of life) becomes the tool through which these initiatives (individuals and collectives) are tracked – sometimes with legal consequences. New technological possibilities are created and shut down at high speed. Something rages, in the high-tech development, and we are still figuring out where this affect is going to go.

Faced with technology's plasticity, we are therefore experiencing the need for a study of technology itself, a kind of technological "education." Now more than ever, the philosophy of technology appears necessary as a way to work through our contemporary predicament. Many have of course been contributing to these debates, not just in philosophy but also in the quickly transforming field of media and technology studies. Rather than cover all of these debates here, this chapter brings together a number of seemingly disparate concerns in Agamben's work, so as to show how an alternative philosophy of technology may begin to emerge from their being considered together. Given technology's intimate link to sovereignty, this profanation of technology is an essential element in the profanation of sovereignty, or the thinking of what I am calling in this book sovereignty's – and by extension technology's – "plasticity."

A New Industrial Politics of the Spirit

A number of years ago, the French philosopher of technology Bernard Stiegler founded a political organization named *Ars Industrialis*. One of the organization's main objectives, in addition to the rethinking of work or industry (to which I will turn in the next chapter), has been the rethinking of technology. As the organization's website puts it, *Ars Industrialis* is "an international association for the promotion of an industrial politics of technologies of the spirit."[8] The manifesto of the group, available online in French, English, and Japanese as well as a few other languages, provides clarification: today, we are living in states in which the life of the mind ("la vie de l'esprit," which can also be translated as "the life of the spirit" – the group takes the phrase from Hannah Arendt) is increasingly colonized by "the demands and the requirements of the market, the law of rapid profit for firms exploiting the technologies of what is called the culture industries, program industries, the media, telecommunications, and finally technologies of knowledge, or cognitive technologies." In response, *Ars Industrialis* affirms that these "technologies of the spirit can and must become a new age of the spirit, a renewal of spirit and a new life of the mind." The technologies that have made possible what Gilles Deleuze, after William Burroughs, called the "society of control" can and must become "the basis of a new epoch of civilization that could bring about the neutralization of the imminent threat of chaos that everyone senses."

Speaking here is a collective of philosophers working in France today: Stiegler, most notably, but also Marc Crépon and George Collins. The theoretical position that they take up not only situates itself after Deleuze; it also rewrites Michel

Foucault's notion of *bio*-power – a power that in the modern age increasingly colonized the life of the people as population, as I will explain further in the last part of this book – as *psycho*-power (and psychopolitics), and more recently (after Maurizio Lazzarato) as *neuro*-power (and noopolitics). Indeed, as Stiegler's book *Taking Care of Youth and the Generations* explicitly states, the contemporary power that should concern us is not so much biopower but psychopower and neuropower, or the ways in which the life of the mind and the brain (and not just biological life) is increasingly saturated by power.[9]

In his book on care, Stiegler discusses a constellation of texts including Immanuel Kant's essay "What is Enlightenment?," Michel Foucault's essay "What is Enlightenment?," and Giorgio Agamben's essay "What is an Apparatus?" For readers familiar with Stiegler's early work, in particular the first volume of the six-volume project titled *Technics and Time*,[10] it comes as no surprise that Stiegler would be interested in a fellow philosopher's discussion of apparatuses.[11] Stiegler's general argument in *Technics and Time* is that philosophy is yet to think technics. Criticizing philosophy's widespread ressentiment against and repression of technics, he offers an overview of some theories of technical evolution (including both lesser-known names such as Bertrand Gille, Lucien Febvre, René Boirel, and André Leroi-Gourhan, and more famous ones such as Martin Heidegger and Gilbert Simondon) in order to develop, in the brilliant second chapter of the book, a discussion of technics in the writings of Jean-Jacques Rousseau. The position that shines through in these chapters as well as in the rest of the book is that contrary to what is generally thought, human beings did not invent technics; it is, rather, the other way round: technics invented human beings (Stiegler of course was not the first to propose this thought).

The human being came about through a technical change in the constitution of the being that preceded it. Thus, the *who* emerges out of the *what*; the question of technics actually *precedes* that of the human.

Given Stiegler's project, it makes sense that he would appreciate Agamben's attempt to think technics. But that does not mean he is *with* Agamben. His reading reveals, rather, that in Agamben's essay, technics is repressed once again in favor of what Stiegler characterizes as an "enigmatic" and "mysterious"[12] praise for the "profanation" of apparatuses that would "bring to light the Ungovernable, which is the beginning and, at the same time, the vanishing point of every politics."[13] Agamben's essay ends with this sentence, and without offering any further explanation of what this "Ungovernable" – which is pitched against both apparatuses and government – might be. In contrast with Agamben's facile opposition in the essay of "two great classes: living beings … and apparatuses,"[14] Stiegler insists on technics and human beings' shared becoming: on the shared processes of individuation through which they both become. As Stiegler's recent work makes clear, this does not mean that he blindly embraces technics as humanity's redeemer. Indeed, if Stiegler's early work insists on undoing the ressentiment against and the repression of technics in thought, his more recent work pairs this insistence on technics with a reflection on the Enlightenment's emancipatory dimension, specifically its relation to education, and the largely negative influence that technics has had on it. Hence, his question, after characterizing Agamben's introduction of the ungovernable as enigmatic and mysterious, about what *mystagogy* may be behind such enigma and mystery.[15]

Like some of Stiegler's other recent works – most explicitly, the volume titled *La télécratie contre la démocratie – Taking Care of*

Youth and the Generations discusses the ways in which technics, and in particular modern technological apparatuses such as the television, are in the process of destroying the contemporary youth's capacity to *pay attention*. In addition, because our present situation is one in which our memory is exteriorized in apparatuses such as televisions, computers, cellular phones, and tablets, human beings become particularly vulnerable to the appropriation – the expropriation and manipulation – of their memory, a state that risks short-circuiting what Stiegler calls, after Simondon, human beings' psychic and collective individuation. Once our memory is taken away from us, and replaced with whatever governments or capital might want to replace it with, our capacity to psychically and collectively individuate ourselves is destroyed. Television is one of the modern technological apparatuses contributing to this destruction, which Stiegler characterizes as a destruction of the spirit.

In response, Stiegler (as well as the other members of the *Ars Industrialis* collective) calls for a new politics of the spirit, in which television might very well – will *have to*, even – play a role.[16] But it is up to us to democratize this modern technological apparatus so that it can become the support of human beings' psychic and collective individuation.

It is here – in other words, precisely where Stiegler demystifies Agamben's closing call for a "profanation" of apparatuses; even if, of course, some enchantment will remain – that his interest in the emancipatory dimension of the Enlightenment comes in. Whereas Agamben's negative view on apparatuses is traced back in *Taking Care of Youth and the Generations* to Foucault's insistence, in his reading of Kant, on the second motto of the Enlightenment that Kant distinguishes – "Argue as much as you will, *but obey*! [emphasis mine]" – Stiegler for his part proposes a return to Kant's first motto: "Dare to know!" What might this educational imperative still mean in the era of "telecracy"? That Stiegler takes this question seriously may be clear from one of *Ars Industrialis*'s projects: the creation of a school of philosophy in Épineuil-le-Fleuriel.[17]

Actuality, Potentiality, Contingency

The first part of this chapter engages the triangulation of Agamben, Kant, and Foucault – in other words, the connection between the technical and emancipatory dimensions of the Enlightenment – that I uncovered in Stiegler's work through a consideration of the close relations between Foucault's and Agamben's engagement with technics and the Enlightenment. In 1986, Agamben gave a lecture entitled "On Potentiality" at a conference in Lisbon organized by the Collège Internationale de Philosophie. Agamben begins the lecture by saying: "I could state the subject of my work as an attempt to understand the meaning of the verb 'can' [potere]. What do I mean when I say: 'I can, I cannot'?"[18] This statement arguably finds its most radical articulation in the essay that closes the edited collection *Potentialities* in which "On Potentiality" was published, namely Agamben's essay "Bartleby, or On Contingency." Uncovering the importance of Herman Melville's enigmatic scrivener Bartleby for the history of philosophy, Agamben argues that Bartleby – a law-copyist who, on the third day of his employment in an office on Wall Street, begins to refuse any and all tasks that are assigned to him by repeating the formula "I would prefer not to" – is a figure of "a complete or perfect potentiality that belongs to the scribe who is in full possession of the art of writing in the moment in which he does not write."[19] In the history of philosophy, this "complete or perfect potentiality" – what Agamben calls, specifically, a "potentiality not-to" – has become eclipsed by another kind of potentiality: one that is always already tipping over into actuality. Bartleby, however, calls this eclipse into question. The scrivener's enigmatic formula – "I would prefer not to" – marks the persistence of that other kind of potentiality – the potentiality not-to – that Agamben is interested in. And this interest has continued all the way to Agamben's most recent work: his short essay "What is a Commandment?" ends with a reference to Melville's enigmatic scrivener.

As the title of Agamben's Bartleby essay indicates, Bartleby is ultimately associated in the essay with contingency. For his definition of this term, Agamben relies on Duns Scotus, who wrote: "By contingent … I mean not something that is not necessary or eternal, but something whose opposite could have happened in the very moment in which it happened."[20] If Bartleby is thus a messianic, savior-like figure, as Gilles Deleuze for example has argued, he does not come

> like Jesus to redeem what was, but to save what was not.… Bartleby comes not to bring a new table of the Law but … to fulfill the Torah by destroying it from top to bottom.[21]

This passage should not be misunderstood: what Agamben has in mind is not the actual destruction of the Law. What he is interested in, rather, is what he refers to as "another use" of the Law, its "deactivation" or "inactivity [inoperosità]."[22] As a figure of the potentiality not-to and more specifically of contingency, Bartleby opens up the possibility of this deactivation or inactivity because he perpetually situates the Law at an aesthetic distance from itself, in the region of its own sayability and its distribution.[23] In other words: in that space where the Law could always also have been otherwise.

The central importance of the notion of potentiality for Agamben's work has already been demonstrated.[24] For the purposes of this chapter, I propose to reread Foucault's answer to the question "What is Enlightenment?" – and specifically, his relation to Kant on this count – through the lens of the tension between potentiality and actuality that lies at the heart of Agamben's project. Much has already been said about the relation of Agamben's analysis of the contemporary political situation to Foucault's work on governmentality and biopolitics. But what about the solutions that Agamben proposes in response to this analysis? What might be the relation of this particular dimension of Agamben's work – his positive politics, as I have called it in this book – to Foucault? Although I will focus on Foucault's "What is Enlightenment?," my general suggestion is that in order to answer this question, one must explore the relation of Foucault's late work on "the care of the self"[25] to Agamben's writings, even if Agamben has also (though mostly for historical reasons) distinguished his work from Foucault's on this count. Indeed, Agamben's most recent publications – in particular, *The Highest Poverty* – have demonstrated this to be the case.

"The Undefined Work of Freedom"

From 1978 until his death in 1984, Foucault repeatedly referred back to Kant's essay "What is Enlightenment?" Kant's essay famously begins with the definition of Enlightenment as "man's release from his self-incurred tutelage,"[26] and follows up with a definition of "tutelage": "Tutelage is man's inability to make use of his understanding without direction from another."[27] "Have the courage to use your own reason!"[28] is thus the first motto of the Enlightenment. Kant insists on human beings' potential to actively make use of their own reason; Enlightenment is defined as human beings' release from the incapacity to do so. At the same time, however, the term Enlightenment refers to a historical period, a present to which human beings are passively exposed. It refers, in other words, not only to an enlightened act but also to an enlightened age. Kant addresses this double-sidedness – human beings' active and passive relation to the Enlightenment – towards the end of his essay, when he raises the question: "Do we now live in an enlightened age?"[29] His answer is, unambiguously, "No."[30] "[B]ut we do live in an *age of enlightenment*,"[31] he continues. With this shift from "an enlightened age" to "an age of enlightenment," Kant manages to combine the active and passive aspects of the Enlightenment: he evokes a historical period that is produced through human beings' actions. Thus, it is not so much the age that is enlightened, and that as such guarantees one's Enlightenment, but one's Enlightenment that produces the age. The final responsibility remains ours.

Although Foucault's essay "What is Enlightenment?" is no doubt the best known of his many engagements with Kant's text, Sylvère Lotringer has recently collected a number of the others in a volume titled *The Politics of Truth*. Since then, Foucault's 1983 lectures on Kant's text have also been published, in both French and English. From these different publications, it appears that for Foucault, the question of the Enlightenment was one that could not be settled. Its answer never quite actualizes in his lectures and his writings. Instead, it is perpetually deferred, like a potentiality that is reactivated in each instance in which it is addressed. It is not difficult to see how this feature of Foucault's engagement with the Enlightenment – specifically, the tension between the actual and the potential that characterizes it – is in fact a central component of Foucault's answer to the question of the Enlightenment.

Indeed, the tension between the potential and the actual around which Agamben's entire oeuvre revolves is equally central to "What is Enlightenment?" Toward the end of the essay, Foucault summarizes the two arguments that he has been trying to make. On the one hand, he has tried to "emphasize the extent to which a type of philosophical interrogation – one that simultaneously problematizes man's relation to the present, man's historical mode of being, and the constitution of the self as an autonomous subject – is rooted in the Enlightenment."[32] On the other, he has tried to emphasize that what connects "us" (Foucault and his audience, his readers) to the "Enlightenment is not a faithfulness to doctrinal elements but rather the permanent reactivation of an attitude – that is, of a philosophical ethos that could be described as a permanent critique of our historical era."[33]

If the first argument could be rephrased as an argument about the human being's simultaneously "passive" relation to history and her or his constitution as an autonomous subject, the second pushes the latter aspect of that argument into an investigation of a more "active" "attitude."[34] Tying this attitude back to the first part of the first argument, it is described earlier on in the essay as

> a mode of relating to contemporary reality; a voluntary choice made by certain people; a way of thinking and feeling; a way, too, of acting and behaving that at one and the same time marks a relation of belonging and presents itself as a task. A bit, no doubt, like what the Greeks called an ethos.[35]

In the closing paragraphs of the essay, Foucault also refers to this attitude as a "philosophical life."[36] What connects "us" to the Enlightenment is the permanent reactivation of this life.

But how is one to understand this "reactivation" exactly, given the obvious tension between the active and the passive, and specifically the actual and the potential, that haunts Foucault's essay? What is certain is that Foucault pitches his understanding of this "reactivation" against Kant. One might suspect that he is attempting to "enlighten" Kant here about something that he considers Kant's essay to be missing (or perhaps better, that he considers Kant to be missing – for Kant's text puts one on the track of it, even though Kant himself might be missing it). Foucault reveals that he wants to transform Kant's enlightened interest in the limits of reason into an investigation of reason's perpetual transgressions. He is interested in how one can "transform the critique conducted in the form of necessary limitation into a practical critique that takes the form of a possible transgression."[37] Foucault points out that such a critique would be both archeological in the sense that it will seek "to treat the instances of discourse that articulate what we think, say, and do as so many historical events" as well as genealogical in the sense that "it will separate out, from the contingency that has made us what we are, the possibility of no longer being, doing, or thinking what we are, do, or think."[38] If the notion of "contingency" in this passage appears to be tied to what Foucault elsewhere in the essay calls the present, one's historical mode of being, Foucault appears to want to push it here toward Duns Scotus's understanding of it as "something whose opposite could have happened in the very moment in which it happened." Such would be an enlightened critique of contingency, the transformation of contingency into the possibility of transgression. Foucault calls such a practice the "undefined work of freedom."[39]

From the closing paragraphs of Foucault's essay, one gathers that it is not entirely certain that such a transformation entails keeping one's faith in the Enlightenment. Rather, to "enlighten" the Enlightenment, to push it towards the potentiality not-to that is central to Agamben's intellectual project, means to question any actualization of the Enlightenment itself, so as to return it instead to the *question* that both Kant and Foucault have as their title. Any enlightened conception of the Enlightenment would thus refrain from presenting the Enlightenment as an answer; instead, the Enlightenment is crucially a question, is defined as a potentiality not-to that permanently resists actualization. Thus, Enlightenment doctrine – the law – is pushed back into the aesthetic[40] regions of its own sayability and its distribution, into those liminal spaces that Agamben is so interested in, where the Enlightenment is always also otherwise: Enlightenment's *infancy*.[41]

Once More, Philologically

This is why Foucault in one of his contributions to a book entitled *Technologies of the Self* asserts that "[t]he question, I think, which arises at the end of the eighteenth century is: What are we in our actuality? … 'What are we today?'"[42] This passage not only reveals – more so than some of the other translations of Foucault's work on the Enlightenment – Foucault's explicit interest in actuality. The shift that one finds from the first question to the second – that is: the shift from "actuality" to "today" – also marks one of the main problems of translation in

Foucault's essay on the Enlightenment, as well as in his lectures on Kant's essay. The problem lies in Foucault's use of the term "les actualités," usually translated as "the present." From the opening paragraphs of Foucault's essay, it is obvious that "the present," "today," is a major concern in his engagement with the Enlightenment. However, to translate "les actualités" merely as "the present" means to lose the notion of actuality that is inscribed in the original French term "les actualités." In French, "the present" is of the order of the actual; to inquire into the present means to inquire into the actual. Foucault's main critique of such a conceptualization of the present will be to insist on the potential, specifically on the potentiality not-to. From this perspective, the present becomes contingent (in Scotus's and Agamben's sense of the word): it could also always have been otherwise. If we are still living in the present of the Enlightenment, the Enlightenment is thus not so much "les actualités" but, rather, potentiality – specifically, the potentiality not-to.[43]

Foucault's obsession with the tension between actuality and potentiality, and specifically with the word actual, is particularly obvious in the French original of his lectures on Kant's essay. Enlightenment is "la question du présent," he states, "c'est la question de l'actualité."[44] Note how the present, "le présent," is immediately translated here into the actual, "l'actualité." "Qu'est-ce qui, dans le présent, fait sense actuellement pour une réflexion philosophique?"[45] Here Foucault establishes once again the connection between the present and the actual, this time through his use of the adverb "actuellement": "What is it that, in the present, makes sense today [actuellement] for philosophical reflection?" At a crucial point in the first lecture, Foucault insists very forcefully on the centrality of actuality for his reflection on the Enlightenment by asking: "Quelle est mon actualité? … Quel est le sens de cette actualité? Et qu'est-ce que fait le fait que je parle de cette actualité?"[46] "What is my present? … What is the meaning of this present? And what causes me to speak of this present?" In each of these cases, "actualité" could just as well have been translated by "actuality." Whereas the reader of the English translation risks encountering a text that is obsessed with the present – an encounter that would not entirely be missed, since the present is obviously a central concern in Foucault's text – the reader of the French original encounters in addition a text that is obsessed with actuality.[47]

At the end of his first lecture on Kant, Foucault evokes specifically the tension between actuality and potentiality that informs Agamben's work. He asks: "Quel est le champ actuel des expériences possibles?"[48] "What is the present [actuel] field of possible experiences?" Enlightenment, for Foucault, will have to do with separating out from the actuality of what one is "the possibility of no longer being, doing, or thinking what we are, do, or think." Enlightened freedom thus comes about not as a state that would be achieved once and for all but as a process, a kind of "work": it is a "patient labor giving form to our impatience for liberty."[49]

Enlightenment is thus inscribed at the very end of Foucault's essay in the aesthetico-ethical practices of self-cultivation that Foucault at this point in his career is analyzing in his work on sexuality. It is theorized here as an "art of existence,"[50] a form of what Foucault in the second volume of *The History of Sexuality* calls the "techne tou biou" or "care of the self."[51] In "What is Enlightenment?," Foucault theorizes Enlightenment as an "art of living,"[52] a practice that becomes part of the practices of the "*cura sui*"[53] that he reveals to be a central concern in classical philosophy. In the Enlightenment essay, the "labor" implied by the "care of the self" is turned into the "undefined *work* of freedom." Enlightenment is a social practice through which one attends to oneself and thus, ultimately, to others.[54]

What thus emerges in my discussion of Foucault's understanding of Enlightenment is a theory of Enlightenment as a biotechnic, a technique of taking care of one's life. Enlightenment is theorized by Foucault as a technique of care-taking. In what follows, I discuss further the place of technics and specifically of technology in both Kant's and Foucault's essays, in order to then turn toward the third text in the constellation that is under discussion here: Agamben's "What is an Apparatus?" Indeed, while Agamben cites the first volume of Foucault's *The History of Sexuality*, specifically its closing section on biopower, as one of his major influences in the introduction to his study of sovereign power titled *Homo Sacer: Sovereign Power and Bare Life*, Foucault's shift in the second volume of *The History of Sexuality* from biopolitics to biotechnics has remained largely unthought in his writings.

The Question of Technology

Early on in his description of the Enlightenment, Kant evokes the curious image of domesticated animals made dumb by their guardians who "have made sure that these placid creatures will not dare take a single step without the harness of the cart to which they are tethered."[55] In his second lecture on Kant's essay, Foucault comments on Kant's use of the word "Gängelwagen" for what is translated in the English version of the essay as "cart."[56] Foucault points out that the German word refers to a kind of walking rack that was used in the eighteenth century to *both* help infants to walk *and* to prevent them from walking wherever they liked. The cart is thus a technical object that *both* enables freedom *and* enforces a degree of obedience.

One can understand why Foucault would have been interested in this word: he considers it to be emblematic of Kant's answer to the question of the Enlightenment. The cart evokes, specifically, the second motto that Kant gives in response: "Argue, but obey!" The curious fact, however, is that Kant in his text rejects the cart as what prevents people from using their own reason. To have the courage to use your own reason means precisely to learn to walk without the help of the cart. Foucault's analysis will show, however, that Kant's enlightened subject nevertheless remains tied to the cart.

Kant's definition of the Enlightenment thus appears to coincide with a rejection of a technical object. To become enlightened means to become independent from technical supplements. It means for the human being to "finally learn to walk alone."[57] Even though the Enlightenment is usually associated with the exponential increase in technological developments, Kant's definition of Enlightenment appears to install a separation between human beings and technology. It is a definition of Enlightenment that is suspicious of the relation of technological development to freedom.[58] This suspicion is echoed in Foucault's essay, which partly aims to show that "the relations between the growth of capabilities and the growth of autonomy are not as simple as the eighteenth century may have believed."[59] Foucault writes:

> And we have been able to see what forms of power relation were conveyed by various technologies (whether we are speaking of productions with economic aims, or institutions whose goal is social regulation, or of techniques of communication):

disciplines, both collective and individual, procedures of normalization exercised in the name of the power of the state, demands of society or of population zones, are examples. What is at stake then, is this: How can the growth of capabilities be disconnected from the intensification of power relations?[60]

In this passage, Enlightenment technology is closely associated with power. It operates in the service of collective and individual discipline. In this sense, it prevents the autonomy that the Enlightenment so prides itself on from coming about.

One should note, however, that the key question to which this insight leads is not a rejection of technology. Foucault asks, rather, how the growth of Enlightenment technologies could be disconnected from the intensification of power relations. One could read this as a version of the genealogical question, formulated elsewhere in the essay, about "the possibility of no longer being, doing, or thinking what we are, do, or think": how could Enlightenment technologies be used otherwise?

In this, Foucault's engagement with the particular problem of Enlightenment technologies appears to differ fundamentally from Agamben's. Although they are not the obvious inter-texts for Agamben's essay, "What is an Apparatus?" clearly refers to both Kant's and Foucault's essays on the Enlightenment. Foucault is, as always, one of the main interlocutors in Agamben's text; but Agamben focuses on the dark side of Foucault's analyses rather than on his late work on the aesthetico-ethical techniques of the self. Agamben speaks towards the very end of his essay of how

the harmless citizen of postindustrial democracies ... readily does everything that he is asked to, inasmuch as he leaves his everyday gestures and his health, his amusements and his occupations, his diet and his desires, to be commanded and controlled in the smallest detail by apparatuses.[61]

It is not only Foucault and his discussion of governmentality and biopolitics that resonates here. One is also reminded of the second paragraph of Kant's essay on the Enlightenment, where Kant criticizes human beings who do not have the courage "to be of age":

> If I have a book which understands for me, a pastor who has a conscience for me, a physician who decides my diet, and so forth, I need not trouble myself. I need not think, if I can only pay – others will readily undertake the irksome work for me.[62]

The echoes of Kant in Agamben's essay allow one to understand that Agamben is also engaging with the Enlightenment in "What is an Apparatus?" Like Kant, he is calling for an emancipation; even more explicitly than in Kant, the emancipation Agamben has in mind is an emancipation from apparatuses – from the apparatuses that command and control "in the smallest detail" the lives of human beings.

In this loaded context, Agamben proposes a distinction between two major classes: "living beings" on the one hand, and "apparatuses" on the other. In addition, he distinguishes a third class, which is produced in the power struggle between living beings and apparatuses: "subjects."[63] Agamben's vision of life's relation to technology is one of a perpetual war between living beings and apparatuses. Foucault's question – "how can the growth of capabilities be disconnected from the intensification of power relations?" – thus appears to become tainted in Agamben by the specter of blind rejection.[64] However, although Agamben explicitly says that he is not interested in "another use" of technology[65] – a statement that appears difficult to pair with his insistence, elsewhere, on "use" and "other uses" unless one understands that the transformative "use" Agamben is proposing is different from one mere "use" that could be substituted for another – "blind rejection" does not appear to describe his position correctly either. Somewhat enigmatically, the closing pages of the essay reveal him to be calling for a "profanation" of apparatuses, meaning a restoration of apparatuses to their "common use"[66] – a call that is worked out in more detail in *The Highest Poverty*, which foregrounds the question of use. In this sense, profanation would function as a "counter-apparatus,"[67] a technique or technology *against* technologies that would halt the destructive progression of modern Enlightenment technologies. It would end the "telecracy" that Stiegler is also warning against. Whereas apparatuses have become part and parcel of what Agamben calls the theological economy of government – a division of power that intends to saturate the entire field of life with the violence of the law – our task is to liberate apparatuses from this arrangement and restore them to their common use. As to what this might mean, exactly, with respect to an apparatus such as the cell phone, which Agamben comes close to rejecting in his essay, remains vague – at least here. And it is precisely on this count that Stiegler attempts to push Agamben further. But what are the realms included in Agamben's work in which the counter-apparatus of profanation might be witnessed in action? What might be the link that is included (and lies occluded) in Agamben's work between the profanation that Agamben is calling for and what Foucault in his late work calls the "art of the self"?

The question might, with some goodwill, not be all that hard to answer. One realm of technical production in which such profanation becomes possible is art. As I have already discussed in Chapter 1, in the opening chapter of *The Man Without Content* Agamben calls for an understanding of art that would do justice to the human being's technical capacities, specifically its uncanny "ability to pro-duce, to bring a thing from nonbeing into being."[68] Such an understanding would in part reconsider art from the position of the creator (rather than from the position of the spectator from where Kant considers it in his *Critique of Judgment*) and return it to its Ancient, political vocation: to pose a danger to the *polis*, to the city-state. In its technical dimension, art is something profoundly dangerous. The tragedy of our time is that art has lost this dimension, and has turned into something that is "merely interesting"; it is "[o]nly because art has left the sphere of *interest* to become merely *interesting*" that "we welcome it so warmly."[69] Aware of the danger that art poses to the city, Plato instead bans it from his ideal republic. A terrifying judgment, at first sight; but at least Plato took art seriously. Agamben theorizes art in the opening chapter of his book as "the most uncanny thing,"[70] as a capacity that inspires "divine terror"[71] because it reveals human beings' essential capacities for production, for "divine" creation and destruction.

In his work on the care of the self, Foucault as well appears to maintain a positive connection between art ("techne") and life ("bios") as a way for the subject to become the author of its own life, to cultivate its own existence. It is here that the connection between biological and psychic life and technics and technology can begin to move from the horrific nightmare of biopower and biotechnology (instantiated in the imagination of film directors such as David Cronenberg, for example) to the more positive promise of biopolitics and biotechnics that can be found not just in Foucault's work on the care of the self but also in the visionary volume titled *Incorporations* edited by Jonathan Crary and Sanford Kwinter, more recent publications such as William Connolly's or Catherine Malabou's books on the brain (titled *Neuropolitics* and *What Should We Do With Our Brain?*), or even cinematic explorations of the figure of the samurai in films by Akira Kurosawa (*Seven Samurai*), Jim Jarmusch (*Ghost Dog*), or Quentin Tarantino (*Kill Bill*).[72] Today, and in line with both Foucault's and Agamben's suggestions, it is the new interest in bioart (which I have already mentioned at the end of Chapter 2) that appears to be one of the most promising realms for such a new discussion of techniques of life. Indeed, couldn't Agamben's reflections on the life of the Franciscans in *The Highest Poverty* not ultimately be read as reflections on a kind of bioart, on the art of living, on a life that would coincide with the rule and vice versa so that the monk's biography becomes indistinguishable from the rule and would provide the rule in its mere telling, through its mere example?

However, does Agamben's philosophy ultimately allow for such a thought/practice? I am convinced that one could push it there. But to what extent is such a pushing also a forcing that in fact covers over problematic aspects of Agamben's thought? In view of these questions, I propose to return to Agamben's essay once more, this time to read it next to the work of a philosopher of technology who is referenced in the first chapter of Agamben's book *Profanations*: Gilbert Simondon. Such a reading will partly unwork the promise of technology I have found in Agamben's thought so as to consider instead some of its more problematic, negative evaluations of technology and the ways in which they are reflected in Agamben's ontology and politics.

Another Turn of the Screw

In the "Best of 2009" issue of *Artforum*, Jonathan Crary recommends Agamben's *What is an Apparatus?* as one of the best books of 2009. Crary's brief recommendation focuses on the twenty-four-page title essay in the collection, arguing that it provides insight in developments that it does not even address, namely the "remaking of the book into an electronic shopping appliance," "the fate of paper and printing," and "the optical properties of illuminated screens."[73] Agamben's essay, Crary argues, takes the reader

> across two millennia of related theological and philosophical problems of governance to a concise account of the current phase of capitalism, with its massive proliferation of apparatuses and its production of "the most docile and cowardly social body" in all of history.[74]

"Apparatuses are inseparable from what makes us human," Crary continues; but Agamben's essay demonstrates that the apparatus is also "what uses us." Contrary to what one might think at first sight, apparatuses thus actually destroy "our capacity to communicate with one another about what we share in common" – in short: "politics."[75]

Crary appears to suggest here – even though his work shows that he knows better – that such a destruction of politics was not yet ongoing before the book was remade into an electronic shopping appliance. The book – printed on paper, and not projected on an illuminated screen – appears to emerge in Crary's short text as something that is outside the history of the apparatus that Agamben outlines. Anyone who has read Agamben's essay, however, will know that for Agamben, this is emphatically not the case. "I shall call an apparatus," Agamben writes,

> literally anything that has in some way the capacity to capture, orient, determine, intercept, model, control, or secure the gestures, behavior, opinions, or discourses of living beings. Not

only, therefore, prisons, madhouses, the panopticon, schools, confessions, factories, disciplines, juridical measures, and so forth (whose connection with power is in a certain sense evident), but also the pen, writing, literature, philosophy, agriculture, cigarettes, navigation, computers, cellular telephones, and – why not – language itself, which is perhaps the most ancient of apparatuses – one in which thousands and thousands of years ago a primate inadvertently let himself be captured, probably without realizing the consequences that he was about to face.[76]

In Agamben's essay, there clearly is no such a thing as a happy age of the book, of paper and printing, before the illuminated screens that Crary mentions. Instead, language itself is presented as an apparatus – a thing through which power operates – in which primates when they first learned to speak became captured.

As might already be clear from the list that was just quoted, Agamben's vision of technology risks taking on, at times, panicky proportions. A few pages later, Agamben, who was a student of Heidegger's, writes:

> For example, I live in Italy, a country where the gestures and behaviors of individuals have been reshaped from top to toe by the cellular telephone (which the Italians dub *telefonino*). I have developed an implacable hatred for this apparatus, which has made the relationship between people all the more abstract. Although I found myself more than once wondering how to destroy or deactivate those *telefonini*, as well as how to eliminate or at least to punish and imprison those who do not stop using them, I do not believe this is the right solution to the problem.[77]

Crary refers to this passage as Agamben's "fiercely unsparing account of the cell phone," a "memorable case in point" of what the book's argument amounts to. Note the violence of the language: Agamben is contemplating not only the "destruction" or "deactivation" of cell phones, but also how to "eliminate" or at least "punish" and "imprison" those who use them. This statement is surprising, given that it is coming from someone whose work has done so much to expose the ways in which the concentration camp continues to function as the matrix of modern power. But perhaps I am taking Agamben too seriously here: many of us have no doubt at one point or another gotten exasperated with cell phones. The solution to the problem that Agamben ultimately proposes is indeed not the destruction of cell phones or the people who use them, but what he calls the "profanation" of these apparatuses.

But what does Agamben mean by this? He does not mean, as Crary correctly observes, "alternative ways to use" apparatuses – here again the question of Agamben's more radical conception of "use" is raised.[78] Agamben calls this a "naïve" solution.[79] Rather, to profane the cell phone would mean to restore it "to the free use of men."[80] "To profane" is thus contrasted in Agamben's analysis to the verb "to consecrate," which "designated the exit of things from the sphere of human law,"[81] their entry into the separate sphere of religion. "Profanation is the counter-apparatus that restores to common use what sacrifice had separated and divided."[82] It is still unclear at this point (at least in this writer's opinion) what exactly such a profanation of the cell phone might look like – and even *The Highest Poverty*, which begins to focus on the question of use, does not yet answer this question. What is interesting, however, is that as such, profanation does not appear to be outside of Agamben's list of apparatuses. He calls it, rather, a "counter-apparatus": an *apparatus against apparatuses*, a book against books, a technology against technologies. In the same way that elsewhere in Agamben's work the messianic – which is inseparable from the theological – leads outside of the vicissitudes of political theology, a technology is supposed to lead outside of the vicissitudes of technologies here. However, it is ultimately left up to the reader to discover how this might be the case.

Ontology

Although profanation — what will save humanity from the apparatus — is thus ultimately presented here as being itself a technology, the vision of technology that dominates the essay is clearly not a very positive one. It is with no small amount of surprise, then, that one finds the first chapter of Agamben's book *Profanations* to revolve around a thinker whose relation to technology could not be more different than Agamben's: Gilbert Simondon. Agamben is not dealing in this chapter, however, with Simondon's thought on technology; instead, it is Simondonian ontology from which he borrows. In line with Agamben's critical practice, Simondon's work is silently adapted in the chapter: his name is mentioned only once, and only after the most obvious borrowings from Simondon have already occurred. Agamben adapts Simondonian ontology in the context of a theory of genius. "In Latin," Agamben begins, "*Genius* was the name used for the god who becomes each man's guardian at the moment of birth."[83] Very quickly in the chapter, this most "intimate and personal god" becomes a figure in the argument for "that which is most impersonal in us: it is the personalization of what, in us, goes beyond us and exceeds us."[84] "From birth to death," Agamben writes, the human being is

> accompanied by an impersonal, preindividual element. Man is thus a single being with two phases; he is a being that results from the complex dialectic between a part that has yet to be

individuated and lived and another part that is marked by fate and individual experience. But the impersonal, nonindividual part is not a past we have left behind once and for all and that we may eventually recall in memory; it is still present in us, still with us, near to us and inseparable from us, for both good and ill.[85]

"Genius is our life," Agamben concludes, "insofar as it does not belong to us."[86]

Although the explicit reference to Simondon only comes later (on page 15, where Agamben observes that "[a]ccording to Gilbert Simondon, emotion is the way we relate to the preindividual"), Agamben is clearly borrowing in this passage from Simondon's theory of individuation. His use of the term "preindividual" to refer to the impersonal element of genius, as well as the language of "phases" that appears in this passage, both evoke the specter of Simondon. However, a close reading of the passage reveals that what is going on might indeed be no more than an evocation: a loose borrowing of terminology that ultimately has very little to do with Simondon's thought.

Agamben theorizes the human being in this passage as "a single being with two phases." It results from a "dialectic" between two parts: one that has yet to be individuated – an impersonal, preindividual, nonindividual part – and one that is "marked by fate and individual experience." His point is, however, that the first, preindividual part is not a part that the individuated human being has left behind and can comfortably recall in memory; it is, instead, something that is still present in the human being, going beyond it and exceeding it. It is that part of one's life that one does not own, the part that escapes. In his other work, Agamben has theorized this part as "the contemporary" ("this unlived element in everything that is lived"[87]);

and also as "potentiality," which in Agamben's reading crucially becomes a "potentiality not-to," a potentiality that would be separated from actuality.[88] Genius is the always-contemporary part of the human being, the potentiality that marks the limit of its actualization as an individual. To be human, according to Agamben, means to be caught up in the dialectic of these two phases of being: the impersonal, preindividual, potential phase and the personal, individual, actual phase. The preindividual, for Agamben, is thus a kind of operative remainder in the individual, the individual's unforgettable[89] that continues to drive the processes of its individuation.

It is upon this theory of the human being as divided between two phases – the preindividual and the individual phase – that Agamben's theory of technology is founded. As I already explained above, Agamben thinks there are "two great classes": "living beings (or substances) and apparatuses. And, between these two, as a third class, subjects. I call a subject that which results from the relation and, so to speak, from the relentless fight between living beings and apparatuses."[90] This sounds like Agamben's version of the "clash of civilizations": living beings are presented as engaged in a fight – a battle or a war – with technologies of all kinds. Subjects are produced in this battle, through the conflict between a living being and the thing that, while it also makes living beings human, uses them: the apparatus. *What is an Apparatus?* thus confirms the conflict that underlies, for example, manifestations of popular culture such as the *Terminator* or *The Matrix* trilogies, in which human beings are involved in a fierce battle against machines.[91] But the point that I want to make is that the fight between man and machine that drives these representations and that Agamben's *What is an Apparatus?* theorizes, can without much difficulty be mapped onto Agamben's adaptation of Simondon: the living being comes down on the side of the impersonal, preindividual, non-individual element in Agamben's theory of the human being; the apparatus is associated with the individual part. Subjects are human beings who are involved in the relentless fight between the preindividual and the individual elements of their being. In short: as Agamben presents it, the individual is a kind of apparatus that preindividual genius resists.

There are a number of differences that separate Simondon from Agamben. First of all, when Simondon develops his theory of individuation, he is not simply talking about human beings. Non-humans are part and parcel of individuation. Second, a process of individuation does not consist of merely two phases; instead, Simondon's theory allows for multiple phases. Third, Simondon insists that the preindividual is not a phase (as Agamben suggests):

> *Preindividual being is being in which there is no phase*: the being in which individuation occurs is that in which a resolution appears through the division of being into phases. This division of being into phases is becoming. Becoming is not a framework in which being exists, it is a dimension of being, a mode of resolution of an initial incompatibility that is rich in potentials. *Individuation corresponds to the appearance of phases in being that are the phases of being.*[92]

Fourth, this division of being into phases – this becoming – is explicitly distinguished by Simondon from a dialectical process.[93] Whereas dialectical becoming changes being by producing its opposite, the phases of being are phases *of being* – being does not turn into something else by passing through them. Rather, it is being that becomes being of phases. So whereas in Agamben, one finds a theory of the human being perpetually caught up in a dialectic of the preindividual and individual phases, in Simondon one finds a theory of human and non-human beings who become through phases. There is no dialectical opposition through which being would become something else; rather, being exists in becoming, as being of phases. Preindividual is simply Simondon's name for an initial, tense being rich in potentials, that then resolves itself into phases.[94]

Technology

Interestingly, these ontological differences between Simondon and Agamben also mark the difference between their thoughts on technology. Whereas Agamben, who understands the human being as caught up in a dialectic between a preindividual and an individual phase, understands subjects to be caught up in a relentless fight between living beings and apparatuses, Simondon's theory of human and non-human becoming through phases does not lead into such a warring vision of man versus machine but thinks instead the shared becoming of human beings and machines. Following Simondon, technology is therefore not what destroys communication and community – and thus, as Crary points out, politics – but what makes them possible. What I want to focus on is not so much Simondon's actual analysis of technical objects, but the ways in which his theory of technology presents what he calls a "technical mentality," a technical mindset or way of thinking that is arguably instantiated in Simondon's ontological or ontogenetic work. In a brief essay titled "Technical Mentality" – which really answers the question "What is Technical Mentality?" and could very well have been titled as such – he argues that technology yields modes of thinking ("coherent and usable schemas for cognitive interpretation")[95] that are capable of forming larger schemas of interpretation. In the essay, he singles out two main conditions, "which can be presented as postulates of the 'technical mentality'":[96] the first is that "the subsets are relatively detachable from the whole of which they are a part"; the second is that "if one wants to understand a being completely, one must study it by considering its entelechy, and not in its inactivity or its static state."[97] How does Simondon derive these postulates from studying technological objects?

Technical activity, Simondon argues, does not produce "an absolutely indivisible organism that is metaphysically one and undissolvable."[98] Instead, "the technical object can be repaired; it can be completed."[99] It is in fact "conceived as something that may need control, repair, and maintenance."[100] For Simondon, this is an essential aspect of the technical mentality, in that it rejects what he calls a "holistic"[101] approach to being; instead, the technical approach is one of careful, detailed examination. The first characteristic of the technical approach is thus that it moves from the set to the subset, and considers the relative solidarity of the subsets to one another. Not their relentless fight, but their solidarity.

Second, being cannot be completely understood in its instability or static state. Instead, one must understand it in movement, as process. In his ontological work, Simondon will speak here of the notion of metastability, which has to do with the potential energy of a system and is very different from the stable state of equilibrium and rest. Simondon comes to this conclusion through his analysis of technological objects such as the stato-reactor of Leduc, which once it has got going becomes capable of maintaining its own speed; of the Guimbal group, which can only be fully understood once all its elements operate together, as a technological regime of functioning. Again, there is no fighting, battle, or war here but instead a solidarity of the technological object's subsets.

It is very much along these lines that Simondon, in the "Complementary Note" to his *Psychic and Collective Individuation*, conceives of the relation between human beings and machines.[102] Indeed, Simondon looks at human beings and apparatuses as involved in a shared process of becoming, thus developing a position that, when considered from a contemporary perspective, can be said to be critical of the popular imagination that informs Hollywood films such as *Terminator* and *The Matrix*.[103] This process does not pitch one side over and against another but needs to be understood, rather, as a metastable system rich in potential – a system that cannot be understood as a static battle of one side against another but needs to be considered instead in its regime of functioning. Technological objects cannot be rejected wholesale out of some concern with living beings that would exist separately from them; rather, the relation between human beings and technology needs to be subjected to a careful, detailed examination that would be able to do justice to the metastability of their relation. These postulates of the "technical mentality," which develop directly out of Simondon's ontological investigations, go radically against Agamben's theory of the apparatus. In response to Agamben's panicky rejection of the cell phone as an apparatus of communication that makes communication, community – in short: politics – impossible, Simondon calls for a different kind of mentality, a different way of looking at the cell phone as part of the human being's shared becoming with technology.

One of the many interesting aspects of Agamben's relation to Simondon is that the critique of identity into which this technical mentality leads in Simondon ("the relation of being to itself is infinitely richer than identity," Simondon writes[104]) is also characteristic of Agamben's work – with the important difference that there, such a critique is opposed to technology, or theorized at the very least as a counter-technological technology. In a book such as *The Coming Community*, for example, Agamben will insist on the revolutionary potential of a non-identitarian singularity – a whatever singularity – as the "enemy of the State."[105] Here again, however, a problematic aspect of Agamben's work is exposed, in that the ontological dialectic he finds between the preindividual and individual phase, which is translated in *What is an Apparatus?* into a relentless fight between living beings and technology, is turned in his political work into a relentless war of whatever singularities against the state.[106] To approach politics from a technical mentality, however, would mean to consider the relation between human beings and the apparatus of the state as a metastable relation that is becoming in phases, relative between different elements existing in solidarity, and rich in potential. It would not pitch one side over and against another but instead explore, through careful examination, their shared becoming.

It is these problematic moments in this thought that have generated the image of Agamben as a thinker against sovereignty who seeks to destroy the law. While there is evidently plenty of truth to this claim, which can be corroborated with evidence from Agamben's entire work, the whole truth is that Agamben's relation to sovereignty and law is much more complicated and must involve a closer consideration, which I have been pursuing in this book, of some of the verbs and nouns that he has used to describe this relation: deactivate, render inoperative, in-operativity, worklessness, *désoeuvrement*, *Aufhebung*, et cetera. The particular poetry of Agamben's relation to sovereignty and law reveals that we are not talking about a simply negative relation of destruction here. In the same way that one of the key notions in his oeuvre, infancy, falls somewhere between silence and speech and marks between these all too easy alternatives a potentiality not-to speak that is crucially different from both, Agamben's relation to sovereignty and law needs to be reconceived along those lines, seeking to expose a third alternative in response to a vicious dialectic that has dominated the spectrum of political possibilities – as well as linguistic possibilities – for too long.

This type of thinking, which is evidenced by the constellation *zoe/bios*/bare life and the close relation between bare life and whatever being/form-of-life, and which Agamben – as I have argued in Chapter 2 – inherits from Walter Benjamin, is developed in Agamben's thought through a reflection on work. It is to that dimension of his thinking that I now turn.

Notes

1   The Ancient notion of "oikonomia," which refers to the *techne* of governing or managing ("nomos," law) the house ("oikos") and has become (as I discussed previously) a key concept in Agamben's work, has a link to technology – though in Ancient times, the technology in question refers to techniques of government and not to what, in modern times, we understand by technology.

2   And one could ask here an even more provocative question: does the camp hold the possibility of such a saving grace? Can the camp be profaned, liberated or retired from its traditional use? Can it be dismantled by a child's play? (One could think here, for example, of Roberto Benigni's *La Vita è Bella*, in which the camp becomes the site of a child's play.) If language is a pharmakon, that is: a cure that at the same time always also risks becoming a poison, then why wouldn't all apparatuses be pharmaka? And if they aren't, does that mean there are *pharmaka*, like the camp for example, that constitute an absolute negativity that cannot be profaned? Is language in that sense different from the camp?

3 I have given a few examples in Chapter 1 of what such a practice might look like.

4 Dimitris Vardoulakis notes this but does not develop it into a reflection on sovereignty's relations to technology (Vardoulakis, *Sovereignty*, 85).

5 I comment on this in François Lagarde's film *Simondon du désert*.

6 See Haraway, *Simians*.

7 To use the term "plasticity" in this context also draws out the nervous, neuronal transformations that the development of technics and technology has accomplished. Bernard Stiegler's recent work focuses on this, taking the research of Maryanne Wolf and Nicholas Carr as two of its central references.

8 See <http://www.arsindustrialis.org/le-manifeste>.

9 See Stiegler, *Taking Care*.

10 See Stiegler, *Technics*.

11 One should note from the beginning the ambiguity of the term "apparatus." In the translations that I am working with, "apparatus" translates both the word for "device" ("appareil," in French) and what Foucault famously calls "dispositif," which refers not so much to a device as to a network established between different elements such as "discourses, institutions, architectural forms, regulatory decisions, laws, administrative measures, scientific statements, philosophical, moral, and philanthropic propositions" (Foucault qtd. Agamben, *WA*, 2). The Italian word in Agamben's title that is translated as "apparatus" is "dispositivo" (the choice was inspired, apparently, not just by the fact that "dispositif" in Foucault is usually translated as "apparatus," but also by Agamben's note "that the torture machine from Kafka's *In the Penal Colony* is called an Apparat" [ibid., 55]). The reference to Kafka reveals much about Agamben's general take on technics and technology: from the get-go, the apparatus that Agamben is trying to define is associated with a torture machine. In "What is an Apparatus?," Agamben uses the term "dispositivo" to refer to both "appareil" and "dispositif." One other obvious lineage of the term "apparatus" is its use by Louis Althusser in his essay on the school as an "ideological state apparatus." Althusser's essay, which pertains to education, is very much within the scope of my own project, even though I do not address it explicitly. Finally, one should note that the obvious inter-text for Agamben's essay on the apparatus is Gilles Deleuze's essay "Qu'est-ce qu'un dispositif?," which marks a powerful engagement with Foucault's thought. I will leave aside here these obvious references in order to explore instead a much less obvious connection, namely the relation of Agamben's essay to Kant's and Foucault's essays on the Enlightenment.

12 Stiegler, *Taking Care*, 299.

13 Agamben, *WA*, 24.

14 Ibid., 14.

15 Stiegler has in his work on aesthetics developed mystagogy's critical function in relation to mystery. See Stiegler, "Proletarianization."

16 See Stiegler and *Ars Industrialis*, *Réenchanter*.

17 *Ars Industrialis* document, "L'école de philosophie d'Épineuil-le-Fleuriel: Un projet de l'association *Ars Industrialis*," sent to me by Bernard Stiegler in personal correspondence. This text is the original proposal for the creation of the school. The school has since been established, and it has been going for several years attracting more and more participants every year, from all corners of the globe.

18 Agamben, *P*, 177.

19 Ibid., 246–7.

20 Scotus qtd. ibid., 262.

21 Agamben, *P*, 270.

22 Agamben, *TR*, 64.

23 In Chapter 1, I distinguished such an aesthetic move from a poetic politics, which would be focused on the actual production of the law. As I see it, there is an aesthetic politics that takes precedence over a poetic politics here.

24 See Durantaye, *Giorgio Agamben*.

25 See Foucault, *Care*.

26 Kant, "Aufklärung," 29.

27 Ibid.

28 Ibid.

29 Ibid., 35.

30 Ibid.

31 Ibid.

32 Foucault, *Politics*, 109.

33 Ibid.

34 Ibid., 105.

35 Ibid.

36 Ibid., 170.

37 Ibid., 113.

38 Ibid., 114.

39 Ibid.

40 As I explained in Chapter 1, I consider this to be an aesthetic issue before it is a poetic one.

41 Of course, as such these spaces do not mark the full relation of plasticity to form. They only capture some of its aspects.

42 Foucault, *Technologies*, 145.

43 John Rajchman comes very close to stating this in his introduction to *The Politics of Truth*. See Rajchman, "Enlightenment Today," in particular 15. Bruno Bosteels also comments on Foucault's use of the term actuality, and briefly notes the connection to Agamben's work that I lay out here, in *The Actuality of Communism*, in particular 59–65.

44 Foucault, *Gouvernement*, 13.

45 Ibid.

46 Ibid., 15.

47 All translations from *Le Gouvernement de soi et des autres* in both this paragraph and the following are mine.

48 Ibid., 22.

49 Foucault, *Politics*, 119.

50 Foucault, *Care*, 43.

51 Ibid.

52 Ibid., 45.

53 Ibid.

54 Ibid., 53. One of the many valuable points made by Jeffrey Nealon in his recent *Foucault Beyond Foucault* – a book that re-examines Foucault's importance *today*, and turns to Foucault's Enlightenment essay throughout its argument – is that this enlightened care of the self should not be understood as theory's version of Nike's "Just Do It" motto. Indeed, as my discussion of the tension between potentiality and actuality in Foucault shows, the "doing" of "care" and the "labor" or "work" it implies might ultimately have more to do with an "undoing" or "unworking" – with the "worklessness" and "inoperativity" evoked by Agamben – than with Nike's sweatshop-tainted imperative. See Nealon, *Foucault*, especially the first chapter.

55 Kant, "Aufklärung," 29–30.

56 Foucault, *Gouvernement*, 28.

57 Kant, "Aufklärung," 30.

58 Many have commented on Kant's suspicion of technology. See, for example, Rutsky, "Spirit."

59 Foucault, *Politics*, 116.

60 Ibid.

61 Agamben, *WA*, 22–3.

62 Kant, "Aufklärung," 29.

63 Agamben, *WA*, 14.

64 Of course, one might argue that Agamben's distinction is ultimately merely analytical, and does not reflect the nuances of his thought on technology. As Anne Sauvagnargues remarked in response to a conference presentation I gave on Agamben and Simondon, Agamben's ultimate interest might simply be modes of subjectivation. Although this point is well taken, it does not adduce the *tone* of Agamben's essay, which is one of struggle and conflict between human beings and machines.

65 Agamben, *WA*, 15.

66 Ibid., 17.

67 Ibid., 19.

68 Agamben, *MWC*, 4.

69 Ibid.

70 Ibid.

71 Ibid.

72 On this point, see George Collins's contribution on the figure of the samurai to the study group on the "Cultures de soi" organized by *Ars Industrialis*: Collins, "Petit Annonce."

73 Crary, [Untitled], 77–8.

74 Ibid., 77.

75 Ibid., 78.

76 Agamben, *WA*, 14.

77 Ibid., 15–16.

78 Crary, [Untitled], 78.

79 Agamben, *WA*, 15.

80 Ibid., 18.

81 Ibid.

82 Ibid., 19.

83 Agamben, *PR*, 9.

84 Ibid.

85 Ibid., 11.

86 Ibid., 13.

87 Agamben, *WA*, 51.

88 See Agamben, *P*.

89 Contrary to what one might expect, the unforgettable in Agamben's work does not refer to what cannot be forgotten. It refers, rather, to everything in individual and collective life that is forgotten all the time, in spite of humanity's attempts at preservation. What makes this forgotten unforget-table, however, is the ways in which it acts upon memory, thus remaining

active within individual and collective life. The subject's relation to the unforgettable is neither one of memory nor of forgetfulness, but one of becoming attentive to its *seemingly* inert and ineffective matter that *in fact* shapes the subject's individual and collective life. See Agamben, *TR*, 39–43.

90 Agamben, *WA*, 14.

91 In these films, of course, matters are much more complicated than any simple opposition of man to machine might have one believe: in *The Matrix*, Neo and his crew move between the real world and the computer program through the use of the very cell phones that Agamben would prefer to see deactivated or destroyed; in *Terminator*, the survival of John Connor, the future leader of the human resistance, depends on a machine that he sent back in time to protect his younger self. Films such as Ridley Scott's *Blade Runner* or Steven Spielberg's *A. I.* can be said to explore this other side of popular culture's technological vision as well.

92 Simondon, *L'individuation*. All translations from Simondon are mine. An English translation of *L'individuation psychique et collective* (translated by myself, Gregory Flanders, Alicia Harrison, with Rositza Alexandrova and Julia Ng) is forthcoming with University of Minnesota Press.

93 Ibid., 224.

94 Ibid., 13.

95 Simondon, "Technical Mentality," 20.

96 Ibid., 19.

97 Ibid.

98 Ibid.

99 Ibid.

100 Ibid.

101 Ibid.

102 Simondon, *L'individuation*, 262–90.

103 That we are also continuing here our dialogue with the Enlightenment that was opened up in the first part of this chapter will immediately be clear from the introduction to Simondon's book on technical objects, where he sets out to criticize the ways in which technical objects have been conceived of as "slaves." See Simondon, *Du mode d'existence*, for example 9. It is a typical emancipatory argument that in this case applies the Enlightenment call for emancipation – its horror of slavery, at least at a metaphorical level (Susan Buck-Morss has emphasized in "Hegel and Haiti" that while "slavery" comes to name everything that is evil for Enlightenment thinkers, they also allowed slavery to continue, ignoring it

in many of their writings). Simondon sets out to liberate technical objects from their age-long state of slavery.

104 Simondon, *L'individuation*, 217.
105 Agamben, *CC*, 87.
106 It is worth noting that Agamben's enemy in these passages is not sovereignty, but the state. This invites us to distinguish between the two, perhaps even to save sovereignty from the state and resituate it on the side of whatever singularity.

6

The Work of Inoperativity

Homo Laborans

The Highest Poverty raises the question of "use," and announces a final volume in the *Homo Sacer* series that will take up that issue at length. It is worth noting, however, that the question of use has been addressed elsewhere in Agamben's work, entering into it as early as *Stanzas* (as Jessica Whyte has noted[1]) through a discussion of Marx, and being further developed in part in *The Coming Community* but then in particular in *The Time That Remains*, *What is an Apparatus?*, and *Profanations*. In addition, "use" as an idea is arguably even more prominent in Agamben's oeuvre if one is willing to recognize its relation to "work." Within such a perspective, it would be necessary to see the intimate relations between use and the notion of inoperativity, deactivation, or worklessness that is central to Agamben's writings. Indeed, one could go so far as to argue that to render something inoperative means to use it in the particular way in which Agamben has defined profanation: to restore something to common use, to the free use of men – and thereby to emancipate it from the economic slavery to which it had been subjected.

To ask "what is use?" could thus return us to another, perhaps more familiar question: what is work? And: why work? And we would be returning to those questions in the midst of an

225

economic crisis, generally thought to have started in 2008, in which there appears to be an ever more desperate desire for work – any kind of work, no matter its conditions. "We are flexible" is, as Catherine Malabou and many others have noted, the motto of the contemporary, neoliberal workforce. Malabou opposes this neoliberal flexibility to plasticity, which – unlike flexibility – is not infinitely stretchable but explodes. Taking my cue from Malabou, I would argue that like her, Agamben is interested in the plasticity rather than the flexibility of work, and starts from work's explosion – its destructive limit – in order to rethink the human being's doings.

In his essay titled "The Work of Man,"[2] Agamben considers the suggestion that unlike architects, carpenters, or musicians, who have a clearly defined kind of work – they build houses, make furniture, or play music – the human being does not have such a clearly defined kind of work. Human beings are, instead, without work. This is a suggestion made by Aristotle in *The Nicomachean Ethics*, where it remains undeveloped.[3] Agamben returns to it in his essay, referencing Hannah Arendt's reflections on work in *The Human Condition* as a key influence,[4] and then again in his more recent writings which develop a discussion of use. Use is of course supremely relevant – perhaps more so than work – in the digital age, where much work is performed and exploited in the form of usership. It is then, perhaps, with a focus on usership and what Franco "Bifo" Berardi and others in the Italian, Autonomist tradition have referred to as the "cognitariat" of users – a cognitariat that embodies today what I called in Chapter 4 the bare life of the proletariat – that the investigation of work today must proceed.[5]

If the question of "use" and the particular economic politics it involves is intimately linked to the question of "work" and in particular "the work of man," that is: the human being's activities, that means that the question of use ultimately also mobilizes the concerns with the human being's potentiality, actuality, and specifically her or his potentiality not-to that I have investigated in the previous chapters. Indeed, what is the type of use, work, or activity – the type of doing – that one could tie to a philosophy of the potentiality not-to, whose greatest hero is arguably Herman Melville's law-copyist Bartleby? What is the type of work that Bartleby's "I would prefer not to" enables us to think? Here too, one senses that the easy way out – opposing work to non-work, activity to passivity, speech to silence – would not do justice to Agamben's thought. If infancy, and the liminal zone between silence and speech in which it operates – the other way of speaking that it opens up – can function like an example, model, or paradigm for one's thinking of work, it appears that one would have to conceive of another kind of work, a "wholly transformed" kind of work (to recall the discussion of Benjamin in Chapter 2) that would carry the negativity of non-work within it – but without succumbing to either the pure negativity of non-work or the full actuality of work. The question to ask then, as I have suggested elsewhere,[6] would be: what constitutes the work of inoperativity? What constitutes the work of worklessness, the activity of deactivation? If inoperativity, worklessness, and deactivation are not simply the opposites of operativity, work, and activation, then what type of doing do they name? How can it be thought?

In his book *Profanations* and elsewhere, Agamben has proposed that the child's play is a good site to develop this kind of thinking. "Study" has also figured in his oeuvre as an example of the kind of work he has in mind. In this chapter, I propose to engage and further this thought through a consideration of inoperativity in two realms that are not alien to Agamben's writing about work: art and cinema. First, I turn to Jeff Wall, whose photographs I began to discuss in Chapter 2, in order to reveal the theory of inoperativity that informs his work. This discussion, and in particular Wall's take on the avant-garde, will lead into legal and political questions that I address, in the second half of the chapter, through a discussion of a contemporary American (US) film: Ethan and Joel Coen's *No Country for Old Men*, based on the novel by Cormac McCarthy. While a discussion of this particular film might appear to be an odd choice for a book on Agamben (a discussion of Godard, as offered in Chapter 3, would certainly seem more appropriate!), there are a number of reasons why I have chosen this particular film: first, because its title – which is a reference to William Butler Yeats's "Sailing to Byzantium" – invites us to consider another figure of inoperativity, not unrelated to the child that Agamben focuses on, namely those who are retired and no longer work. Much of Agamben's vocabulary when he theorizes inoperativity and use is about "with-drawal" (literally, "re-tirement") and thus suggests that retirement may be a fruitful place to think through inoperativity. I choose the topic of retirement also in view of our contemporary moment, specifically the problematic of care that dominates our day, and with an eye on the rapidly aging populations in Western democracies – a fact that, as Bifo has noted, is not receiving the philosophical attention it should. Thirdly, I am interested in *No Country for Old Men* because it marks a specific American (US) imagination, associated in the film with the genre of the Western, in which the theologico-political questions that are central to Agamben's work are played out. This focus on the US and its politics will return in the next chapter of this book, where I will look at Agamben's treatment of the US in his political writings.

Taking my cue from a political cartoon that parodies the film's official poster, I analyze *No Country for Old Men* as a political film that targets the ways in which the Bush government responded to the September 11 terror attacks, by declaring a state of exception – by heightening nationalist discourse, suspending civil liberties, extending surveillance mechanisms, and so on – in the hope that final security could ultimately be achieved. The film's representation of the confrontation between the retiring sheriff Ed Tom Bell (played by Tommy Lee Jones) and the hit man Anton Chigurh (Javier Bardem) reveals such a hope to be theological, and suggests moreover that it inspires a work of justice that is profoundly misled and produces the opposite of what it hopes to produce.

I argue that *No Country for Old Men* works through such a theological practice of justice not in order to abandon it altogether but in order to "retire" it: in order to lead it into a realm of "non-work" from where it could be practiced otherwise. From this perspective, it is the film's retiring sheriff who will provide the key to the film's politics. However, the sheriff's retirement cannot be disentangled from the retirement of the other characters in the film: Llewelyn Moss (Josh Brolin), a retired welder; Carla Jean Moss (Kelly Macdonald), Llewelyn's wife who works at Walmart but is declared "retired" by her husband after he finds a satchel full of money (the declaration can be read as an instance of tragic irony, since Carla Jean will be "retired" or "killed" by Chigurh at the end of the film); and in particular Anton Chigurh, the hit man who at the end of the film is the only one still standing ("el último hombre," "the last man," to recall Llewelyn's words early on in the film) – the only one who is not retired, but whose prime activity consists in "retiring" or "killing" other living beings. It is by analyzing the film's play with retirement that *No Country for Old Men*'s "worldly meaning"[7] as a work of art – its significance for human beings in the world of today – can be revealed, and that some political aspects of Agamben's critique of work can be uncovered.

My aim in this chapter is thus to ultimately bring the question of retirement, which is central to the Coen brothers' film, together with the critique of political theology that the film develops. Through the linked discussion of both the film and Jeff Wall, I seek to further, with concrete examples, the elusive thought of inoperativity and use that is a central component of Agamben's work.

Inoperativity and Play

In an interview with Arielle Pelenc, Jeff Wall observes that his "work has been criticized for lacking interruption, for not displaying the fragmentation and 'suturing' which had become *de rigueur* for serious art, critical art since the 1960s."[8] He points out, however, that by the middle of the 1970s, he "felt that the 'Godardian' look of this art had become so formulaic and insti-tutionalized that it had completed its revolution, the plus was becoming a minus, and something new was emerging."[9] This "something" he found in films like Robert Bresson's *Mouchette* (from 1967) and Jean Eustache's *La Maman et la Putain* (1973). Contrary to the "jump cuts" of earlier radical cinema, these films preserved the classical codes of cinema and transferred "the energy of radical thinking away from any direct interrogation of the medium and towards increasing the pressure or intensity they could bring to bear on the more or less normative, existing forms which seemed to epitomize the medium."[10] "They accepted,"

Wall says, "what the art form had become during its history."[11] "They accepted technique, generic structure, narrative codes, problematics of performance and so on, but they broke away from the decorum of the dominant institutions."[12]

Wall's description of this aesthetic is particularly illuminating, and worth quoting at length:

> There is a lot that could be said about a kind of internalized radicalism in the work of these filmmakers and others working between, say, 1955 and about 1980, an almost "invisibilized" intensity as far as any disruption of the classical codes is concerned. What happened was that the "outside," as you call it, did get inside, but in doing so it refused to appear directly as an outside, disruptive element. It dissembled. It appeared to be conventional, appeared to be the same as (or almost) the conventionalized "signs for the real" that make up ordinary cinema.... So, the new form of the threshold was not a drastically broken-up surface like in Godard, but a self-consciously, even ironically, even manneristically normalized surface. This is – or seems to be – a more ambivalent approach to the idea of critique and auto-critique than an openly contestatory one. This apparent ambivalence, this technique of mimesis and dissembling, this "inhabitation" didn't satisfy anyone who demanded avant-gardist criteria of overt, antagonistic confrontation.[13]

Wall is clearly searching for words here, developing a poetry of his aesthetic practice. Against "overt, antagonistic confrontation," he embraces a practice that does not "destroy" technique, genre, narrative code, the problematics of performance, et cetera but aims to overcome them – to work through them, traverse them – by making them appear the same and not the same, the same and yet wholly other. Everything is in place in Bresson's or Eustache's films, he argues, but the very way in which it is in place has become intensified, charged, inhabited by a dissembling element. As Wall explains, this element does not enter the work of art as a visible disruption. Instead, the element accomplishes a taking apart or unworking of the work that he appears to think of as more subversive than the visible interruption of the jump cut. The idea of a mimesis that would dissemble resonates here with the idea of *désoeuvrement* that Agamben often uses in his discussions of inoperativity.

As if all of this wasn't already interesting enough, Wall characterizes this unworking in explicitly legalo-political terms. Speaking about the way in which his work can be approached as a site for an "aesthetic and libidinal gaming with tradition, a site of the transgression of its rules and laws" (as Pelenc puts it), he states that

> [t]ransgression is the beginning of authentic existence, the origin of art's truth and freedom. But modern societies are constitutional; they have written, deliberately, their own foundations, and are continuously rewriting them. Maybe it is a sense that it is the writing of laws, and not the breaking of them, that is the most significant and characteristic act of modernity. Avant-garde art certainly operated this way, writing new laws as quickly as it broke any old ones, thereby imitating the constitutional state.… I feel that art develops through experimentally positing possible laws or law-like forms of behavior, and then attempting to obey them.[14]

Instead of merely destroying laws, art also posits laws – it participates in what Benjamin in "Critique of Violence" calls "law-positing" violence. Wall in fact does not believe that there can be such a thing as "pure law-breaking activity": that is a "romantic fiction of the radical avant-garde,"[15] he states. His work does not aim to transgress law; instead, it aims to transgress the "institution of transgression" by "liberat[ing] what previously had to be seen as the anti-liberating elements in art."[16]

A few remarks are in order. First of all, Wall's comments resonate with the take on sovereignty that I develop in this book. The point is not, as I have argued, to destroy it; the question of sovereignty *today* is *not* whether it should stay or go. Instead, it is about liberating or better unworking something within sovereignty, a plastic – explosive – element that will enable it to go in new directions. My suggestion has been that political phenomena such as Occupy and the Arab Spring are indications of this explosive element. Like Wall, I do not believe in a pure law-breaking activity. Benjamin's "divine" or "pure" violence is certainly not that, as I have shown in Chapter 2; Agamben's call for an anomic, political action is also not a call for an action that would destroy the law (I will return to this in detail in the final part of this book). What both are aiming at, rather, is the separation of life from law that would make a truly political action possible. This separation is not one that will come from an outside. Instead, it begins to leak from within, transforming the entire apparatus in which it works. Of course, and this is the second point that needs to be made, the very term "work" is under pressure in such a context, for what we are confronting here is characterized by Wall – and Agamben is in line with Wall on this count – as a dissembling of what is assembled. However, this pressure does not amount to the abolition of assembly.

The reason why I find Wall's discussion of his aesthetic practice so interesting is not simply because it uses legalo-political language; it is also because it ultimately tackles the key term of this chapter, "work," and begins to think it otherwise. For Wall, the artwork appears to unwork the work it is doing, not by destroying "tradition" or "the law" but by liberating those very elements in order to enable them to begin to leak from within. His aim is not the broken-up surface; it is the norm – *but different*. The aim is, emphatically, to make the familiar appear strange without taking recourse to the very obvious intervention of the jump cut. The strange is not visible in this particular way in Wall's work. Instead, he operates much more subversively, uncannily unworking the manneristic surface of his photographs.

Throughout Agamben's work, the term "inoperativity" or "*désoeuvrement*" explicitly appears, and scholars have recognized that it is a key term in his thought.[17] As such, it becomes associated there with different figures: with the already mentioned Bartleby, for example, who prefers not to execute any and all tasks that are assigned to him and thus unworks the organization of the Wall Street law office where he is employed.[18] Or one can think of Saint Paul, whose letters propose a theological notion of "inoperativity" that will be crucial for the community Agamben is trying to think. But rather than focus on such figures who, as these examples already illustrate, risk widely differing, I propose to turn instead (and it is something of an impossible focus, of course) to the "work" of "inoperativity" itself. For it is clear that, in spite of its name, inoperativity is *doing* something. What is this something so that it can begin to resonate in Agamben's work not just as an aesthetic but also as a political practice?

One thing that can be noted, in spite of the seriousness associated with the notion, is that in Agamben's work, inoperativity comes in close proximity to "play" ("study" and "festivity" are two others that are associated with it). In *State of Exception*, for example, Agamben writes: "One day, humanity will play with law just as children play with disused objects, not in order to restore them to their canonical use but to free them from it for good."[19] (He notes in that same book that this does not mean

234

to destroy law but to render it inoperative, to deactivate it.) The sentence summarizes Agamben's understanding of law after it has been disentangled from mythical violence and can be said to *critically* evoke Claude Lévi-Strauss's analysis of mythical thought as "a kind of intellectual 'bricolage'" in the opening chapter of his classic *The Savage Mind*.[20]

"There still exists among ourselves," Lévi-Strauss writes,

> an activity which on the technical plane gives us quite a good understanding of what a science we prefer to call "prior" rather than "primitive" could have been on the plane of speculation. This is what is commonly called bricolage in French.[21]

According to Lévi-Strauss, the bricoleur – unlike the engineer, who "is always trying to make his way out of and go beyond the constraints imposed by a particular state of civilization"[22] –

> make[s] do with "whatever is at hand", that is to say with a set of tools and materials which is always finite and is also heterogeneous because what it contains bears no relation to the current project, or indeed to any particular project, but is the contingent result of all the occasions there have been to renew or enrich the stock or to maintain it with the remains of previous constructions and destructions [les résidus de constructions et de destructions antérieures].[23]

If we take this into account, it begins to become clear what the relation between bricolage and inoperativity might consist in.

Just like bricolage, inoperativity does not aim to go beyond ("outside," to recall Wall's comments on this aesthetic practice) a particular state of civilization. Instead, it chooses to *accept* this state only *in order to completely transform it from within*. Thinking of law and sovereign power as inoperative would mean to continually reconstruct them from the same materials. As

Lévi-Strauss writes – and this resonates both with Benjamin's discussion of means and ends in "Critique of Violence" and with the title of Agamben's *Means Without End* – in such bricolage "it is always earlier ends which are called upon to play the part of the means."[24] A thought and practice of inoperativity would continually be working with the "remains and debris" of laws and sovereignties: "in French, 'des bribes et des morceaux', or odds and ends in English, fossilized evidence of the history of an individual or society."[25] Thus, mythical thought "builds up structures by fitting together events, or rather the remains [résidus] of events, while science, 'in operation' [en marche] simply by virtue of coming into being, creates its means and results in the form of events."[26]

Silently echoing William Wordsworth's famous line that the child is father of the man, Agamben conceives of such a tireless reordering as "play." Inoperative law-making would consist of playing with the law as with disused objects, not in order to restore it to its canonical use but in order to liberate it from its definite and determinate purpose for good. As will be clear from what I wrote above, such liberation does not entail a nihilistic destruction of the law. Instead of trying to break out of the realm of law and sovereign power, inoperativity would accept structures of government in order to intensify them with an invisible disruption (this is what Wall's aesthetic theory showed us). Adding pressure to the law, it would leave sovereignty in place while at the same time suspending it. This is the epochal opening that Agamben's thought represents, the contemporary light within which Lévi-Strauss's "science of the concrete" can gain new meaning.

In this book, I theorize such an understanding of sovereignty as "plastic": it would account for sovereignty's form-giving, form-receiving, and form-exploding capacities. Once again, Agamben's term of preference – "play" – would mark the explosive, limit-capacity of sovereignty's plasticity, the activity where its violent, mythical appropriation is resisted and something new can begin to become possible.

Agamben's own term for the play with law that he describes – compared to play with disused objects, to liberate them from their traditional uses – is "profanation." By "profane," Agamben means "the free use of men"; to profane something means to restore it to the free use of men. But restore from where? The answer is not surprising, given Agamben's other work: profanation removes something from the sphere of the sacred. This does not mean, however, that it restores this something to its "natural" use; instead, the thing has become profaned. In his text "In Praise of Profanation," Agamben compares this "passage from the sacred to the profane" to "play":

> play frees and distracts humanity from the sphere of the sacred, without simply abolishing it. The use to which the sacred is returned is a special one that does not coincide with utilitarian consumption. In fact, "profanation" of play does not solely concern the religious sphere. Children, who play with whatever old thing falls into their hands, make toys out of things that belong to the spheres of economics, war, law, and other activities that we are used to thinking of as serious. All of a sudden, a car, a firearm, or a legal contract becomes a toy.[27]

Thus a "new dimension of use" is opened up. Children have the capacity to do this; and philosophers have it as well. Unfortunately, today "[p]lay as an organ of profanation is in decline everywhere."[28] Part of Agamben's project will be to restore it.

As have already stated, one of the key references that Agamben gives in his work for the development of this kind of thought is

Arendt's book *The Human Condition*. In the prologue to this book, Arendt famously states the project of the book to be "to think what we are doing."[29] Arguing that modern times have saddled human beings with an impoverished notion of work that reduces all of their activities to "making a living,"[30] only in order to then take their labor away from them, her book proposes to provide the categories for a richer understanding of our doings. These categories turn out to be labor – "the activity which corresponds to the biological process of the human body"[31] – work – "the activity which corresponds to the unnaturalness of human existence" and "provides an 'artificial' world of things"[32] – and action – "the only activity that goes on directly between men without the intermediary of things or matter" and "corresponds to the human condition of plurality" that is "*the* condition of all political life."[33] These categories can of course be challenged, but that does not take away any of the conceptual force of Arendt's project – a project that gains new resonance today, in the midst of an economic crisis in which human activities once again risk being reduced to "making a living."

In a later passage in the book, Arendt restates her general argument, but now she adds to it a fourth category that at this point in my discussion should not come as a surprise: play. "The same trend to level down all serious activities to making a living is manifest in present-day labor theories," Arendt writes in 1958, "which almost unanimously define labor as the opposite of play."

> As a result, all serious activities, irrespective of their fruits, are called labor, and every activity which is not necessary either for the life of the individual or for the life process of society is subsumed under playfulness. In these theories, which by echoing the current estimate of a laboring society on the theoretical level sharpen it and drive it into its inherent extreme, not even

the "work" of the artist is left; it is dissolved into play and has lost its worldly meaning. The playfulness of the artist is felt to fulfill the same function in the laboring life process of society as the playing of tennis or the pursuit of a hobby fulfills in the life of the individual.... From the standpoint of "making a living" every activity unconnected with labor becomes a "hobby."[34]

To be sure, this passage should not be misread as a plea for "play" or for "hobbies." What Arendt criticizes is the fact that activities that are being called "play" or "hobbies" are thereby stripped of their seriousness: their "worldly meaning" is dissolved under the sovereignty of labor as the only serious and meaningful human activity.

In a footnote on page 127, Arendt points out that underlying the opposition between labor and play that she analyzes, is the "real" opposition between necessity and freedom, with labor being linked to necessity and play to freedom. Again, it goes without saying that play is not Arendt's idea of freedom. If anything, her book challenges the construction of freedom as play and insists instead on freedom's "work," more precisely on the "action" that is the condition of all political life.

Even if their thoughts also remain significantly different – it should be clear from the above that Arendt, unlike Agamben, could never accept Melville's Bartleby as a political hero – it should now also come as no surprise that a more positive notion of play, or of what in this context one could also more generally call "non-work," appears in the philosophy of Agamben. While he has explored it mostly from the perspective of the child's play, I propose to approach it here from the retirement of the elderly in order to see what such a consideration might reveal to us about the politics of inoperativity in Agamben's work.

"You Can't Stop What's Coming"

If one does a quick Internet search for images of *No Country for Old Men*, the first few results are likely to include a political cartoon by R. J. Matson, first published in *The New York Observer*, that borrows heavily from the film's official poster.[35] The left half of the image features the Republican heavy-weights George Bush senior, John McCain, and John Warner – the three of them grouped together above the film title. The right half of the image is filled by one of the film's taglines: "You Can't Stop What's Coming." The immediate message of the cartoon is clear: McCain, who ran for president against Barack Obama, is being told by Bush and Warner that he is too old for the job. The cartoon could perhaps also be read more broadly, however, as a critique of the policies of George Bush junior, who was president when this cartoon as well as McCarthy's novel and the Coen brothers' film first appeared. Indeed, any of the film's other taglines – "There Are No Clean Getaways," "There Are No Laws Left," and "Nothing You Fear … Can Prepare You For Him" – could serve just as well to sum up the ways in which the Bush government responded to the September 11 terror attacks.

"What's Coming" in the film's official poster – and the political cartoon preserves this part of the original image – appears to be a tiny, darkened figure running in the foreground, carrying what looks like a gun in the left hand, and a briefcase in the right. Judging from the film, this figure is most likely Llewelyn Moss, a sympathetic, all-American Vietnam veteran who comes upon a satchel full of money while he is hunting in the desolate landscape of West Texas, close to the US–Mexican border. It is the money of a drug deal gone wrong. Moss decides to hold on to the money, but both the Mexican drug sellers and the American buyers are on his tracks. As if things weren't already complicated enough, the Americans also hire a hit man called Anton Chigurh to get their money back.

No Country for Old Men comes to revolve around the struggle between Moss and Chigurh, a struggle that ends abruptly before the end of the film, when Llewelyn is killed by the Mexican drug dealers. This makes for an at first sight uncomfortable series of closing scenes, in which the film appears to continue beyond its central storyline for much longer than it should. However, in the wake of this initial discomfort there quickly emerges the question of whether the struggle between Moss and Chigurh was really the central story of the film, or if there was, perhaps, another story going on whose significance was eclipsed by the struggle between Moss and Chigurh that took up most of the viewer's attention.

Like several of the Coen brothers' other characters, Chigurh is the embodiment of an unstoppable "drive" – beautifully evoked at the beginning of the film when a handcuffed Chigurh steps into a police car that speeds away on an empty desert road – a man who continues even when all available roads are blocked, and who belongs to an almost superhuman realm of endurance. It might thus turn out that "what's coming" in the film is not the tiny Moss running in the foreground of the film poster, but Chigurh, the embodiment of a principle of evil by which Moss as well as everyone else in the film becomes hunted and haunted. Starting with the monologue that opens the film, Chigurh is presented as a figure of an unnamable terror against which one is ultimately incapable of protecting oneself. What constitutes the particularly terrorizing aspect of Chigurh is not so much that his "work" consists of the fact that he puts people forever out of work; it is that he does this *not* in order to make a living, *but* out of principle. In the end, the satchel full of money is only of secondary importance to Chigurh; it is what he was hired to retrieve, but it does not constitute the meaning of his life. What counts, for him, is not so much the money, as the killings that his being hired to retrieve the money makes necessary. Killing people is the quasi-monastic "rule" according to which Chigurh lives (as Carson Wells, a hit man hired to hunt Chigurh, puts it) – a rule of death rather than a rule of life. Death is the principle of Chigurh's life, the motor or drive of his operations.

Such a figure of a categorical imperative gone wrong[36] becomes highly resonant in a time – the post-9/11 moment – and place – the United States – when the protection against the sudden and supposedly irrational death of terror, and specifically suicide bombing, had become the government's main occupation. If the suicide bomber, as Talal Asad in a recent book *On Suicide Bombing* explains, already challenges the value of life that is pivotal to the Western philosophical, moral, and political tradition, at least the suicide bomber's imperative can still be constructed as hypothetical (they blow themselves up because of the promise of the seventy-two virgins in the afterlife; they blow themselves up because of America's role in international politics; they blow themselves up out of resentment against the Western, capitalist world; and so on). Chigurh represents a more extreme figure of this construction: a man who does not kill because of anything that is exterior to himself, but because he must do so, because that is the reason for his life.

I would argue that Matson's political cartoon perceptively invites one to consider *No Country for Old Men* not only as a story set in West Texas in the 1980s, but also against the background of current political events, specifically as a story about the struggle between terror and government. How should governments deal with terror? What is the government's relation to terror, what is the relation between state terror and the terror of suicide bombing? What should be the philosophical, ethical, and political values according to which one governs in a time of terror? *No Country for Old Men* addresses these questions through its representation of a struggle that has remained out of my focus so far, namely the confrontation between Chigurh and sheriff Ed Tom Bell.

The Sheriff and Chigurh

It is perhaps difficult to notice upon a first viewing, but sheriff Ed Tom Bell has both the first and the last word in *No Country for Old Men*. The film begins with a moving monologue in which the sheriff (who will only appear in the film a while later) recalls the men who have preceded him as sheriffs in West Texas – he mentions both his father and his grandfather – and reflects upon the differences between their times and his. Whereas back then, some sheriffs did not even need a gun to maintain law and order, in Bell's time even a gun risks not being enough to protect one from the evil that is out there. A gun might save one's body, the sheriff suggests, but it cannot save one's soul – and it is one's soul that is at risk if one ventures out into today's world. These thoughts, which are initially spoken over people-less images of West Texas, come to accompany the scene of Chigurh's arrest, thus creating the suggestion that Chigurh is a figure of the soul-threatening evil that the sheriff's monologue evokes.[37]

Although the viewer might not entirely realize it yet, the sheriff – he who is supposed to preserve the peace in West Texas – is thus introduced in the film not as the strong arm of the law, but as a highly precarious figure who is profoundly disturbed by Chigurh. In the face of terror, the sheriff emerges as a figure of a heightened vulnerability, a vulnerability that becomes all the more pressing because the sheriff also represents the law and order that are supposed to keep us safe. In the figure of the sheriff, it appears to be law and order themselves that are under threat, faced with a terror that the humanist presuppositions upon which they are built can barely contain. As Judith Butler in a similar context has noted, this raises the question of how government is going to respond to such destabilizing terror and to the sense of heightened vulnerability that it produces. In her opinion, "final control is not, cannot be, an ultimate value" when it comes to responding to terror, because control is inevitably disrupted by other processes that traverse it, and of which it is a part.[38]

Something of Butler's point about the impossibility of final control shines through in *No Country for Old Men*'s closing scene, which features the sheriff's face, looking strangely childlike and intensely aged at the same time, at a loss after the sheriff has just recounted two dreams about his long-dead father to his wife. The first, which involved his father giving him money which he then lost, he can barely remember; the second, however, featured his father riding ahead of him on a mountain pass into the cold, dark night, shielding a light and fixing a fire up ahead to receive the sheriff whenever he would get there. This light and fire can easily be read as the light and fire of justice: as the dream of final control that is projected up ahead, with the sheriff's long-dead father protecting it until the sheriff will get there himself, in other words: until the sheriff himself will have died. One does not have to be a psychoanalyst to understand the dream's significance: only in death will the sheriff's work of justice be completed. Final justice is not a part of this world.

It is no coincidence that this dream comes to the sheriff in the early days of his retirement, after he has given up on the quest for justice because he feels "overmatched" by the world of today. Indeed, this is one of the ways in which *No Country for Old Men* establishes a link between the particular kind of politics towards which it gestures and the sheriff's retirement. As the sheriff explains in a conversation towards the end of the film, "I always felt that when I got older, God would come into my life. He didn't." This confession reveals the theological assumption behind the sheriff's life-long work of justice, namely the fact that he operates within the belief – or more precisely, on the basis of a "feeling" – that when he got older, God would step in, presumably to complete the work of justice that the sheriff as a young man took up. God did not step in, however, and this radical absence of transcendence brings into sharp relief not only the fact that the sheriff's work, even though he is retiring, is hardly done – an unfinishedness that is arguably the condition of all retirement; for which one of our works is ever really completed during our lifetime? – but also the bitter failure of all of the sheriff's life-long attempts at preserving law and order. One gets the distinct sense that the confrontation with Chigurh, which is the broader context within which the story of the sheriff's retirement is being told, leaves the sheriff defeated: disillusioned with the project of justice to which he has dedicated his life – in vain.

However, this vanity only depends upon the theological assumption that the work of justice could somehow be completed once and for all. Indeed, if one of the mottos of truth and justice cited in the film is "to dedicate oneself daily anew," the sheriff responds that he will dedicate himself twice daily, or even thrice daily, not realizing that such multiple dedications are not going to solve the problem. It is precisely this theological dedication to truth and justice, a dedication that operates on the assumption that final truth and justice will ultimately be realized, that the film's representation of the sheriff's retirement, of his becoming retired, allows the viewer (and perhaps also the sheriff) to work through. In this sense, Chigurh can be read along more positive lines as the active agent of such retirement, as the one who retires; retirement thus reveals itself in the film as a kind of premature death, a dying without dying that only anticipates an even more radical falling out of work that will arrive when the sheriff meets his father again. It is part of the magic of film that it allows the viewer to experience this without actually dying, through the encounter with the otherwise horrific figure of Chigurh. Although Chigurh's final "victory" over Moss might be disturbing, especially given the fact that the seemingly last good man (another "último hombre") in West Texas, sheriff Ed Tom Bell, is retiring, it may actually be necessary to read these two figures together, with Chigurh as the agent of a retirement that actually teaches the viewer something about the sheriff's work of justice in response to figures of terror such as Chigurh.

Such a reading is suggested by the close affinity, and intimacy even, between the sheriff and Chigurh that *No Country for Old Men* develops. Continuing the references to Judith Butler's work earlier on, one might say that the close connection between the sheriff's heightened vulnerability and the terror of Chigurh reveals something important about the relation between government and terror. Consider, first of all, a number of scenes in which this connection is established. There is, to begin with, the sheriff's voice at the beginning of the film, which accompanies the images of Chigurh's arrest. This initial weaving together of the figures of Chigurh and the sheriff is further developed later on in the film, when the sheriff visits Llewelyn Moss's trailer home in search of Moss and his wife, Carla Jean. Chigurh has visited the trailer only minutes before, and the Coen brothers have the sheriff sit down in the exact same spot where Chigurh had been sitting (which is almost the exact same spot where, the evening before, Moss joined his wife on the couch). Like Chigurh, the sheriff sees himself reflected in the dark glass of Moss's television, their mirror images perfectly overlapping if one were to superimpose these two shots. When the sheriff pours himself a glass of milk from the bottle that stands sweating on the living room table – a sign that the sheriff and his colleague, deputy Wendell (Garret Dillahunt), only just missed their man – this mirroring of images goes beyond the level of reflection, and Chigurh enters into the sheriff's constitution, thus further undermining any easy opposition of Chigurh and the sheriff, and instead exposing a certain affinity, intimacy, or similarity even between both, as well as between what these two figures stand for: government and terror.

The contamination of these two categories that are all too easily constructed as opposites becomes uncannily clear through the fact that the sheriff, even though he appears to be at a complete loss in the confrontation with Chigurh, nevertheless seems to understand some profound things about Chigurh and his mode of operation. In a conversation with Moss's wife Carla Jean later on in the film, the sheriff talks about a man who was paralyzed by an accident involving a captive bolt pistol – a kind of air pressure gun that is used to put cattle to death. As he is explaining how this type of gun works – by firing a piece of metal into the animal's skull that is then sucked back into the gun, leaving no bullet nor exit wound – the viewer realizes that this is Chigurh's signature weapon. The film (unlike McCarthy's book[39]) leaves it unclear whether the sheriff actually realizes this as well; but *No Country for Old Men* rises above the limitations of its characters' understanding, and reveals an intimate connection between the sheriff and Chigurh.

Finally, towards the very end of the film, after Moss has been killed in a motel room in El Paso, the sheriff returns to the scene of the killing and finds the lock cylinder of the motel room door blown out – a sure sign, as by then the viewer knows, that Chigurh has visited the premises. There follows a magisterial, expressionist series of shots in which both the sheriff and Chigurh are shown to be reflected – and possibly see each other reflected as well – in the copper-colored inside of the blown-out lock, with the sheriff standing outside of the door, and Chigurh inside. Given that this reflection occurs in the inside of a lock that has been blown out, the door (which can thus no longer be closed) represents a threshold in disintegration, a border that is no longer a border, where the sheriff practically fuses with Chigurh and vice versa. Given this fusion, it is perhaps no surprise, then, that when the sheriff finally steps into the room, Chigurh turns out to be gone; but he remains spectrally present, as the sheriff repeats one of his signature gestures – making sure that he does not get any of Moss's blood on his boots – when he leaves the room.

Even though the sheriff might not realize it, *No Country for Old Men* thus reveals to its viewers a strange contamination between government and terror that is also one of the leitmotifs in a film that came out just a year after *No Country for Old Men*, and whose central madman, according to Michael Wood's review essay in *The London Review of Books*, "resembles the slouching killer of the Coen brothers' *No Country for Old Men*":[40] the Joker (Heath Ledger) in Christopher Nolan's *The Dark Knight*. "This is what happens," the Joker explains in a memorable confrontation with Batman, "when an unstoppable force ['You Can't Stop What's Coming'] meets an immovable object": they will not kill each other; instead, "you and I are destined to do this forever." Earlier on in the film, the Joker puts it even more emphatically: "I don't want to kill you. What would I do without you? You complete me."[41] Of course, the "immovable" outlaw Batman hardly resembles the precarious sheriff from *No Country for Old Men* even if Batman will, at the end of the film, join sheriff Bell in retirement. My point is that in this case as well, the film reveals the contamination between two opposite forces, and raises the challenge of how it might become possible to escape the peculiar deadlock of such a situation.

Many have noted that this is also the political deadlock in the post-September 11 world, in which an ever-increasing state violence confronts an intensified terror by which it is contaminated. As the Bush government's response to the September 11 attacks has shown, the attempt to completely control terror only ends up producing more terror: even conservative scholars now agree that the US is less safe today than it was before the September 11 attacks. The very idea that government could ever be completely done with terror, in the sense that final control and justice would have been achieved, is – as *No Country for Old Men* makes its viewers realize – a theological assumption that risks producing precisely the opposite of what it attempts to bring about. In *No Country for Old Men*, it is the sheriff's retirement – a term that is, significantly, associated with Chigurh as well – that provides a way out of this deadlock, by having the sheriff realize the essentially unfinished, human nature of a work of justice that cannot be completed through divine intervention.

Thus, *No Country for Old Men* leaves the viewer with something like a politics of retirement – a phrase that rings false given the passivity usually associated with retiring. However, it is precisely this association that is being drawn into question – because the politics of retirement actually accomplishes something: it manages to break with government's deadlock relation to terror. That is the work of its worklessness.

The Politics of Retirement

By exposing the theological assumptions behind sheriff Ed Tom Bell's life-long work of justice – his expectation that when he grew older, God was going to step in to finish the job – *No Country for Old Men* draws attention to Bell's retirement and invites the viewer to rethink the work of justice through its representation of this retirement. The work of justice is indeed a work to which one dedicates oneself daily anew, *but without the theological promise of final justice being accomplished at the end of the line.* To practice justice otherwise, as a work that turns final control into its ultimate value (to recall Butler's reflection on September 11 once more), is bound to have adverse effects and to produce only more of (or intensified instances of) the terror that escapes it. This is not a cynical message that would lead to the abandonment of justice; retirement is, in this sense, not the same as "non-work," as Agamben is at pains to point out. Retirement in *No Country for Old Men* functions as site for the viewer to think through another kind of work, another way of practicing justice that would liberate government and terror from the deadlock in which they have arrived. In this sense, an otherwise horrific figure such as Chigurh might reveal itself to be an active agent of the retirement that the film is inviting one to think: a limit-figure who invites one to imagine the work of justice, as well as the work of government, from an impossible position, as a position from which power is always partly withdrawn.

Ultimately, the politics of retirement might thus mark a situation in which "the power of the people" – another kind of sovereignty – could be revitalized through the withdrawal of executive power. In her book *Bad for Democracy: How the Presidency Undermines the Power of the People*, Dana D. Nelson has admirably shown how the rise of executive power in the US – culminating in the messianic, superhero-figure of Obama – has steadily undermined the power of the people, an evolution that is captured most succinctly, perhaps, in George Bush junior's post-September 11 admonition to the American people "to go shopping" while the government would deal with the situation at hand.[42] Like the American economy, American democracy has become eroded, and it may require an act of retirement from the executive in order for the principles of the American con-stitution and the spirit of American democracy to be restored.

It is through the politics of retirement that government may be able to liberate itself from the terror by which it has become contaminated – even if actual terror will, of course, persist. Indeed, if there is one figure of retirement in *No Country for Old Men* – in addition to the retired welder Llewelyn Moss, his retired wife Carla Jean, and the retiring sheriff Ed Tom Bell – it is without a doubt Chigurh himself, who practices retirement actively and has turned the killing of people into the rule of his life. Chigurh is, like the Joker, an extreme figure of retirement, in which government risks becoming absent altogether and entering into the realm of a certain death. It is part of the power of *No Country for Old Men*, however, that it allows one to pass through such extremes without losing one's life, thus experiencing – if only for a brief moment – government's most radical outside: the outside in response to which power today attempts to govern, but has not yet learned to govern in the proper way.

All of this of course does not mean that the three old Republicans represented in the political cartoon discussed above should somehow have triumphed over Obama. It doesn't mean that George Bush junior and Dick Cheney should somehow be restored to power. I am challenging, rather, Cheney's repeated attempts since Obama was inaugurated to return from his retirement – his refusal to learn from the ways in which he was removed from power. It is from this removal, from a certain temperance of and withdrawal from power, that much can be learned – by anyone in power, including Obama – in a precarious time of terror of all kinds.

By framing this conclusion within the context of Agamben's critique of work, my aim was to draw out the political aspects of that critique, the way in which it ties up with Agamben's politics of withdrawal that I began to confront in the opening pages of this book. Along the way, however, I have also tried to develop a critique of such a politics of withdrawal – I have tried to show, more precisely, how it links up with a positive politics that amounts to more than passive retirement. Thus, through my reading of *No Country for Old Men* in this context I have tried to ultimately draw out the "operation" of "inoperativity," a peculiar "activity" that must be grasped if one does not want to lose sight of the politics of "potentiality" that is key to Agamben's work. To do so would mean to lose sight of the specific sovereignty that his work theorizes: one that is not beyond work, but works otherwise, in a "wholly transformed" way.

★

In closing, and as a transition to the third and final part of this book, we must of course ask: what remains of politics in such a politics of retirement? Doesn't the politics of retirement partly risk retiring politics, getting rid of politics altogether? Doesn't it weaken politics, take away its vitality, bring it in such a close proximity to death that it risks bringing the end of politics altogether? Such questions, while valid, would also reveal the poverty of a political imagination that is unable to think politics outside of the fortifications of a theologico-political sovereignty in which it has become caught up. It is in part to confront the charge of "weakness" – even if, of course, a "weakening" of politico-theological sovereignty is what I have pursued – that I insist in this book on using the term sovereignty for the politics I theorize. If the politics of retirement I have laid out here comes very close to the monks' form-of-life that Agamben theorizes in *The Highest Poverty*, it is worth noting that there too, form-of-life is not entirely separate from sovereignty but takes place within sovereign structures, with a superior, sovereign power "conferred on the abbot defined as 'lord and father.'"[43]

In fact, it is the continued attachment to the term sovereignty within a weakening critique of theologico-political sovereignty that is often perceived as leftist "horizontalization" (as opposed to the right's attachment to hierarchical verticalization), that will enable me, in the final part of this book, to bring some aspects of verticalization back in, as a way to reinforce the "power" of the politics I theorize here – but without, I hope, flipping back into the pitfalls of political theology.

Notes

1 Whyte, "Use."

2 See Agamben, *WM*.

3 See Aristotle, *Nicomachean Ethics*, 10–11.

4 See Arendt, *Human Condition*.

5 For an overview of the movement, see Lotringer and Marazzi, *Autonomia*. Agamben's relation to the French Situationist Guy Debord is also meaningful in this context, given Autonomism's relation to Situationism. Others have already discussed this relation. See, for example, Murray, "Beyond Spectacle."

6 Boever, "Bio-Paulitics."

7 Arendt, *Human Condition*, 128.

8 Pelenc, "Conversation," 10.

9 Ibid., 11.

10 Ibid.

11 Ibid.

12 Ibid.

13 Ibid.

14 Ibid., 16.

15 Ibid., 17.

16 Ibid.

17 Note, for example, the term's inclusion in Murray and Whyte, *Agamben Dictionary*.

18 It is no coincidence, I think, that Melville's story has become associated with Occupy, given the fact that the story is set on Wall Street. Some of the pitfalls of this association may begin to become clear when one compares Bartleby with that other, less passive hero of Occupy, V from Alan Moore's *V for Vendetta*.

19 Agamben, *SE*, 64.

20 Lévi-Strauss, *Savage*, 17. For the French original, see Lévi-Strauss, *Pensée*. On Agamben's relation to Lévi-Strauss, see also Murray, *Giorgio Agamben*, 26–7.

21 Lévi-Strauss, *Savage*, 16 / *Pensée*, 30.

22 Lévi-Strauss, *Savage*, 19.

23 Lévi-Strauss, *Savage*, 17 / *Pensée*, 31.

24 Lévi-Strauss, *Savage*, 21.

25 Ibid., 22.

26 Lévi-Strauss, *Savage*, 22 / *Pensée*, 36.

27 Agamben, *PR*, 76.

28 Ibid.

29 Arendt, *Human*, 5.

30 Ibid.

31 Ibid., 7.

32 Ibid.

33 Ibid.

34 Ibid., 127–8.

35 See <http://politicalhumor.about.com/od/johnmccain/ig/John McCain-Cartoons/No-Country-for-Old-Men.-1ke.htm>.

36 The only reason why Immanuel Kant could put forward the categorical imperative as a moral standard is because the imperative presupposes, as Kant's examples in *Groundwork of the Metaphysics of Morals* abundantly make clear, the value of life. See Kant, *Groundwork*, 31–3. However, one must also ask, as Jacques Derrida does in his course on the death penalty, to what extent death is already written into Kant's imperative. Derrida notes that Kant defends the death penalty in the name of life, as evidence of the human being's rationality. Chigurh would be this tendency, fully realized as a kind of Kantian monster. See Derrida, *Death Penalty*, 123ff.

37 This is confirmed by Chigurh's first killing in the film, which follows shortly after his arrest and constitutes the most brutal scene in the film.

38 Butler, *Precarious Life*, xiii.

39 See McCarthy, *No Country*, 105–6.

40 See Wood, "Rev."

41 Nolan, *The Dark Knight*.

42 See Nelson, *Bad for Democracy*.

43 Agamben, *HP*, 53.

Part III: Politics

7

Agamben in America

From Auschwitz to America

I began this book with a discussion, in largely negative terms, of a short text that Giorgio Agamben published in *Le Monde* in January 2004, and in which he explained his decision to cancel a class he was set to teach at New York University a few months later. Titled "No to Bio-Political Tattooing," the text criticizes a new regulation requiring everyone traveling to the United States with a visa to be fingerprinted and put on file when they are entering the country. Agamben refuses to undergo such exceptional and inhumane measures, which he considers to go one step further in what he claims Michel Foucault calls "the progressive animalization of man." As I explained in Chapter 1, he considers the measures to be indicative of our contemporary biopolitical situation. Here as elsewhere in his work, Agamben turns to the United States to provide evidence for his thesis that the paradigm of modern politics is not the Greek city-state – Athens – but the camp – Auschwitz. America thus comes to figure in his work not only as Athens's antithesis, but also as a contemporary instantiation of Auschwitz.

As I pointed out in my first chapter, such a figuration continues to encounter resistance.[1] Anticipating such resistance,

259

Agamben insists in the *Le Monde* piece that his comparison of the visa regulation to Auschwitz is not historical but philosophical: he is trying to draw a logical parallel between the regulation and the tattooing at Auschwitz (in both cases, human beings' biological life becomes the locus of their political existence; "tattooing" becomes the most efficient way to manage life – never mind that in the case of fingerprinting, no actual tattooing is involved).

"Athens," "America," "Auschwitz": each of these proper names of course refers to a highly specific historical configuration, and it is very difficult, if not impossible, to mobilize them in a *merely* philosophical way. A version of this problem arises with Carl Schmitt's claim about all significant concepts in the modern theory of the state: he writes not only that they are secularized theological concepts, but adds that this is the case *both* historically *and* structurally.[2] How does history compare to structure in this argument about secularization? How does one secularize a structure? The question has perhaps received less attention in the context of these particular debates than it deserves.[3]

Nevertheless, Schmitt's work and Agamben's use of it are very helpful in the larger context of the argument for plastic sovereignty that I have developed in this book. For the structure Agamben's philosophical argument focuses on when he uses the name "Auschwitz" or even the already more abstract term "camp" is that of what Schmitt calls a "state of exception." Analogous to the miracle in theology, this notion refers to a situation in which the normal rule of law is suspended in the name of an emergency. After Schmitt, Agamben associates such a state with the operation of sovereignty. In an article in *The New York Review of Books* in which Agamben is referenced, Mark Danner uses the phrase "state of exception" to refer to the

American political situation post-9/11.[4] One does not have to make the comparison with Auschwitz to show that in post-9/11 America – a constellation whose main features Judith Butler observes to be "heightened nationalist discourse, extended surveillance mechanisms, suspended constitutional rights, and developed forms of explicit and implicit censorship," as I have already recalled – the normal rule of law is under attack. Using the phrase "state of exception" to capture this situation enables one to draw this out: on the one hand, *without* giving up on the structural comparison with Auschwitz, which is arguably an extreme articulation of the state of exception; but, on the other, *with* the advantage of avoiding the identification of contemporary America, or indeed any state of exception, with Auschwitz. The notion of the "state of exception" is, in this sense, a theoretical notion – a paradigm, to stay within Agamben's conceptual vocabulary – that can be mobilized in a variety of contexts. The same can never be true of "Auschwitz."

In this chapter, I propose to look in a bit more detail at some political theoretical debates about the state of exception. Due to post-9/11 political developments such as the ones Butler points out – developments that led Danner to speak in the *NYRB* of "our state of exception" when referring to contemporary America – pessimistic thinkers of the political such as Schmitt but also Niccolò Machiavelli and Hobbes have gained new importance for critical, political thinking. This is largely because some of their key texts – *Political Theology* (Schmitt), *The Prince* (Machiavelli), and *Leviathan* (Hobbes) – set up helpful frameworks to understand the extraordinary use of power in the aftermath of the 9/11 attacks. For many, Schmitt's infamous dictum that "sovereign is he who decides on the exception"[5] seemed to be proven true once again after 9/11: it appeared that the US – and arguably the rest of the world – once again found itself under the rule of a monarch who exercised power sovereignly, from a position partly above and even against the law. *The Prince* and *Leviathan* are treatises that theorize such a use of power, and it is thus the Schmittian, Machiavellian, and Hobbesian aspects of contemporary power that gained much critical scrutiny in the first decade of the twenty-first century.

In each of these cases, the history of political theory has arguably also produced a "solution" for the problematic, theologico-political exercise of sovereign power that these thinkers theorize. Consider, for example, Hobbes's theory of the Leviathan, that "Mortal God"[6] whose rights (as listed in Chapter XVIII of the second part of Hobbes's text) leave little doubt about the extent of the absolute, indivisible power that Hobbes theorizes. In his *Second Treatise of Government*, John Locke responded to this problematic aspect of Hobbes's theory by arguing that as long as human beings do not have a common power to turn to in the case of a conflict between the people and the sovereign, they continue to live in the very state of nature (characterized, in *Leviathan*, as a state of war of all against all) that Hobbes wanted to overcome. And so Locke proposed a separation of powers – to simplify, a division between the legislative and the executive – that was meant to keep the executive in check. The question in terms of sovereignty then became: which one of these different powers qualifies as "the highest"?

In the case of Machiavelli, one could read Machiavelli's own book *The Discourses*, in which Machiavelli discusses the separation of powers, as a similar, "Lockean" response to the sovereignty theorized in *The Prince*. In the case of Schmitt, the challenge is centered around his relation to Benjamin, whose "Critique of

Violence" quite probably triggered Schmitt's *Political Theology*, as I discussed in Chapter 2.

I will be focusing in this chapter on the Hobbes/Locke configuration, because Locke's proposal for a separation of powers could arguably be the first recourse for anyone who wants to criticize the talk about the Hobbesian features of contemporary power (others have suggested the work of Jean-Jacques Rousseau[7]). If it is indeed true that something like the Hobbesian Leviathan has returned upon the scene of contemporary politics, then one answer could be to reinforce once again the separation of powers: it would consist, once again, of mobilizing Locke against Hobbes, and choosing the one over the other. It would once again be a question of horizontalizing the verticality that Hobbes theorizes.

However, there are number of problems with such an approach: the first is that the separation of powers has evidently not been able to prevent the growth of executive power and specifically the theologico-political exercise of sovereignty. It is worthwhile noting, as others have done, that executive power has grown excessively since the birth of the US, and has without a doubt – and in spite of the system of checks and balances – become the most powerful of the three branches of government. The current US president Barack Obama is the most powerful president in US history. If the system of checks and balances could not keep this development – the production of a kind of executive "monster," a Leviathan in this sense of the word – balanced and in check, then it might be necessary to revise it. Second – and this is the part of the problem that I propose to focus on – a close reading of Locke's treatise reveals that even in theory, it by no means brought about the end of the kind of sovereignty – absolute, indivisible power – for which Locke criticized Hobbes.

In this sense, the return of sovereignty that we are witnessing today arguably marks the return of the Hobbesian power that, in Locke, did not disappear but merely went underground.

I begin this first political-theoretical chapter with a discussion of the place of America in Agamben's oeuvre: even though the US is often the target of Agamben's political criticisms, Agamben actually spends very little time discussing US political history. What are the episodes that he focuses on? Which conclusions do they enable him to draw with respect to a positive politics that could be practiced against the state of exception that he considers America to exemplify? I then turn to Locke's *Second Treatise* in order to expose its hidden, Hobbesian element: here, both Locke's and Hobbes's use of the phrase "the silence of the law" will take up a key place in my argument. Exposing the Hobbesian core of Locke's treatise will reveal that the treatise does not constitute an effective response to the problems of sovereignty, and specifically to sovereignty conceived as the power to decide on the exception. This will lead into the third stage of my argument, where I state that the transition from Hobbes to Locke does not present a softening of power, as is often thought, but power's intensification.

It is indeed Hobbes who, parallel to his insistence on absolute and indivisible power, maintains a space where the subject is free – a supreme power *of* life – thus highlighting in particular sovereignty's explosive and resistant plasticity. Locke's theory of government saturates that space with power, thus turning freedom into a mere correlative of the deployment of power (to recall Michel Foucault's work on governmentality and biopolitics). It is in this light also, I argue, that Foucault's statement in *The Birth of Biopolitics* that "Locke does not produce a theory of the state; he produces a theory of government" needs to be understood.

In conclusion, this chapter returns to Agamben's theorization of a positive politics. Read through the lens of the debate between Locke and Hobbes, Agamben now appears to argue for a reappropriation of the spaces of political possibility that Hobbes's political theory (unlike Locke's) preserves. On this count, Friedrich Nietzsche's critique of biopolitics in *On the Genealogy of Morals* – specifically, his insistence on a political *life* – will become supremely relevant (this importance of Nietzsche was launched in Chapter 1, when I noted Agamben's proximity in his work on aesthetics to Nietzsche's critique of Kant). And yet, in the final instance, Hobbes's insistence on the silence of the law as the place of freedom will not be of much help either to sum up the concept of plastic sovereignty that I have developed in this book. Indeed, Agamben's *The Kingdom and the Glory* demonstrates, as others have shown, that theologico-political sovereignty and governmentality (Hobbes and Locke) operate in tandem, and that the solution of the power-machine they constitute requires another critical move. *Silence*, as I have insisted throughout the previous chapters, *is not infancy*. As long as one remains caught up in the vicious dialectic between law and its outside, between speech and silence, it will remain impossible to dismantle the logic of the state of exception – often associated with sovereignty – that has been the political focus of this book. And while it might thus be necessary, today, to pass through Hobbes in order to challenge the Lockean governmentality that has become the order of the day – and in which new, and what Butler calls "petty," sovereigns operate – such a passing truly needs to be a passing, that is: a moving *through* that ultimately must not remain stuck in the illusions of a freedom-outside-of-the-law that plague it.

If Nietzsche, in the last instance, will enable me to capture the explosive dimension of the plastic sovereignty that I have tried to theorize in this book – he criticizes relentlessly the "sovereign and universal" legal order that intends to "[prevent] all struggle in general" and that would thus be "a principle hostile to life" – the move from the dialectic between law and its outside, speech and silence, to political infancy is a shift from this power of life to a truly political sovereignty that would form itself around its own living contestation.[8] It is from the aesthetic redistribution of this dialectic that another politics becomes possible.

In the next two chapters, I will develop this point first, from the point of view of aesthetic theory (Chapter 8), and second, through a close reading of what I will call an aesthetico-political formation of infancy (Chapter 9): the actual realization, in the form of a literary work, of the politics of infancy that Agamben theorizes.

Reading America

Although the relevance of Agamben's work for the contemporary political situation in the US should be evident to any reader of his work, and in particular to those who had the patience to follow the arguments of this book, it remains a curious fact that Agamben spends very little time in his work actually discussing the US legal and political system that much of his writing appears to criticize. In *Homo Sacer: Sovereign Power and Bare Life*, perhaps Agamben's most influential book in the US, the legal and political analysis focuses on Auschwitz – and while it also ranges widely (and problematically) outside of that focus, American history is not what this book is about. That part of the discussion appears to have been deferred to another installment of the *Homo Sacer* series, a short little volume titled *State of Exception*. Even there, however, the discussion of America is delegated to the small print, where the US features (next to France, Germany, Italy, and the United Kingdom) in a "brief history of the state of exception."[9]

"The place … of a theory of the state of exception in the American constitution," Agamben begins, "is in the dialectic between the powers of the president and those of Congress."[10] Using the terms that I have set up above in my presentation of Hobbes and Locke, it is in the dialectic between the executive and the legislative branches of power that it can be found. As an example, Agamben takes the Civil War. He recalls that Abraham Lincoln "decreed that an army of seventy-five thousand men was to be raised and convened a special session of Congress for July 4th."[11] "In the ten weeks that passed between April 15 and July 4," Agamben continues, "Lincoln in fact acted as an absolute dictator":[12]

> "Whether strictly legal or not", [Lincoln] declared, the measures he had adopted had been taken "under what appeared to be a popular demand and a public necessity" in the certainty that Congress would ratify them. They were based on the conviction that even fundamental law could be violated if the very existence of the union and the juridical order were at stake.[13]

Following Schmitt's definition of the sovereign as "he who decides on the exception," Agamben is interested in this particular case because it presents Lincoln's sovereign, executive eclipse of the law (Congress). For Agamben, this Civil War situation marks a moment in US political history when the separation of powers is challenged, and the systems of checks and balances abolished. And his argument is that such a way of governing – the exceptionalist way – has gradually become the norm. Dana Nelson's research on the growth of executive power in the US (which I already mentioned in the previous chapter) largely confirms this point, even though Nelson has a much stronger belief in American democracy than Agamben.

The second example that Agamben discusses is that of Woodrow Wilson, who is very much a part of the history that Nelson in her book sketches out. So is Agamben's third example, Franklin Roosevelt. Roosevelt's New Deal

> was realized by delegating to the president ... an unlimited power to regulate and control every aspect of economic life of the country – a fact that is in perfect conformity with the already mentioned parallelism between military and economic emergencies that characterizes the politics of the twentieth century.[14]

Criticizing the New Deal – generally considered in a positive light by those "on the left" – Agamben risks appearing here in favor of a liberal (and even neoliberal, given how the New Deal has reappeared in recent discussions of the US economy) separation of politics and economy.[15] But that is, of course, not really the point: he is interested, rather, in the *logic* of Roosevelt's intervention, which – even though it may have done a lot of good – is that of the state of exception. The provocation of Agamben's discussion of the New Deal is that structurally, Roosevelt's intervention can thus be compared to Adolf Hitler's rise to power in early twentieth-century Germany. As was perhaps to be expected, former US president George W. Bush stands at the end of the exceptionalist history of American power that Agamben describes.

Again, one should remember that this is a philosophical (in Schmitt's terms: structural) and not a historical argument. It is worth noticing, however, that according to such an argument, the socialist intervention of the New Deal is "similar to" the way in which fascism rose to power.[16]

From this short series of examples, it will be clear that one actually learns very little about the history of American democracy by reading Agamben's text. Instead, it is the exceptional moments that are being recalled, and that are transformed into the paradigm of how American power operates. The exception thus becomes, quite literally, the rule – while the principles of American democracy are forgotten. If the argument is indeed structural instead of historical, this means that our focus should not be on Agamben's beef with America, but on the structural problem he finds in American politics: that is, on the logic of the state of exception. So what, then, is this logic of the state of exception that Agamben takes issue with?

Distinguishing the state of exception from the state of siege and martial law with which he considers it to ultimately have very little in common, but still comparing it to political phenomena such as civil war, insurrection, and resistance, Agamben develops his theory of the state of exception in response to the question: "[W]hat does it mean to act politically?"[17] Indeed, this becomes the key question of Agamben's short book, revealing his intent to move towards a positive politics, an articulation of political action.[18] For Agamben, the phrase "state of exception" appears to mark a certain perversion of politics: a "lasting eclipse" that politics has suffered because "it has been contaminated by law."[19] Agamben's criticism of the New Deal appears to resonate here: he appears to advocate for a political sphere that would be separate from law. Within the regulation/deregulation debate, he thus appears to come down on the side of deregulation. At this point, a question arises: isn't the problem with the state of exception precisely that there isn't enough law, that the law is no longer capable of keeping politics in check? Not a problem of politics' contamination by the law, in other words, but a problem of a lack of law?

Not according to Agamben. Indeed, the problem with the state of exception is hardly that there isn't any law left. Following Schmitt, Agamben theorizes the state of exception as a situation in which the normal rule of law is *suspended*. For Agamben, such a theory marks Schmitt's attempt to bring all possibility of anomic or extra-legal, political action within the law, through the paradox of sovereignty ("I, the sovereign, who am outside the law, declare that there is nothing outside the law"[20]). The state of exception thus marks the law's maddening capacity to suspend itself, through the miracle – or, as some might prefer, the trickery – of sovereignty. The law is thus not abolished. The problem is, rather, that of the law's suspension, its political overcoming into meaningless force. In this sense, the law is "the legal form of what cannot have legal form."[21] In such a situation, as Agamben notes, the difference between the legal and the illegal – with the latter coming in close proximity to politics – enters into deconstruction.

Agamben characterizes this maddening logic according to which the law becomes capable of suspending itself through its appropriation of politics, as the logic of a "machine." To dismantle the state of exception would mean to jam this machine not by calling for more law or for less law but by reasserting the difference between law and politics, and rediscovering politics. It means, along Benjaminian lines (the connection between Agamben's politics and the politics of divine violence is very close, as I have shown in Chapter 2), to break up the connection between the juridical and the political that Schmitt's work establishes. In

270

the closing paragraphs of *State of Exception*, Agamben can thus urge his readers "[t]o show law in its nonrelation to life and life in its nonrelation to law."[22] Doing so "means to open up a space between them for human action, which once claimed for itself the name of 'politics.'"[23] Evidently, there is a politics of life that is being proposed here – at a distance from law, and from the sovereign politics over life that operates through the state of exception.

This means that with respect to the American situation, Agamben's position appears to be a highly peculiar one. He is not so much arguing for a restoration of the legislative branch of power as a power that should exercise more authority over the executive branch. Rather, he appears to be calling for the undoing of the executive's eclipse by the legislative, so as to separate politics from law and reopen the space of a properly political action, one that would not take place in relation to the law. (As will be clear, this is not simply an argument for an unbridled executive either.) How can one argue against the law's eclipse of politics, that is: for the liberation of politics from law, and against the state of exception (the political suspension of the law), at the same time?

In these two arguments, we are confronting the central ambiguity of Agamben's work, the double bind that one has to grasp (I borrow the notion of the double bind from Gayatri Chakravorty Spivak's important book on aesthetic education; she takes it from Jacques Derrida[24]) in order to acknowledge the promises and pitfalls of his aesthetico-political project. On the one hand, the problem Agamben sees with politics is that law has come to coincide with life, thus defusing life's political potential. As a result, we can no longer think any politics outside of the law. On the other, the current political situation he criticizes is one in which the law is eclipsed by political power, in which political leaders think they can act outside of the law in order to preserve the law. The dynamics in both cases are clearly different: in the first, law eclipses politics; in the second, politics appears to eclipse law. Agamben's response – his call for a separation of life from law, for a non-relation between life and law – works against law's eclipse of politics, it liberates politics from the hold of the law; but the trap that this sets up is that such a separation of life from law appears to flip into a state of exception, an eclipse of law by politics. Obviously, that is not where Agamben wants to go either.

And so it turns out to be necessary to think the separation of law from life as a third possibility, a *real* state of exception that Agamben proposes and that would be a true rediscovery, even reinvention, of politics. As I will discuss in more detail in the next chapter, Agamben takes this idea of a real state of exception from Walter Benjamin, who theorizes it in his "Theses on the Philosophy of History." In the end, the question becomes how to theorize this real state of exception and the new politics it marks. My thesis in this book has been that the real state of exception is Benjamin's name for the plasticity of sovereignty, the force he calls (in German) "waltend": that gives form in addition to receiving it, and that can explode form as well. As the "Critique of Violence" essay demonstrates, Benjamin thought this plasticity in its anomic, extra-legal – which is not the same as anti-legal – dimension. As a theorist of the state of exception, Schmitt came very close to it – but he always returned its force within the law, as the paradoxical, legalo-political capacity to suspend the law. What we need here, once again, is an extra turn of the critical screw.

Foucault, Hobbes, Locke

There is a passage in his 1978–9 lecture course at the Collège de France titled *The Birth of Biopolitics* where Michel Foucault states the following:

> [T]he last of the theories of the state is found in Hobbes, that is to say, in someone who was both a contemporary and the "supporter" of a type of monarchy that the English precisely got rid of at that time. After Hobbes, there is Locke. Locke does not produce a theory of the state; he produces a theory of government.[25]

Although Hobbes still figured prominently in Foucault's 1975–6 lecture course titled *"Society Must Be Defended,"*[26] what Foucault becomes interested in during his subsequent courses – specifically, *Security, Territory, Population* and then also the already mentioned *The Birth of Biopolitics* – is not a Hobbesian theory of the state, but Locke's theory of government. The difference that Foucault makes between Hobbes and Locke can thus be mapped onto the analytical distinction that structures all of these lecture courses, namely between sovereignty ("Hobbes") and governmentality ("Locke"). Whereas the former is concerned with territory and operates by forcefully imposing laws upon subjects – Foucault famously argues that sovereignty is defined by the ancient right to take life – the latter is concerned with security and operates through *laissez-faire*, by subtly organizing the lives of the population in such a way that the people's very freedom ultimately becomes no more than a correlative of the deployment of power. In contrast to sovereignty, governmentality is not defined by the right to "take" life but by the right to "make" it – to generate and foster life so that it becomes saturated into its most intimate regions with what Foucault called biopower. Racism and sexuality are two topics that Foucault mentions, both in *The History of Sexuality* and in the final lecture of *"Society Must Be Defended,"*[27] as crucial sites for the investigation of biopower.

As many in Foucault's wake have pointed out (see, for example, Wendy Brown's work on governmentality[28]), the distinction between sovereignty and governmentality is overdrawn in Foucault's lectures. Brown suggests that Foucault may have insisted on the distinction for tactical reasons: as we all know, it is sometimes useful to overdraw a distinction in order to get a point across. There are many moments in the lectures, however, where Foucault notes that the transition from sovereignty to governmentality is not so much a chronological transition from one homogenous type of power to another; as he sees it, sovereignty and governmentality form a power triangle with discipline,[29] and he is merely analyzing governmentality's more dominant role in late modern power practices. This insight has informed some very powerful recent political analyses: for example, Agamben's *Homo Sacer* trilogy — which ranges from an analysis of the continued importance of sovereignty in *Homo Sacer: Sovereign Power and Bare Life* to the analysis of governmentality in *The Kingdom and the Glory* — and Judith Butler's analysis of the Guantánamo Bay detention camp.[30]

This casts an interesting light on Foucault's association of the distinction between sovereignty and governmentality with the distinction between Hobbes and Locke. The transition from Hobbes to Locke was, of course, a chronological one; but reading that transition through the lens of Foucault's point about the triangular relation of sovereignty to governmentality and discipline, one might begin to wonder about the continued activity of sovereignty within a predominantly governmental power practice. In other words: in what ways does Hobbes continue to remain active in Locke's theory of government?

Reading Locke critically, as many have already done, one can easily see that although his theory of government contains a strong rejection of Hobbes – Locke writes, for example, that "absolute monarchy, which by some men is counted the only government in the world, is indeed inconsistent with civil society, and so can be no form of civil-government at all"[31] – Locke's treatise also leaves intact the very type of power that the Hobbesian sovereign wields. Consider, for example the infamous chapter 14 from *Second Treatise of Government*, in which Locke, the champion of the separation of powers, talks about the "prerogative." He uses this term to refer to the "power to act according to discretion, for the public good, without the prescription of the law, and sometimes even against it."[32] Such a use of executive power – outside and sometimes even against the legislative – is necessary, because when the law is designed, it is "impossible to foresee, and so by laws to provide for, all accidents and necessities that may concern the public."[33] And so to be able to protect the people when such emergency situations or states of exception occur, "there is a latitude left to executive power, to do many things of choice which the laws do not prescribe."[34] Clearly, Locke in no way provides a solution to Hobbes when it comes to preventing the state of exception. Rather, Hobbesian sovereignty – the absolute, indivisible power that Locke attacks in Hobbes – continues its life within Locke's theory of government. It is this particular life that has returned to the surface of modern politics today – a politics that prided itself on having left Hobbes behind.

The Biopolitics of Government

Locke's *Second Treatise of Government* thus does not constitute an effective response to the problems of Hobbes's theory of sovereignty that it takes on. Although the theory of the separation of powers is of course an important step towards solving these problems, the fact that Locke's theory leaves room for what Locke calls the "prerogative" indicates that Locke ultimately preserves the very power that his theory is trying to overcome. It indicates, in other words, that the system of checks and balances is precisely what its name suggests: a system that does not overcome Hobbesian sovereignty, but keeps it balanced and in check. It is a mere stopgap intended to circumscribe and curtail a power that ultimately, in emergency situations and states of exception, exceeds it. With the theory of the separation of powers, humanity is still virtually living under Hobbesian sovereignty. The problem of Hobbesian sovereignty is not solved in Locke but merely transformed. Sovereignty lives on – anachronistically, spectrally – as the dwarf in the puppet of governmentality: as the sovereign prerogative that animates the field of governmentality. This is why, as Agamben's *The Kingdom and the Glory* suggests, a simple call for the separation of powers will not solve the problems of biopolitical sovereignty. It is also why Butler, in response to the contemporary problems of sovereignty she analyzes, cannot merely end with a plea for a revalidation of the legislative.[35] This is probably also the place to point out, as Sora Y. Han has done in an article that is very critical of Agamben's work, that when it comes to the separation of powers, "the judicial," that is: the supreme court – "the third term of constitutional democracy" – entirely disappears from Agamben's argument, thus leaving a critical agent in the relation between law and political power out of the picture.[36]

As for "who shall be the judge?" of whether a particular situation qualifies as an emergency situation or a state of exception, Locke appears to suggest that it is the legislative that decides. The legislative is, for him, emphatically "the supreme power" – with the exception that it can also, as we have seen, provide the executive with the power of the prerogative, which thus appears to exceed the legislative. Displacing the political question of deciding on the state of exception onto the ethical question of whether the executive's extra- or even counter-legal actions are really for the benefit of the people (in addition to the question of whether the executive's actions under normal circumstances contribute to the public good), Locke suggests both in the chapter on the prerogative and at the very end of his text, that God should be the judge of this: "He alone, it is true, is judge of the right."[37] According to this rationale, the former US president George W. Bush could *not* be taken to court for the decisions he took in the aftermath of the September 11 terror attacks; he claimed, after all, that God was on his side. However, Locke also suggests immediately after raising this theological solution at the end of his text that "*in a matter where the law is silent or doubtful,* and the thing be of great consequence, I should think the proper *umpire,* in such a case, should be the body of the people [first emphasis mine]."[38] The rationale in the closing pages thus seems to be that since it is the people who ultimately placed their trust in the executive, it is they who should be the judge of the validity of its actions. The people here become the sovereign's true (political) god – the true holds of sovereign power. According to such a rationale, Bush *could* be taken to court if the people decided he should be. "Sovereignty," or "the highest, supreme power," is evidently torn here between different powers – legislative and executive, the people and God.

The phrasing that Locke adapts – "in a matter where the law is silent or doubtful" – is interesting for a number of reasons. Locke uses the phrase to refer to a judgment, namely the people's judgment on the executive's use of power in exceptional (but also in normal) circumstances. However, Locke's evocation of matters in which the law is silent also recalls his earlier description of the prerogative, as a power with which the executive might be invested by the legislative in those cases that Locke refers to as "impossible to foresee":[39] "accidents and necessities that may concern the public,"[40] "future events"[41] that cannot possibly be mastered by the totality of the law. Locke is thinking here, in other words, of cases that the legislators, when they designed the law, could not have foreseen and about which the law therefore has nothing to say. He is thinking of matters in which "the law was silent,"[42] as he states in the chapter on the prerogative. In such situations where the law is silent, the prerogative enables the executive to speak, outside of the law and sometimes even against it. The executive is supposed to fill the void of this silence with brute – unbalanced and unchecked – power/ speech. Whereas Locke thus appears to recognize that the law, because it always attempts to regulate something that it cannot in its entirety foresee – namely life – by definition remains silent upon a number of issues – life is in this sense both the law's target and limit – he calls upon the very power that he criticizes in Hobbes to deal with life's unexpected accidents and necessities. It is here that one encounters the hidden, biopolitical motivation of Locke's theory of government – and the reason why Foucault is interested in Locke more so than in Hobbes – namely the fact that Locke's theory of government attempts to saturate the entire field of life – even those regions where the law is silent – with power.

One finds a very different vision in Hobbes. When Locke speaks about the silence of the law, he is in fact silently quoting Hobbes. In a fascinating chapter of his *Leviathan* titled "Of the Liberty of Subjects," Hobbes writes that "the greatest liberty of the subjects dependeth on the silence of the law."[43] This means that Hobbes, for all his insistence on sovereign power, ultimately acknowledges a gap between life and power – marked by the zone where law is silent – where the greatest liberty of the subject exists. Although Locke recognizes this zone as well, his theory of the prerogative intends to saturate even this zone with power: to make even the accidents and necessities that the law could not possibly foresee – what I have called here the accidents and necessities of "life," which I have also associated with "freedom" – a part of an economy of power.

This is precisely the argument that Foucault develops in his lecture courses *Security, Territory, Population* and *The Birth of Biopolitics*: biopolitical governmentality, which emerges in the age of Enlightenment, operates not by imprisoning subjects but by granting them freedom, a freedom that becomes part of a balancing game – an economy, to go back to the key term of the second part of this book – of power. The key question for government thus becomes, as Foucault explains early on in *The Birth of Biopolitics*, how not to govern too much; government needs to become "frugal," it needs to find the proper balance between "too much" and "not enough" government, lack and excess.[44]

Thus, in Locke, the only liberty that is possible is a liberty within the law. In Hobbes, on the other hand, the greatest liberty exists where the law is silent. It is in this silence that the subject knows its greatest freedom. Reading the debate between Hobbes and Locke about the silence of the law through the lens of Foucault's lectures on biopolitics and governmentality reveals that the history of biopolitical governmentality only properly takes off with Locke, and can be understood as a history of making the law speak even where it is silent: of filling this free space of silence with power talk so that life in its entirety becomes saturated with power. So that one's very life – in addition to one's sexuality, as Foucault has convincingly shown – becomes no more than an effect – a discursive effect – of power. That is the freedom-within-the-law that Locke theorizes.

Hobbes, Nietzsche, and Beyond

> … in order to then bring to light the Ungovernable, which is the beginning and, at the same time, the vanishing point of every politics. (Giorgio Agamben, "What is an Apparatus?")[45]

The significance of such a reading is not only that Locke did not save humanity from Hobbesian sovereignty – this will be obvious to any critical reader of Locke. It is also that, from a Foucaultian perspective, Locke's theory of government represents an intensi-fication of biopower. It appears that after September 11, it might thus not be Locke who provides the solution to the complex interplay of sovereignty and governmentality in contemporary manifestations of power such as the Guantánamo Bay detention camp. One could argue, in fact, that Hobbes and his insistence on the brute conflict between sovereign power and life, as well as on those regions where the law is silent and subjects are still properly free, may be more helpful.

Indeed, might not the very return of sovereignty within the field of governmentality after September 11 also mark the return of a political potential, namely the possibility of the existence of a zone where the law is silent, and life exists in a productive tension with the legal and political apparatus, in the state of its rediscovered and *properly* political potential? The return of a politics of life? Might not the Hobbesian zone where the law is silent mark a zone of what I have called, in Chapter 6, the inoperativity or *désoeuvrement* of the law that leads away from the biopolitical saturation of life with the legal and political talk characteristic of contemporary societies of the spectacle?[46] Might humanity not be in need, if it is to overcome its current political impasse, of a "barbaric" return to Hobbes in order to save it from Locke's "civilized" theory of government? Of a type of human action that would truly be outside of the law (that is: unlike in a state of exception, which marks the law's political capacity to legally be suspended)?

While these are all the right questions, the issue I want to address is that they are ultimately not covered by Hobbes's theory of freedom as existing in a zone where the law is silent. Indeed, such a theory is still one step removed from "a productive tension with the legal and political apparatus" or "the inoperativity or *désoeuvrement* of the law" that I have just mentioned. If Lockean governmentality is a politics of speech that seeks to make power speak even where the law is silent, thus killing the politics of life, Hobbes's theory of freedom depends on a silence of the law that, through the outside it evokes, is ultimately complicit with the type of sovereign power that Hobbes also theorizes. Hobbes's theory of sovereignty and his theory of freedom go hand in hand, the one mirrors the other. The problem that presents itself here is that while many may be critical of Hobbes's theory of sovereignty, they remain romantically attached to his theory of freedom, and without realizing that the one actually feeds the other (this problem is particularly pressing in art theory, as I will discuss in the next chapter). It is thus the theory of freedom that needs to be transformed in order to ultimately transform the theory of sovereignty – and this without slipping into a Lockean governmentality where freedom would become a mere discursive effect of power. That is the challenge, and one finds it addressed in the solution that the questions I raised above evoke.

Those questions are relevant even for those who, after all has been said and done, would still stick with Locke because "at least he got rid of Hobbesian political theology."[47] Nothing could be further from the truth. There is, first of all, Locke's important recourse to the theological – even if he also displaces it, as I have noted, turning the people into a political god – in the debate about who is to judge whether the executive has rightfully declared a state of exception. Secondly, it is by no means certain that Locke's theory of the separation of powers marks an exit from theology. In the wake of Agamben's recent work on governmentality, I would argue that the shift from absolute, indivisible sovereignty in Hobbes to divided and balanced governmentality in Locke parallels the transformation in theology from the absolute and undivided power of the sovereign God in the Old Testament to the divided and balanced Trinitarian power of the Father, the Son, and the Holy Spirit in the New Testament. Agamben analyses this transition as a transformation from political theology to what he calls "theological economy": a theological division of the divine household into Father, Son, and Holy Spirit so as to guarantee God's operations on earth while preserving God's essential unity.[48] Of course, Agamben's analysis of the New Testament situation of government as an economy becomes particularly relevant with respect to Locke, whose insistence on property as the supreme value for government has made him not only the father of modern capitalism, but also of what came to be known as political economy. It is an economy that is just as theological as it is political – which is one more reason to be critical of Locke's presumed relevance today.[49]

★

In what is perhaps his most biopolitical text, *On the Genealogy of Morals*, Friedrich Nietzsche deplores the ethical and political history that has made human beings "calculable, regular, necessary" – in short: "secure," even from their own future.[50] It testifies to a type of work, evoked by Locke in his theory of the prerogative, of mastering even those future events that the legislative could not foresee when it made the laws: accidents and necessities all become part of a balancing game of power. As a result, human beings – indeed, life itself – become "necessary, uniform, like among like, regular, and consequently calculable": "with the aid of the morality of mores and the social strait-jacket, man was actually *made* calculable."[51] Nevertheless, what such a history of biopolitical production will arguably lead to is the emergence of what Nietzsche calls "the *sovereign individual*" who is not bound by her or his promises but has the "*right to make promises*" should she or he freely will to do so.[52] It is a question, in other words, of becoming the agent of the means of biopolitical production, and of thus returning a calculable, uniform, and regular humanity to the "struggle between power-complexes" that power's attempt to *prevent* struggle – to *overcome* the gap between life and power – has tried to root out. Such a preventive politics would in Nietzsche's view operate according to "a principle *hostile* to life."[53] *On the Genealogy of Morals* counters such an "administrative nihilism"[54] with an insistence

283

on the human being's instinct to freedom, its will to power – and, I would argue, its right to make promises should it freely will to do so.

What Nietzsche – or at least my Nietzsche – invites readers to see, in other words, is *not two but three* things: first, he draws attention to the history of biopolitical production, to the genealogy of how ethical and political subjects are produced. There is an ethical and political *work* that goes into the production of subjects who exist in perfect alignment with power, whose lives can no longer produce the accidents or necessities that power might not have anticipated. By exposing this work, Nietzsche attempts to return human beings not simply to a state *before* such production, but *after* such a thoroughly saturated life – a state in which a sovereign subject who is the agent of her or his own life will come into being.

This is, I would argue, the second insight that Nietzsche's book yields: it puts its readers back in touch with that region where according to Hobbes the subject's greatest freedom exists, that zone where the law is silent, and life's difference from power – and its own power of life – is revealed. If Locke tried to be done with such a zone, Nietzsche returns it to one's attention, arguing that it is from that very region that political agency becomes possible.

But added to that is the point about becoming the subject of one's own biopolitical production (a point that the Nietzschean philosopher Peter Sloterdijk also makes at the end of his "Rules for the Human Zoo," as I discussed in Chapter 2): the human being is not bound by its promises but has the "*right to make promises*" should it freely will to do so.

It is thus Nietzsche who, after all has been said and done, puts us in touch with the plastic sovereignty that I have theorized throughout this book: a sovereignty that gives, receives, and explodes form.[55] It is in this sense, I would argue, that Nietzsche can be understood as "the philosopher with the hammer": for the hammer does not just explode things into destruction. In the smithy, it is part of a process of form-giving and form-receiving, one that – as Daniel Heller-Roazen in the extraordinary seventh chapter of his book *The Fifth Hammer* has shown – is not as far removed as one might think from the history of aesthetic theory.[56]

In the end, such a move towards Nietzsche might be described as an attempt to save the modality of the verb "can" from its progressive actualization in the biopolitical era. This is the most important contribution that Barack Obama's first election campaign brought: it put the American people back in touch (but for how long?) with their political potential, with the meaning of the verb "can." The question is, however, how to safeguard that potential from becoming entirely appropriated by power. If today, the phrase "Yes, we can!"[57] has gained so much popularity, then Agamben notes – in another distinctively "American" moment in his writing – that it is likely because its meaning – the potentiality not-to that it captures – has become appropriated by another one, namely "I give myself the order to obey."[58] Going back to my discussion of both Kant's and Foucault's "What is Enlightenment?" essays in Chapter 5, the question is how to disentangle Kant's imperative to know – dare to know! – from the second imperative that his essay delivers: "Obey!"

One way might be for the people to shout that motto of potentiality back at whoever is in power, as a means to remind them that the motto speaks of a potentiality that not only put them in power but can also get them out. This path is powerfully documented in the documentary film *The Square*, which I mentioned in my Prologue. It is in this way that the gap between life and power – the silence of the law, and the very power of life that it marks – that Hobbes still recognized as the site of the subject's greatest freedom can become a site of leverage within contemporary politics, a democratic tool to mark the disruption of biopolitical governmentality by the plastic sovereignty of life.

However, while such an interruption may pass through the silence of the law that both Hobbes and Locke evoke, this does not sum up the full scope of plasticity, and plastic sovereignty, as I have theorized it here. Indeed, if I have moved with these reflections into the outer extreme of a freedom that would be outside of the law, plasticity evidently ties that explosive limit firmly to the concept's form-receiving and form-giving dimensions, thus pushing a theory of freedom based in the silence of the law elsewhere. This elsewhere, as I have sought to argue, is not the elsewhere of power talk that, through my reading of Locke, I have presented here as Hobbes's "opposite." It is, rather, an elsewhere in-between the silence of the law and power talk, namely the zone – marked out from the opening pages of this book – of infancy, which is neither silence nor speech and relates to both those actualities as a potentiality not-to. It is this potentiality not-to – which is central to Agamben's work – that, in these pages, I have brought in productive conversation with Catherine Malabou's notion of plasticity, as two philosophical concepts that are capable of breaking the vicious dialectic between law and violence that haunts the politics of the state of exception that has been central to this book.

Next to the horizontality of silence and the verticality of speech, there is the other dimension of infancy that unworks speech without regressing to the pitfalls of silence. This is the particular kind of silence of the remainder, the left-over, and the rest, that is central to Agamben's dismantling of the logic of the surplus. The greatest freedom of the living being depends on what we can now call *the sovereign infancy of the law*, which is neither its absence (silence) nor its suspension through brute political speech. It is, properly speaking, the law's sovereign left-over with which Agamben invites his readers to play.

It is then, perhaps, no coincidence, that it is in *Hamlet* – possibly Shakespeare's most famous drama of sovereignty – that "the rest" becomes associated with, is even identified with, "silence." But the question remains: what silence?

Notes

1 For a recent example, see Seymour, "Purgatory."
2 See Schmitt, *Political Theology*, 36.
3 Structuralism's relation to history has of course received plenty of discussion in other contexts.
4 See Danner, "After September 11."
5 Schmitt, *Political Theology*, 5.
6 Hobbes, *Leviathan*, 114.
7 See Whyte, "'The king.'"
8 Nietzsche, *Genealogy*, 76.
9 Agamben, *SE*, 11.
10 Ibid., 19.
11 Ibid., 20.
12 Ibid.
13 Ibid.
14 Ibid., 22.
15 In my Prologue, I have discussed, however, how such an insistence on the separation of the political and the economic also characterizes new sovereign emergencies such as Occupy. In the case of liberalism and neo-liberalism, the argument is made from the point of view of the economy. I am making the argument from the view of politics. And the two positions are, of course, in spite of appearances, very much in tension with each other.
16 In such a perspective, "orange juice" begins to look surprisingly similar

to "Agent Orange," to recall Bruce Robbins's contribution to an issue of *Occasion* on the welfare state. See Robbins, "Orange Juice." Robbins, of course, would never agree with this equation – and I don't think anyone else should either. We are confronting here the old tension between history and structure, as introduced into this chapter by my discussion of Schmitt.

17 Agamben, *SE*, 2.

18 In a recent paper, Adam Kotsko has argued that Agamben's book *The Highest Poverty: Monastic Rules and Form-Of-Life* is his most explicit and extensive attempt to date to answer this question. See Kotsko, "Saint Paul."

19 Agamben, *SE*, 88.

20 Agamben, *HS*, 15.

21 Agamben, *SE*, 1.

22 Ibid., 88.

23 Ibid.

24 Spivak, *Aesthetic Education*.

25 Foucault, *Birth*, 91.

26 See Foucault, *"Society Must Be Defended,"* 87–114.

27 Ibid., 239–64; Foucault, *History*, 135–59.

28 Brown, *Regulating Aversion*, in particular the Introduction and ch. 4.

29 Foucault, *Security*, 107.

30 Agamben, *HS*; Agamben, *K*; Butler, *Precarious Life*, 50–100.

31 Locke, *Second*, 48.

32 Ibid.

33 Ibid., 84.

34 Ibid.

35 Butler, *Precarious*, 86.

36 Han, "Strict Scrutiny."

37 Locke, *Second*, 123; see also 87.

38 Ibid., 123.

39 Ibid., 84.

40 Ibid., 81.

41 Ibid., 84.

42 Ibid., 86.

43 Hobbes, *Leviathan*, 146.

44 See Foucault, *Birth*, 27–50.

45 Agamben, *WA*, 24.

46 In Agamben's *Homo Sacer* trilogy, the terms *inoperativity* and *désoeuvrement* are used to refer to operations that do not destroy the law but render it inactive, thus liberating the law from its link to violence. Agamben himself

has situated these terms in a long tradition of theological, philosophical, and political thought. See Agamben, *TR*. The phrase "society of the spectacle" is of course borrowed from Guy Debord's work on this topic, which is a crucial reference for Agamben's thought.

47 I use the term political theology to refer to the transcendental position that the sovereign in Hobbes takes up with respect to the law. Although Hobbes's work marks an important step in the secularization of power, that secularization did not affect the structure of power, which in Hobbes remains theological.

48 See Agamben, *K*. The point about preserving unity is central and already anticipates, to a certain extent, the continuation of Hobbesian politics in Locke.

49 I have explored the biopolitics of the New Testament, specifically of Saint Paul's letters, in Boever, "Bio-Paulitics." My reading of Paul in this context differs substantially from Agamben's. Whereas Agamben turns to Paul as a critic of biopower, I argue that Paul's letters mark an important step in biopower's intensification.

50 Nietzsche, *Genealogy*, 58.

51 Ibid., 59.

52 Ibid. In her plenary address titled "Capital/Punishment" at the American Comparative Literature Association conference on 21 March 2014, Judith Butler raised the question of this other, "positive" type of promise and whether it might lie occluded in Nietzsche's work. Her attempt was to think affinities, affiliations, and ultimately communities of the promise that would lie beyond the economy of debt in which the Nietzschean promise risks remaining caught up.

53 Nietzsche, *Genealogy*, 76.

54 Ibid., 79.

55 Nietzsche is of course usually only read as a proponent of explosion.

56 See Heller-Roazen, *Fifth Hammer*.

57 Agamben, *C*, 58; in English in the original.

58 Ibid.

8

Sovereignty's Glitches

The idea of creation links the political decision simultaneously to God and to the artist. (Paul W. Kahn, *Political Theology*)[1]

Two States of Exception

I will now return to the problematic of the state of exception, covered through a discussion of political thought in the previous chapter, from the point of view of aesthetic theory in order to see how this might further our theorization of a politics that would be beyond the exceptionalist power that Agamben criticizes. As I have already noted, the notion of the state of exception enters into Agamben's work through his discussion of the German legal theorist Carl Schmitt, who proposed in his book *Political Theology: Four Chapters on the Concept of Sovereignty* that "[s]overeign is he who decides on the exception."[2] The state of exception – the English has "exception" but Schmitt uses the word "Ausnahmezustand" or "state of exception," in the original German – is a situation or state in which the law is suspended in the name of an emergency situation. In his work,

Agamben argues (taking his cue from Schmitt) that sovereignty's key activity – one might even say, its rule – is the generation of such states of exception. It is in such states that bare life, which he considers to form a couple with sovereign power, is produced. (As I discussed in Chapter 2, Agamben adapts the notion of "bare life" from Walter Benjamin.) The production of bare life is thus another key activity of sovereign power. While the concentration camp marks perhaps the most extreme realization of this activity, the state of exception is also operative in some of the achievements of Western political history that many may value the most: as I have already discussed in Chapter 2, Agamben takes on human rights, for example, as one of those sites where bare life is generated.

The question that drives these final three chapters on politics is what kind of thinking, and ultimately doing, can effectively dismantle the logic of the state of exception – and by "effectively," I mean: without falling into the trap of reproducing its logic. In this chapter, this question arises out of a discomfort I began to feel reading philosophical theorizations of the politics of art and aesthetics, both those of Agamben and those of other thinkers, that seemed to reproduce if not the logic then at least the poetry of the state of exception. In his book *The Century*, for example, Alain Badiou theorizes art as "forcing a thinking to declare, in its area of concern, *the state of exception*"[3] – and he values this positively. Theorizing riots and uprisings in his book on the Arab Spring, Badiou writes in a long paragraph on political organization about the "Subject of the exception,"[4] using this phrase to refer to a subject constituted by the organization emerging from nihilistic rioting and pre-political turmoil. Once again, the exception appears to be valued positively, as a pre-political state of revolution.

I am certainly not the only one to have noted these resonances of Badiou's thought with theories of the state of exception. In an early response to Badiou's *Being and Event*, Jean-François Lyotard already suggested that Badiou's theory of the Subject begins to strangely "mirror" Schmitt's theory of the sovereign as he who decides on the state of exception.[5] It is not that Lyotard is blaming Badiou for everything that is wrong with the state of exception – but still, what to make of these resonances? Are we confronting two different states of exception here? A pharmacology of the state of exception (to recall Stiegler's terminology)?

Let me give just two others examples before I return to Agamben. When Steve Corcoran characterizes the connection between aesthetics and politics in his introduction to *Dissensus*, a collection of Jacques Rancière's writings, he proposes that in Rancière's work "art and politics can be understood, such that their specificity is seen to reside in their contingent suspension of the rules governing normal experience"; they find each other in the fact that both depend on "an innovative leap from the logic that ordinarily governs human situations."[6] These sentences, which seek to capture the similarity of art – aesthetics – and politics, could have been drawn from Schmitt's theory of sovereignty. Particularly striking is Corcoran's use of the verb "suspend": in the state of exception, crucially, the law is not destroyed but merely suspended. This is why it is an intra-/extra-legal possibility where the law begins to flirt with its own (political) illegality.

The problem that I am confronting here is widespread in art theory and aesthetic theory. When, in his *Toward a Lexicon of Usership*, art theorist Stephen Wright seeks to define what he calls "escapology" as the theory of practices that would escape all kinds of capture – all kinds of apparatuses of capture – he writes that escapology "is the theory and practice of suspending the operations of all these mechanisms of capture."[7] In what way, then, is the politics of art and aesthetics and the "suspension" it promises any different from the politics of the state of exception? In what way is the attachment to a politics of art and aesthetics that "suspends" a secret promotional campaign, in the supposedly critical and progressive sphere of the arts, for the very politics of the state of exception that many of the same people working in the arts are, politically, against?

Given the state of exception's intimate relation to sovereignty, these questions ultimately target sovereignty, and art's and aesthetics' relation to sovereignty. It is no coincidence, given the ambiguities of the politics of art and aesthetics that I laid out above, that it is precisely in some contemporary reflections on the politics of art and aesthetics today that one can find criticisms – which, granted, do not necessarily amount to a plea for sovereignty – of, for example, the "horizontalism" that has been touted as one of the main features of the Occupy Movement.[8] Indeed, it seems that our entire imaginary of the artist, the curator, the art school, gallery, or museum, is at least vaguely complicit with the imaginary of exceptionalist sovereignty, in the sense that artists, curators, art schools, galleries, and museums are all supposed to be people or institutions that stand out in a world in which, especially today, "flatness rules": the kind of world that is described by sociologist Pascal Gielen in his introduction to a recent book on art institutions in the neoliberal world of "today's networked society," in which everything has become "democratized" and the mediocre is dominant.[9] In many ways, this seems to be a valuable political position that restores some of the verticality of exceptionalist sovereignty into a horizontal world – of both neoliberalism *and* Occupy.

Philosophically, it is a valuable position as well as it goes against much of the trending work on the "democracy of objects," proposing a "flat ontology" that resonates both with the rising popularity of studies in posthumanism – and that could, politically, be on the side of either neoliberalism or Occupy. If Gielen can speak of the neoliberal world of today's networked society, it is worth noting that this networked society is the key model of many anti-neoliberal developments in today's society as well.

The question, as I see it, is how aspects of this verticality – this sovereignty – that Gielen and co. praise can be maintained – in response to the risks of a world in which flatness rules – without thereby falling into all of the traps that exceptionalist sovereignty sets up. The point is not to choose for either of these dimensions – horizontal or vertical – but to enter into the game of their dynamic relation and arrive through that at a politics with elements of both. The horizontal and the vertical are political tendencies or forces that each have their virtues and keep each other in check; alone, each one of them would create a meaningless politics of either a lack or excess of power. If we want to avoid being caught up in the swings of the pendulum that is suspended between both, it will be important to think – and practice – both of them together and to consider what politics might emerge from that. The challenge, once again, is not to think *sovereignty and its other* – two "opposites" that risk both being caught in the logic of suspension – but to think instead *another sovereignty*, one that would allow for the play of different tendencies.

As several critics have noted, the problem of art's and aesthetics' exceptionalist politics and its complicity with the politics of the state of exception has arisen in Agamben's work and it continues to be an issue in his most recently published writings.[10] This problem is, arguably, twofold. First of all, critics have struggled to understand what Agamben means by the state of exception and how it can function as a paradigm for understanding contemporary Western politics (I have sought to address this issue in the previous chapter). The second issue is that critics struggle to understand Agamben's proposed "solution" to this problem, specifically the ways in which this solution would be different from the state of exception it seeks to dismantle (this is the issue I will take on in this chapter as well as the next). Agamben has addressed this second issue explicitly in a few pages in *The Time That Remains*, his commentary on Saint Paul's "Letter to the Romans." There, he seeks to distinguish between the state of exception's suspension of the law and what he proposes in response to it: the messianic deactivation of the law. That the two are not entirely separate is evident from how Agamben introduces this discussion: "How should we think the state of the law under the effect of messianic *katargesis* [unworking, *désoeuvrement*]?" he asks at the beginning of the section, "What is a law that is simultaneously suspended and fulfilled?"[11] Interestingly, it is Schmitt who helps him answer this question. For insofar as Schmitt, with his conservative theory of the state of exception, is ultimately "an apocalypticist of the counterrevolution,"[12] "he cannot help but introduce some genuinely messianic *theologoumena* into it."[13] It is, in other words, from Schmitt's theory of the state of exception that the state of exception's messianic undoing emerges: Schmitt's theory already includes the seed of such an undoing. Agamben's messianic deactivation of the law unworks the state of exception and "absolutizes" the suspension that is its mode of operation.

In the case of such fine distinctions, where the poison also turns out to be part of the cure, nomenclature is important, and Agamben takes care in his work – in particular in his choice of verbs – to write these distinctions in discrete ways. Instead of "suspend," the verbs that are used to characterize this absolutization of the state of exception are "deactivate" and "unwork," or the phrase "render inoperative"; Agamben thus speaks about the messianic "inoperativity" of the law. If the state of exception is the site where bare life is incessantly produced, what we find in the messianic deactivation of the law is what Agamben calls, in *The Coming Community*, "whatever being" (see Chapter 3). "Whatever being" operates in Agamben's work as a messianic counterpart to "bare life": if the latter is life in a state of exceptionalist suspension, the former is life in a state of messianic deactivation. Associated with this are different models of the political (if we can still call it that): the camp, in the case of bare life; and the coming community – a new *polis* – in the case of whatever being. If bare life is perpetually caught up in the violent (hylomorphic) dynamic between the simple fact of living and its form (*zoe* and *bios*; matter and form of life), whatever being's life and form of life are indistinguishable – it is form-of-life. *Homo sacer* is the figure that is most closely associated with bare life. The monk has emerged in Agamben's work as its most elaborately developed counterpart. Although I am setting up two opposing models here, the ambiguity of these figures remains. As I have considered in Chapter 6, Agamben's *Flamen Diale* can arguably be understood *both* as a *homo sacer and* as a monk.[14]

One final question that circulates here is how the two opposing models I have laid out relate to the concept of sovereignty that Schmitt, in his book, was theorizing. My answer has been that in these two models, there are competing aspects of sovereignty – the highest power – in play. While Agamben's criticism of the state of exception of course challenges what he perceives to be the essential operation of sovereignty – producing bare life – he also finds in it another operation that effectively "deactivates" sovereignty's capacity for "suspension." Rather than reading this as a rejection of sovereignty, with all of its implications, I read it as a pluralization of the concept, more specifically (and after Malabou) as a theorization of its plasticity, in which sovereignty's form-receiving, form-giving, and form-exploding capacities would be able to coexist. While this coexistence is not always possible in Agamben's work – there are moments, as I have already discussed, where the negotiation of plasticity fails and gives way to an all too easy logic of opposition that risks producing more of the state of exception rather than effectively challenging it – plasticity marks something like a possibility (though I would hardly call it "messianic") in Agamben's work that deserves to be pursued, beyond a logic of simply opposing sovereignty to its "other." Whether we like it or not, sovereignty is here to stay. It seems then that rather than opposing it, the more valuable path would be to pursue its deconstruction, and to find – and here is where Malabou goes further than Derrida – what other formations it might enable. At this point, as will be clear, we may indeed be going further than Agamben himself, who insists on a potentiality not-to that would not flip over into actuality. Such a potentiality not-to is indeed, as I have argued, the first, aesthetic moment of sovereignty's pluralization. But I do not limit myself to that first moment in my reading of Agamben's work. Instead, I tie to it a second, poetic moment where actual formations of another sovereignty are considered. Part of what I begin to accomplish in this chapter is precisely that: a consideration of formations that would be neither "sovereign" (in the theologico-political sense of the word) nor its other (a binary that reproduces the logic I seek to contest), but attuned to the dynamic of sovereignty that I have sought to draw out in this book. In my final chapter, I call such formations "formations of infancy."

In his "Critical Introduction" to Agamben's work, Leland de la Durantaye has already noted that the ambiguity of the state of exception in Agamben's work can be traced back to a doubleness of the state of exception in the work of Walter Benjamin, namely the distinction that Benjamin makes in his "Theses on the Philosophy of History" between the state of exception that has become the rule and a real state of exception that would end this situation.[15] In what follows, I start from a discussion of Benjamin's real state of exception to consider not so much what it is, but in what ways it might be different from the state of exception that has become the rule. I pursue this consideration through a reflection on what could be considered one possible articulation of a state in which, as in the state of exception, life is exposed at its limits: poverty. Benjamin has written about poverty, and the issue has become a key concern in Agamben's recent work as well. My focus for this investigation will be the domain in which I find the logic of the state of exception most often reproduced in the guise of an alternative politics, namely the realm of art and aesthetics, and I will be returning here to a number of the references in art and aesthetics that already appeared in previous chapters. Thus, I will ultimately seek to outline another politics of art and aesthetics that would break with the logic of suspension familiar to us through the state of exception, and move instead toward its deactivation. This will involve, in the end, thinking sovereignty as image, and specifically thinking the glitches of the image of sovereignty – thinking sovereignty as what Hito Steyerl in her work has called a "poor image." It will involve thinking a poor, precarious sovereignty – contradiction in terms – and the peculiar power that it wields.

Exception and Poverty

In his eighth thesis on the philosophy of history, Walter Benjamin draws a famous lesson from what he calls "the tradition of the oppressed," namely that "the 'state of emergency' in which we live is not the exception but the rule."[16] If we conceive of history on the basis of this insight, "[t]hen we shall clearly realize that it is our task to bring about a real state of emergency" – and he concludes, in 1940, that "this will improve our position in the struggle against Fascism."[17] What is the real state of emergency to which Benjamin refers? Presumably, it would be a state of emergency that would end the "fake" state of emergency that has become the rule: the tradition (rule) of the oppressed (those living in emergency conditions). But how, exactly, would this be accomplished?

Benjamin's seventh thesis anticipates the point about the tradition of the oppressed with the claim that "[t]here is no document of civilization which is not at the same time a document of barbarism";[18] in the ninth thesis, Benjamin's call for a real state of emergency becomes associated with "the angel of history," who wants to "make whole what has been smashed" but cannot because his wings have become caught in the storm of progress.[19] What we call progress is barbaric. It furthers a tradition of oppression – the rule of a state of emergency – that needs to be stopped. It is time to set free the wings of the angel of history and bring about a real state of emergency. The story – if indeed there is one – mobilizes familiar Benjaminian themes, from the messianic angel of history to the barbarism of civilization and progress that permeates almost all of his work (even if he is also enthusiastic about the developments that modernity brings).

I propose to consider here an example of the state of oppression that Benjamin is writing about, namely the state of "poverty," which he has discussed elsewhere. I would like to show – taking my cue from an argument that Alexander García Düttmann develops in a text titled "Making Poverty Visible – Three Theses" – that poverty is a key site to investigate not only the "fake" state of emergency that Benjamin mentions (poverty and its relation to the tradition of the oppressed) but also the "real" state of emergency that Benjamin calls for in his struggle against fascism (poverty and the angel of history, if I can put it this way). In his article, which takes its cue from Agamben's work on sovereignty and bare life, Düttmann considers that in poverty, as in the concentration camp, "human life reache[s] a limit that teaches us something about the human being."[20] I think I agree, even if the comparison of poverty to "the camps" may raise some hackles (see Chapter 1). I would like to pursue further the politics of that consideration. This will help me make sense of Benjamin's real state of emergency and its operation.

Benjamin writes about poverty in a text that Düttmann also discusses, "Experience and Poverty." It begins with the barbarism of civilization and progress: "With this tremendous development of technology," Benjamin writes, "a completely new poverty has descended on mankind."[21] This new poverty is what he calls "the poverty of experience."[22] Developing a theme that readers perhaps know best from his essay "The Storyteller: Observations on the Works of Nikolai Leskov" (discussed in Chapter 2),[23] Benjamin diagnoses this poverty in people's loss of the ability to communicate experiences – their withdrawal into silence. "[T]he reverse side of this poverty," he notes, "is the progressive wealth of ideas that has been spread among people,"[24] which he characterizes as a kind of carnival of deathly superficiality. It marks, Benjamin concludes, "a new kind of barbarism."[25]

But which barbarism? Whereas barbarism in the seventh thesis on the philosophy of history refers negatively to the tradition of the oppressed that he writes about in 1940, in 1933 he uses the term "to introduce a new, positive concept of barbarism" that captures how the poverty of experience "forces" the barbarian "to start from scratch."[26] It is from the state of emergency that technological development has brought, that a new human being is born. Poverty of experience does not mark people's

> yearning for new experience. No, they long to free themselves from experience; they long for a world in which they can make such pure and decided use of their poverty – their outer poverty, and ultimately also their inner poverty – that it will lead to something respectable.[27]

How are we to read this passage? It seems to be caught between the nostalgia with which the text opens, and the excitement that Benjamin also appears to be feeling about the new, positive barbarism. Like barbarism, "poverty of experience" is characterized by the ambiguity that can also be found in the state of emergency: split between the fake and the real, there appears to be some cure that can be found in what is otherwise diagnosed as a poison.

At the end of his text, Benjamin famously proposes Mickey Mouse as the "dream" in which this "miraculous" reinvention of the human being can take place and where, in fact, a satire of technological development can begin. In the life of Mickey Mouse, "in which a car is no heavier than a straw hat and the fruit on the tree becomes round as quickly as a hot air balloon," "nature and technology … have completely merged," and in this miraculous fusion – which shows a modern life that is simple rather than full of "endless complications" – the poverty of experience has been overcome into a new barbarism of laughter that restores "a little humanity to the masses."[28] There is something like an *experience of poverty* that opens up here, in contrast to the *poverty of experience*, one that could be read as an anticipation of the digital age in which minds and bodies have become so integrated with technological devices that we no longer know where mind or body end and technology begins. But whether this situation has restored humanity to the masses and is to be met with laughter remains to be seen.

It remains to be seen, in other words, whether it is a mere furthering of the state of emergency – the poverty of experience – that Benjamin links to the tradition of the oppressed, or whether it is able to bring about a real state of emergency – an experience of poverty – that would end this tradition. I will now turn to two theorists of the image working in Benjamin's wake to further explore this problem.

Sontag and the Outside

At the end of her famous *New Yorker* essay "Looking at War: Photography's View of Devastation and Death" (2002), which condenses the argument of her book *Regarding the Pain of Others* (2003), Susan Sontag turns to a Jeff Wall photograph: "Dead Troops Talk (A Vision after an Ambush of a Red Army Patrol, near Moqor, Afghanistan, Winter 1986)." The photograph seems to Sontag "exemplary in its thoughtfulness, coherence, and passion"[29] when it comes to its representation of war. The reasons she quotes may surprise the reader: if Wall's image can function as an example, it is because it is "[t]he antithesis of a document."[30] It shows a made-up event, inspired by other representations of war,

> in the tradition of nineteenth-century history painting and other forms of history-as-spectacle that emerged in the late eighteenth and early nineteenth centuries – just before the invention of the camera – such as tableaux vivants, wax displays, dioramas, and panoramas, which made the past, especially the immediate past, seem astonishingly, disturbingly real.[31]

However, even if Wall's photograph is realistic, Sontag emphasizes that "the image is not": "Dead soldiers don't talk."[32] But in Wall's photograph, "they do."[33]

"One could fantasize," she concludes her essay, "that the soldiers [represented in Wall's image] might turn and talk to us. But no, no one is looking out of the picture at the viewer … These dead are supremely uninterested in the living."[34] As Sontag puts it in the powerful closing lines of her essay, "Why should they seek our gaze?"

> What would they have to say to us? "We" – this "we" is everyone who has never experienced anything like what they went through – don't understand. We don't get it. We truly can't imagine what it was like. We can't imagine how dreadful, how terrifying war is – and how normal it becomes. Can't understand, can't imagine. That's what every soldier, and every journalist and aid worker and independent observer who has put in time under fire and had the luck to elude the death that struck down others nearby stubbornly feels. And they are right.[35]

The paragraph sums up her criticism of the "society of the spectacle" analysis that she struck down earlier on in the essay:

"[t]o speak of reality becoming a spectacle is a breathtaking provincialism," she argues there – those who are in the middle of the wars represented on television "do not have the luxury of patronizing reality."[36] War thus remains, in Sontag's analysis, outside of the frame of the various images she discusses: it is an obscene event that withdraws from representation and can exist only in the experience of those who have put in time under fire and had the luck to elude death.

Sontag's argument can be criticized from a number of perspectives. First of all, it is worth noting her insistence, in her critique of the "society of the spectacle" analysis, on a reality that is outside of the image. Against the theory that there is nothing outside of the image, Sontag insists on the reality of that outside. To call reality a spectacle

> universalizes the viewing habits of a small, educated population living in the rich part of the world, where the news has been converted into entertainment ... It assumes that everyone is a spectator. It suggests, perversely, unseriously, that there is no real suffering in the world. But it is absurd to identify "the world" with those zones in the rich countries where people have the dubious privilege of being spectators, or of declining to be spectators, of other people's pain.... [37]

One can disagree here with Sontag's understanding of the "society of the spectacle" analysis, or of that other famous theoretical analysis that resonates here – Jacques Derrida's "there is nothing outside of the text," "il n'y pas de hors-texte"[38] – but this simplified view of her opponents does have the advantage of clarifying Sontag's own position: reality is not a spectacle. *There is* something outside of the text.

Now, consider what ethical (and, ultimately, political) arguments this position enables Sontag to make. First of all,

Sontag's insistence on reality, on an outside, leads her to argue that only those who have been in a war can know what it is like. But on what grounds can one claim to "have been in a war"? She writes that it means to have put in time under fire and escaped with your life. There are at least two potentially risky consequences of such an argument. First, when this kind of argument is pushed to the extreme, one cannot but arrive at the logical conclusion that only those who have died in war know what it is really like. This is, by now, a well-known position in testimony studies: Agamben has argued in his book *Remnants of Auschwitz: The Witness and the Archive* that it is only the *Muselmann*, the extreme concentration camp prisoner in the zone of indeterminacy between life and death, who is the camp's true witness – the one that can no longer witness.[39] Again, following this logic all the way through, one would have to conclude that there are no "true" witnesses to the Holocaust, or to any other genocide for that matter – because the true witnesses of the Holocaust are dead, and if there are any survivors of a genocide, it means there was no real genocide (for clearly, *someone* survived).[40]

Secondly, if the condition for knowing what war is like is to have put in time under fire, one wonders whether a hierarchy of experiences is created here and whether, for example, someone who has lost a limb under fire knows better what war is like than someone who has not. Even the dead soldiers in Wall's photograph are not safe from this risk: some have lost limbs, others have been disemboweled, some have lost their head – does that mean any one is "more dead" than another? I am not trying to be facetious: if to have been in a war is the condition for knowing what war is like, surely there are gradations to "being in a war," and I wonder how Sontag values such gradations when it comes to knowing what war is like.

I am asking in part because of a related political position that Sontag develops in another, earlier text from 1995 titled "A Lament for Bosnia: 'There' and 'Here'" that I have already discussed in Chapter 1. I pointed out that in that essay, Sontag's "harshest words … are reserved for the intellectuals, who have become 'morosely depoliticized.'"[41] Sontag criticizes those who are "a creature of 'comfortable upper-bourgeoisie apartments and weekend country houses,'" and "loath to leave them."[42] Instead, she wishes intellectuals would engage – on site. As I discussed, Bruce Robbins takes issue with Sontag's words, pointing out that "very few" of Sontag's readers are "likely to enjoy the time, the personal autonomy, and the disposable income necessary for even one or two trips to Sarajevo, let alone nine."[43] One can hear this politics resonate in "Looking at War," in the argument that only those who have put in time under fire can know what war is like: in the same way that one must go to Sarajevo to be politically engaged, one must have put in time under fire to be able to talk about war. Everyone who did not does not have a clue.

Arise, Ye Image People!

I recall these issues because I encountered them again in a more recent text of image theory, Hito Steyerl's "The Spam of the Earth: Withdrawal from Representation," first published in the journal *e-flux* and then republished with a set of Steyerl's other *e-flux* pieces in her book *The Wretched of the Screen*. The book as a whole deals with the status of images in contemporary digital culture. In "Spam of the Earth," Steyerl characterizes the contemporary media landscape as a "zone … of exception, which seems dangerous to enter."[44] "[P]ictorial representation –

which was seen as a prerogative and a political privilege for a long time – feels more like a threat."[45] In a situation or state in which everybody has truly become famous for fifteen minutes thanks to a culture of "mutual mass surveillance, which adds to the ubiquitous urban networks of control, such as CCTV, cellphone GPS tracking and face-recognition software," "now many people want the contrary: to be invisible, if only for fifteen minutes. Even fifteen seconds would be great."[46]

Steyerl has begun to notice that in such a state, "many people have started actively avoiding photographic or moving-image representations, surreptitiously taking their distance from the lenses of cameras."[47] If "representation" used to be "the primary site of contestation for both politics and aesthetics"[48] – think, for example, of Gayatri Chakravorty Spivak's discussion of this issue in "Can the Subaltern Speak?" (Steyerl wrote the introduction for this text's German translation[49]) – today, the issue may have become "withdrawal from representation."[50] Today,

> many people ... walk away from visual representation. Their instincts (and their intelligence) tell them that photographic or moving images are dangerous devices of capture: of time, affect, productive forces, and subjectivity. They can jail you or shame you forever ... and, moreover, once these images are online they will never be deleted again.... The old magic fear of cameras is thus reincarnated in the world of digital natives. But in this environment, cameras do not take away your soul ... but drain away your life. They actively make you disappear, shrink, and render you naked ... In fact, it is a misunderstanding that cameras are tools of representation; they are at present tools of disappearance. The more people are represented, the less is left of them in reality.[51]

It is from this optic – one for which Sontag would likely have had some sympathy, given how it resonates with her own characterization of the contemporary world as "saturated, even hypersaturated, with images" – that Steyerl approaches the actual topic of her text: image spam. Where does this approach lead her?

One could ask, as she points out, who the people are who are "portrayed in this type of accelerated advertisement," that is: image spam. One would then find that these people are not "actual humans" but "ideal" types, "addressed to the vast majority of humankind" that they do not show.[52] One could then interpret image spam "as a tool for the production of bodies," "as an instrument of coercive persuasion as well as of insidious seduction."[53] Steyerl characterizes this as the "traditional Cultural Studies" approach.[54] She, by contrast, is after something else:

> What if actual people ... were not excluded from spam advertisements because of their deficiencies but had actually chosen to desert this kind of portrayal? What if image spam thus became a record of a widespread refusal, a withdrawal of people from representation?[55]

If photography can be conceptualized "as a form of civil contract" (as, for example, in the work of Ariella Azoulay, to which Steyerl refers), then this choice could be read as a "breaking of the social contract."[56] She concludes that it is, perhaps, in this way that "a people" can be represented: visually, "in negative form"; philosophically, as an event that escapes representation; politically, as a community that sets itself apart from the stereotype of its national or cultural representation.[57] Her text ends with the suggestion that image spam people may thus liberate people from the representations from which they suffer: "Go off screen, they [the image spam people] seem to whisper. We'll substitute for you. Let them tag and scan us in the meantime. You go off the radar and do what you have to."[58]

The ending raises some questions about who is being referred to in the title of Steyerl's book: "the wretched of the screen." One assumes that the title refers to the image spam people who substitute for us and for this deserve "our love and admiration." But it could also refer to us, those damned into what Steyerl characterizes as the exceptional contemporary media land-scape, in which withdrawal from representation presents itself as an aesthetic and political strategy.[59] In such a reading, "we" are the rubble from which, as one of Steyerl's interlocutors has noted, the "angel of history" is being pushed away.[60] Indeed, those questions of interpretation – who are the wretched of the screen? – are bound to haunt those "extraterrestrial forms of intelligence" evoked at the beginning of Steyerl's text who will, from the future, consider image spam and seek to find in it "a true portrait of our times and ourselves."[61] One reading could consider image spam as an actual, truthful representation of what human beings look like (documentary image). Say these extra-terrestrials are familiar with the cultural studies approach Steyerl references, they may come up with another reading that draws out the way in which image spam operates "as an instrument of coercive persuasion as well as of insidious seduction" (image spam's "positive" plasticity). This may lead them in the end to Steyerl's (Deleuzian) conclusion, namely that "the people are missing" (spam as "negative" image). With the move from the theorization of the contemporary media landscape as a state of exception to the reading of image spam as a zone in which the people are missing, Steyerl seems to have moved from "excep-tion" to "refuge":[62] if representation as she discusses it at the beginning of her text names an ubiquitous practice that violates actual people who are internally excluded in it, the representa-tion of image spam as she discusses it at the end of her text has been turned into a representation from which the people have actively chosen to withdraw.

In this case too though, and here is where I will be looping back to Sontag, there are some ethical and political consequences. A brief note on the phrase "the wretched of the screen": it is a reference, of course, to "The International" – the song of the First and Second International written by Eugène Pottier in Paris in 1871 – which calls on "the wretched of the earth" – in the original French in which the song was composed, "les damnés de la terre" – to "rise."[63] (Many probably know the phrase as the title of a book by Frantz Fanon – indeed, that is the only reference that is cited in the texts about Steyerl's book that I consulted. "The International" is effectively elided in the reception of Steyerl's book. The same goes for Fanon's book.[64]) In the song, "damnés" is taken to refer to "the poor": "prisoners of want," as one translation has it; "galley-slaves of want," in another. But in Steyerl's discussion of image spam people, the phrase begins to take on strange meanings. If it refers to us, who are violated by the image, then no problem: we are "the poor" referred to in her title, and we should rise in reaction to our situation. If it refers to the image spam people who, in the image, substitute for us, then the "poor" are the image spam people who are doing the violent work of "imaging" for us. In view of the reference to "The International," this second reading seems problematic. Translated back into that context, Steyerl's conclusion – written by an artist – would be something like: "the poor work for us and for this they deserve our love and admiration." Going back to Benjamin's language: the real state of emergency that Steyerl proposes against the fake state of emergency of the contemporary media landscape risks ending up furthering the tradition of the oppressed, this time with image spam people in the role of the oppressed.

310

Again, one could object that I am being facetious: image spam people are not real people. The concern with their well-being that I am voicing is similar to being concerned about the oppression of characters in a film or a novel. It is the acumen of a high postmodernist sensibility mixed in with an American (US) culture of political correctness: in the US, *even characters are easily offended*. Soon they will be suing! *Even fictional beings deserve rights* – as opposed to love and admiration, which are nice but do not change their enslavement. My concern, however, is with the *logic* or structure of the move that Steyerl performs, and with whether the real state of emergency that is being declared in her text in any way constitutes an alternative to the fake state of emergency that her text seeks to contest. In what way, structurally speaking, is the real state of emergency that Benjamin calls for in the eighth thesis on the philosophy of history different from the fake state of emergency that he criticizes in the same thesis? It seems to me that it will not do to simply substitute image spam people for real people in the ubiquitous representations from which we suffer, and announce – with reference to Benjamin – that the end of fascism has arrived. For the logic of fascism would continue, with the only difference being that image spam people now carry its horrific burden.

Let me, given the reference to "The International" earlier on, develop a brief parallel to a nineteenth-century situation: the way in which human beings were caught in the violence of factory work, one of those emergency situations (as I have argued elsewhere[65]) in which "human life reache[s] a limit that teaches us something about the human being." Benjamin would no doubt characterize this as a fake state of emergency that marks only one of many moments in the tradition of the oppressed. What would it mean to declare a real state of emergency on this situation, and truly subvert the logic of fascism that is operative here? Consider the image spam people solution: we replace the human beings who are working under these conditions with machines, and the problem is solved. They will substitute for us. We can withdraw from work, go off the radar, and do what we have to do while they take care of business. In such a view, machines would simply substitute for human beings without any real transformation in our conception of the conditions of factory work. Am I mounting a defense of "machine rights" here? No. I am arguing that as long as there is no real transformation in our conception of the conditions of work, the risk remains that somewhere, a human being is doing the work of the machine, under exactly the same conditions, which have remained unmodified.[66]

As an aside, it is worth recalling that when Benjamin in his essay "Critique of Violence" (1921) discusses the violence of a strike, he is not calling for the end of work or the replacement of the workers in factories by machines. Instead, he argues for a transformative politics – which he calls, at the end of the essay, "waltend," translated as "sovereign" – a strike after which people would go back to work – to what he calls (as I have already mentioned in Chapter 2) "a wholly transformed work," "eine gänzlich veränderte Arbeit."[67] Instead of substitution, Benjamin gives us transformation.

While I am not mounting a defense of "machine rights" here, I will say that I do wonder about the conception of machines that the mere substitution of machines for people on the factory floor perpetuates. In his work on technical objects, the French philosopher of technology Gilbert Simondon (whose work I discussed in Chapter 5) has challenged the view of the machine as some kind of galley-slave that would liberate us from labor, arguing instead for the co-individuation of human beings and technology that appears to be much more attuned to the contemporary digital age that Steyerl in her text is analyzing.[68]

I thus wonder, at the end of the day, about the conception of image people that Steyerl's argument perpetuates. For even though she is dealing with a particular kind of image people – image spam people – "image people" are probably at least equally present in Steyerl's life as they are in mine. Like Sontag, and like Steyerl, I *know*, of course, that those image people – say, people living in Iraq, China, or Sudan – are "real"; but given that they are really no more than images to me, it seems we should be careful not to shift the violence of representation from which we suffer *onto them*. Such care involves unworking the violence of representation *even for* image spam people, however absurd that might seem.[69]

Note that I am not using the verb "liberate" – at least for now. In what follows, I move away from the insistence on the "outside" that haunts both Sontag's text and Steyerl's text on spam. Instead, the verb I use is "unwork," which I present, in the final part of this chapter, as a near-synonym for "use"; and this will become – in close relation to poverty – the key term in my discussion of the politics of a real state of emergency that would truly dismantle the fake state of emergency from which we *all* suffer. People *and* image people – which are ultimately, as will become clear, *one* people.

Image and Poverty

In my discussion of Steyerl's book title, "the wretched of the screen," there is one other reading that I have not yet considered, namely that the wretched of the screen that Steyerl is referring to may be the images themselves. Not so much image spam *people* – always still caught up in the politics of humanism, as I have argued above – but *images*. After all, what is projected onto the screen is not people but images. And something changes, I think, when this move from image people to images is accomplished.

Indeed, the grounds for such a reading are established earlier on in Steyerl's book, in a text titled "In Defense of the Poor Image," in which Steyerl writes that "[p]oor images are the contemporary Wretched of the Screen."[70] What does she mean by "the poor image"? The poor image, she writes in the text's first paragraph,

> is a copy in motion. Its quality is bad, its resolution substandard. It is a ghost of an image, a preview, a thumbnail, an errant idea, an itinerant image distributed for free, squeezed through slow digital connections, compressed, reproduced, ripped, remixed, as well as copied and pasted into other channels of distribution.[71]

Two components of "poverty" are worth noting here. First of all, by "poor images," Steyerl is referring to images that are, technically speaking, "poor"; secondly, a key component of what constitutes an image's poverty is its use: how it is copied, distributed, circulated, et cetera. These two components, however, arguably allow for very different ontologies, which are not fully accounted for in the text.[72]

According to a first reading, the poor image *is* poor: it is technically poor, it is an image that is of a bad quality. According to the second reading, however, the original of the image that is circulated is not necessarily poor; it *becomes* poor through being compressed, reproduced, ripped, remixed, et cetera. While use may thus render it poor, this second reading still includes the suggestion that somewhere, outside of this sphere of use, an original "rich" version of the image exists. The first understanding of the poor image does not allow for such a possibility. Steyerl does not account for this difference when, toward the end of her text, she states that the poor image, "[b]y losing its visual substance … recovers some of its political punch and creates a new aura around it. This aura is no longer based on the permanence of the 'original', but on the transience of the copy."[73] This argument – which echoes Benjamin's essay on the work of art in the era of mechanical reproducibility[74] – is true for her first understanding of the poor image; but it is not necessarily so for the second.

What both understandings of poverty share is that neither undermines the compliment that I have heard film or photography students make about each other's work: "you make such strong images!" The poor image, as Steyerl discusses it in this text, seems to exclude bad – ugly, weak – images. She is writing about strong images that either *are* poor from a technical perspective or *become* so through circulation. Most of the poor images she discusses (with the exception of the image reproduced on page 4 of the *e-flux* version of her text) are "art" images that *reappear* as poor images in the realm of circulation: Chris Marker's film essays or "rare prints of militant, experimental, and classical works of cinema as well as video art."[75] Such examples enable her to discuss a third component of "poverty": marginalization. The fact that these images reappear as poor images

reveals the conditions of their marginalization, the constellation of social forces leading to their online circulation as poor images. Poor images are poor because they are not assigned any value within the class society of images – their status as illicit or degraded grants them exemption from its criteria. Their lack of resolution attests to their appropriation and displacement.[76]

I guess that from the perspective of the general viewer, this is probably true; but reading this in the context of the art institute where I teach, I also wonder about how marginalized Marker or some of the other artists that Steyerl mentions really are. Is this an argument about art and its marginalized place in society? About certain kinds of art and their marginalized place in society? Does Steyerl's definition of the poor image reproduce a distinction between "underground" and "mainstream" that would separate certain kinds of film, photography, or other visual art from others? This is, once again, the question of hierarchies. What does it take to qualify as a poor image? Are some images more poor than others? Is there some kind of elite of poor images that make Steyerl's cut? On the basis of what criteria are other images left behind? Aren't those the truly poor images, then – the ugly, the weak? And doesn't Steyerl's argument, at the level of its logic, risk reproducing the very issue she is trying to contest? Won't there always be a poorer image than the one she is defending? And doesn't this require a different kind of defense?

Steyerl's discussion of "the afterlife of many former master-pieces of cinema and video art"[77] culminates – via a discussion of Juan García Espinosa's manifesto "For an Imperfect Cinema" – in a short little section about "reality." Considering the regret some people may feel due to the fact that the poor image "is not the real thing" (she is referring to "the original" she mentions in the implicit engagement with Benjamin in the previous section of her text), she counters by asking, "please, anybody – show me this real thing."[78] This echoes a statement she makes elsewhere:

"Whoever is not an image raise their hand."[79] What is key to the poor image is that it "is no longer about the real thing – the originary original. Instead, it is about its own real conditions of existence" – the image's circulation. "In short," she concludes, "it is about reality."[80]

Something very interesting is happening here: Steyerl both undermines the recourse to the real thing – an original that would exist outside of or as separate from the poor image – *and* insists on reality, the reality of the thing's circulation ("its own real conditions of existence"). This effectively undermines the position she develops in the text on image spam: there, you will remember, she insists on the existence of real human beings who withdraw from the representations of image spam people who no longer resemble in any way actual human beings. In her discussion of the poor image of image spam – a poor image if there ever was one, unless bad images are not allowed in the club of poor images? – Steyerl in other words answers her own plea from earlier on in the book. Show you the real thing? Why, it is those people who, according to the argument you develop in your text on spam, have withdrawn from the image! However, it is Steyerl's point at the very end of the text on poor images that enables one to unwork what I consider to be the "error" of her text on spam: if there is no such original, and if all that matters is the conditions of existence – circulation, compression, ripping leading to poor technical quality – then it hardly matters whether we are talking about images or real people. We are concerned, instead, with conditions of existence.

It is, as I have tried to argue, at this level that a real state of emergency can be declared – one that would surpass the fake state of emergency, caught up in the logic of reality versus representation that both Steyerl in the image spam text and Sontag in "Looking at War" reproduce. If the concern is no longer reality versus image but conditions of existence, we will not try to substitute human beings by image spam people or machines but instead we will seek to change conditions of existence. It is the logic of substitution that needs to be challenged in order for oppression to stop. It will not do to put someone or something else into the position of the oppressed. That is an all too easy solution that only realizes freedom for some while maintaining the state of oppression for others. Presumably Benjamin – and both Sontag and Steyerl are clearly working in his tracks for their approach to the image – was after something else when he presented the real state of exception to us as a task.

Politics of Art and Aesthetics

Returning to the reading of Jeff Wall's work that I presented in the previous chapters, I am doubtful that Wall can be mobilized as an example of the aesthetic of the outside (if I can call it that) that Sontag is proposing. Certainly when Wall is reflecting on the politics of art, and noting that the Godardian aesthetic of the jump cut to violently disrupt the image had become "formulaic"[81] by the mid-1970s, it is not that aesthetic of the outside that he is after. Instead, as I already discussed in Chapter 6, he is interested in a moving away "from any direct interrogation of the medium and towards increasing the pressure or intensity they [artists] could bring to bear on the more or less normative, existing forms which seemed to epitomize the medium."[82] This involves "accept[ing] what the art form had become during its history": "they accepted technique, generic structure, narrative codes, problematics of performance and so on, but they broke away from the decorum of the dominant institutions."[83]

The description certainly resonates with Sontag's description of "Dead Troops Talk." And yet, the aesthetic – and aesthetic politics – that Wall draws from it seems very different: he does not end up insisting on an outside of the image, the outside that Godard with the jump cut somehow tried to bring in; instead, he insists more on the inside: technique, generic structure, narrative code, et cetera. The point, which takes us back to my discussion of Vande Veire in Chapter 1, was to accept these and strive for their uncanny inhabitation by what undermined them. Politically, these different aesthetics mark the shift from an avant-garde aesthetic that seeks to break laws – thus always dialectically imposing new ones – to letting these laws be, reorienting its (that is: the aesthetic's) forces instead toward a moving away from the decorum of dominant institutions. In his work, Wall sought to transgress "the institution of trans-gression" by "liberat[ing] what previously had to be seen as the anti-liberating elements in art"[84] – technique, genre, narrative.

I want to suggest that what Wall captures here, through his discussion of two different kinds of aesthetics, is the political difference between the two states of exception – the fake one and the real one – that I am trying to capture in this chapter. And it marks, in fact, the difference between the politics of Godard's jump cut, and the politics of music in Godard's *Notre Musique* – which incorporates the outside in an entirely different way – that I discussed in Chapter 3. On the one hand, there is the avant-gardist law-breaking/law-making that ultimately only substitutes one law for another and never really manages to create a real state of exception that would effectively end the situation that it seeks to contest. On the other, there is an aesthetic that seeks to liberate (now I will use the word, after Wall) the law in art and to make artwork starting from there. As I showed in the previous chapters, Wall importantly characterizes such a liberation as an unworking, a *désoeuvrement* or deactivation that resonates with the poetics of Agamben's messianic deactivation of the law, the real state of exception.

Wall's aesthetic intervenes, then, exactly in the problem that I raised at the beginning of this chapter, namely how to break with art and aesthetics' secret promotional campaign for the state of exception's politics of suspension? How to push art and artists from such a politics to a politics of deactivation, unworking, inoperativity?[85] If making another kind of art is the first step in this project, it is worth noting how this coincides with a moving away from what Wall calls the "decorum of dominant institutions," which shows that Wall's aesthetic is a political (as opposed to a merely legal or legalo-political) project: letting the law be, and practicing it even (for any law-breaking is also a law-making), the focus is instead on moving away from the dominant institutions that have sought to capture – institutionalize – power. At a distance from these institutions, then, and without claiming to break laws, artists arguably discover a new kind of doing that may truly deserve the name of politics: an activity that is separate from the law and dominant institutions but thinks of itself as engaging these entities through its aesthetic play.

In this context, and here I take my cue from both Steyerl and Agamben, it seems that the notion of playful yet serious "use" – of "using the law" or "using the dominant institution" – in close relation to my discussion of the term "unworking" in Chapter 6 – may be promising. In her discussion of poor images, Steyerl mentions as a key characteristic of the poor image, the way in which it is being "used." It is worth repeating her definition of the poor image to foreground this aspect of her thought. The poor image

> is a copy in motion. Its quality is bad, its resolution substandard. It is a ghost of an image, a preview, a thumbnail, an errant idea, an itinerant image distributed for free, squeezed through slow digital connections, compressed, reproduced, ripped, remixed, as well as copied and pasted into other channels of distribution.[86]

It is, Steyerl argues, as poor images that certain precious works of art – in the interview with Daniel Rourke from which I have already quoted, Rourke and Steyerl talk about Chris Marker and Alain Resnais's film on dead statues – "[come] back in form of a YouTube file replete with artifacts, cut up and dispersed in fragments across the web to live again – if only for another while."[87] This reanimation of the rare work of art as a poor image – art's second life, so to speak – is something like what Agamben calls a "profanation." Removed from the hallowed sphere of the museum or the archive, where the artworks can only be viewed, screened, or touched with extreme care (if at all!), the rare films that Steyerl mentions are profaned in the digital age as poor images, for all of us to "use." They are thus removed from the sacred sphere of the museum and (in Agamben's parlance) restored to "the free use of men."[88] In his text "In Praise of Profanation," and this is key for my argument, Agamben explicitly distinguishes such a profanation – a removal from the sphere of the gods – from a secularization that, in his view, "does nothing but displace the heavenly monarchy onto an earthly monarchy, leaving its power intact."[89] As such, secularization only furthers the state of exception of the heavens on earth. Profanation, however, deactivates it. Like the angel of history, it brings a real state of exception.

Reading Steyerl and Agamben together, one can thus characterize poor images as profane images. As I have already noted, "use" is a key problem in Agamben's work, and the assessment of its particular politics requires some care. In Chapter 6, I discussed the importance of "use" for the contemporary digital era. In his analysis of our times, and in particular of the high-tech devices governing our lives, Agamben notes that he is not interested in "another use" of technology – that would amount to a mere substitution of one use for another, and as such it would change nothing about the logic of the particular power he is criticizing. What he is after, specifically, is something more radical: another kind of use, a "common use" that would transform our notion of use without, however, entirely abolishing it. Instead, it offers a wholly transformed use (in the same way that Benjamin's strike would have us return to a wholly transformed labor). This common use, which "would think life as that which is never given as property but only as common use,"[90] is approached in his book on Franciscanism, but ultimately deferred (in the final paragraph of its preface) to "the final volume of *Homo Sacer*."[91] Its definition, however, can already be stitched together with the discussion of the real state of exception that I have developed here, as well as my remarks on deactivation, unworking, and inoperativity in the previous chapters.

Before Steyerl's and Agamben's discussions of use are equated with the horizontalism, flat ontology, or democracy of objects that I evoked in the first section of this chapter, let me insist on the ontological point that I made in my discussion of Steyerl earlier on: Steyerl's poor images are still strong images – it is their bad technical quality, or their circulation, that renders them poor. Rather than an argument for a democracy of images, then, that would make all images equal – and thus erase the verticality associated with artists, curators, art schools, museums, galleries, et cetera – she maintains this verticality but has it unworked through technology or use. With respect to Agamben, I have already discussed at the end of Chapter 4 how a sense of sovereignty is still maintained in the form-of-life of Franciscanism that Agamben praises, and in which the free use of men – common use – is a central category. So it appears that here as well, the dimension of verticality – sovereignty – is at least partly maintained. Indeed, the monks "reverse" and "absolutize" the state of exception: when all is normal, they consider their existence to be beyond the law; it is only in emergency situations that they take recourse to it. However, it is with this state of exception as it is with sovereignty among the monks: reversed and absolutized, its operation is one of de-activation rather than suspension, and in this way it manages to effectively constitute a "messianic" (according to Agamben) alternative to political theology. Here, of course, I have sought to present this "messianic" alternative as the profaning politics of art and aesthetics – I will admit that I find the notion of the profane much more promising in this context than that of the messianic, which is too caught up in the Judeo-Christian tradition and lacks the profane's broader appeal, evident from the category of "use."

Given use's inevitable proximity to the state of exception – the intimacy of the contrast between deactivation and suspension that it marks, evident, for example, in the intimate distinction between profanation and secularization on which Agamben insists – I would like to propose, in moving toward closing, an alternative (and entirely speculative) rereading of the notion of the state of exception. Etymologically, the word exception refers to a being taken outside, a paradoxical mode of being captured by being located outside (from the Latin "ex-capere").

The phrase that circulates as its near-synonym but has, at least to my ears, more positive associations – the state of emergency – is said to equally come from the Latin: emergency comes from "ex-mergere," a movement out of a sinking or dip. In view of Agamben's criticism elsewhere of the notion of "energy," from the Greek "energeia," as naming a kind of potentiality that is always already tied to an activity, specifically a work ("ergon" – "en-ergeia" literally means "in-work"), I want to propose an apocryphal, *Greek* etymology for the state of emergency, as a state where one would, rather than move out of a sinking or dip (the Latin "ex-mergere"), move out of work (the neologism "ek-ergein" instead of the common "en-ergein"), and toward a practice of use, which thus reveals itself as a form of retirement. I have argued in this chapter that it is between these two options, which can be identified with the state of exception and the real state of exception – a state of emergency or unworking – that the aesthetics and politics of sovereignty are caught up.

The politics of art and aesthetics is all too often still conceived of as a politics of the exception that would suspend "the rules governing normal experience" and mark "an innovative leap from the logic that ordinarily governs human situations" (to recall Corcoran's characterization of Rancière's politics of aesthetics). With Steyerl's poor image, however, we arrive instead at a politics of use that unworks this state of exception and proposes in its stead a state of emergency – a notion that I have "ripped" here to mean a state of moving out of work, into use. I imagine that some may find scandalous this profanation of the term emergency through a speculative etymology that no serious philologist would likely back up. But serious philology was not the point of the play I have performed: my intention was to use philology itself to operate next to the avant-gardist

324

aesthetic politics of law-breaking and law-making to propose instead an aesthetic politics that would let the law be. It is only from a certain acceptance of the law, and the inhabitation of its plural plasticity – a free and common, sovereign use of the law by people, rather than just another use of the law – that a politics on the other side of the state of exception will become possible – one that would not have to give up on sovereignty.

Coda: Sovereignty's Glitches

In the interview with Daniel Rourke from which I have already quoted, Steyerl points out the following:

> One of the biggest misunderstandings about digital information is that it is replicated identically, without loss or transformation. But anyone who works with such information knows that digital practice is constituted – like perhaps any technology – by malfunction. One has to constantly convert information in order to work with it across different platforms and softwares and on the way it is reformatted, translated, compressed or sometimes even blown up, it is enhanced or diminished: it changes. It changes its format or container or outlook or context.[92]

Again, the ontologies that are assumed here are multiple. There is, first of all, digital information, which works just fine – even if, presumably, glitches may already occur within it. There is, secondly, the replication of such information which comes, in Steyerl's experience, with loss or transformation: going back to her theory of the poor image, one could arguably speak here of digital's information being rendered poor through the replication that constitutes the information's use. Presumably, there are replications that do not produce such poverty, where information is replicated identically – but that is not what interests Steyerl. Finally, consider the list of verbs that Steyerl uses to characterize what happens to digital information under the conditions of "use": reformat, translate, compress – these are, arguably, ways in which digital information can receive form, in which it is being formed. However, Steyerl also mentions that images can be blown up. Here, she may simply be referring to the fact that they can be enlarged in the transfer; but given that she is talking about malfunction in this context, surely "blown up" in the sense of "explode" is in play here as well (use does not only give form; it also explodes it). One aspect of digital information's plasticity that is not mentioned here is its capacity to resist formation: it presumably gives form as well, resists whatever forces to which it is exposed, so as to remain, at some degree, the digital information as which it entered into use. In other words, and even if Steyerl does not talk about this, there is a limit to the information's poverty, a limit beyond which it can no longer circulate while remaining the "same" information. At this point, there would no longer be a value in the use for the use would have destroyed the very object on which it operates – it would have used it up. Circulation would have become consumption.

In this way, one could arguably speak of the plasticity of digital information, or of the plasticity of the poor image – even if Steyerl does not make these different features of digital information or the poor image explicit. While such plasticity may be typical of the contemporary era, in which digital images circulate or "tumble" at high speed, Steyerl points out that that these kinds of "poor" images are not new:

We already see it in a certain genre of wood cuts from the floating world or ukiyo of the Edo period. The ukiyo was the world of fleeting beauty and the hardship of sex work. It was also the world of countless cheap images being reproduced by printing presses, of whores, wrestlers, actors and idols, a world which was essentially fluid and full of unstable reproductions. It was considered "low" art, disposable, defined by circulation and affect.[93]

It is probably in this passage that the connection between her reflection on digital information and its glitches and her theory of the poor image becomes most clear.

The passage also proves, however, that what Steyerl has to say about digital information as a poor image is not limited to our time – indeed, images have been circulating for much longer than we have had Tumblr. More specifically, when it comes to the sovereignty that has been the central concept in this book, it is worth noting that it has always been difficult to disassociate from images and their circulation, whether those are metaphors that circulate through the text of a work of political theory or the actual visual representations that might accompany them. One of the most famous visual representations of sovereignty that I discussed in Chapter 6 is the frontispiece of Thomas Hobbes's *Leviathan* (1651), which is meant to visualize the indivisible, absolute power that Hobbes is at pains to theorize as a real unity of all. However, the art historian Horst Bredekamp has written an entire book about the image's reproductions and transformations from one edition of Hobbes's text to the next, leading Bredekamp to speak of "sovereignty's brothers," of a family of sovereigns.[94] Thus, the frontispiece of Hobbes's book is arguably already something like what Steyerl calls a "poor image" – with all of its deep ontological implications. For in this case, and in tension with the project that Hobbes in his book is trying to pull off, sovereignty's image would not refer back to some original unity that would precede the image's reality of circulation. No. Instead, sovereignty would have always already been a poor image – an image that is of a bad technical quality, and that is recirculated for widespread (democratic) use. In her discussion of digital information, Steyerl notes that digital information may share the fact that it is constituted by malfunction with "perhaps any technology." In this sense, the frontispiece of Hobbes's book as a poor image would be saying something about the technology – "the artificial man" – of sovereignty that it represents, for like this technology the image would be constituted by malfunction. Sovereignty would, as a technology, be haunted by poverty and malfunction, just like its image. Both the image and the technical object of sovereignty would, in other words, be thought here starting from their glitches, their malfunction – from how they receive, give, and explode form. And the key category in which this ontology of error would be exposed would be use.

How different this is from Badiou's discussion in his book *The Century*, in the paragraphs immediately following his theorization of art as "forcing a thinking to declare, in its area of concern, *the state of exception*" that I discussed earlier on, of Malevich's "White on White." Badiou, too, is interested in thinking a difference of the image – a difference that Steyerl calls "malfunction" or "poverty" – but he arrives at an entirely different position:

> *White on White* is – within the field of painting – the epitome of purification. Colour and form are eliminated and only a geometrical allusion is retained. This allusion is the support for a minimal difference, the abstract difference of ground and form, and above all, the null difference between white and white, the difference of the Same – what we could call the vanishing difference.

We find here the origin of a subtractive protocol of thought that differences from the protocol of destruction. We must beware of interpreting *White on White* as a symbol of the destruction of painting. On the contrary, what we are dealing with is a subtractive assumption. The gesture is very close to the one that Mallarmé makes within poetry: the staging of a minimal, albeit absolute, difference; the difference between the place and what takes place in the place, the difference between place and taking-place. Captured in whiteness, this difference is constituted through the erasure of every content, every upsurge.[95]

It could not be more different from the poor image – we move, in fact, from the difference of the *poor* image to the *pure* difference of Badiou's Malevich – and this difference resonates with my criticism of Badiou's use of the state of exception. Just to be clear: the problem here is not the insistence on difference, which Badiou and Steyerl in fact share; where they differ is in their characterization of that difference as "pure" (Badiou) versus "poor" (Steyerl). Whereas the former is arguably complicit with sovereignty, as evidenced by Badiou's flirtation with the state of exception in his characterization of politics, the latter (as I see it) breaks with the exceptionalist conception of sovereignty and thinks a precarious sovereignty and its poor power.

Moreover – and this is a second, related criticism that I want to develop – given the language of purification in the passage I quoted from Badiou, some may argue that the Malevich reading has "biopolitical" overtones and risks beginning to sound like an expression of the "internal racism of purification" that Foucault attacks in *"Society Must Be Defended."*[96] One should note, however (and in a way Badiou's entire book revolves around such a pause), that Badiou's subtraction turns biopolitics inside out – as Lyotard notes in his critique of Badiou, Badiou's state of exception is not exactly Schmitt's, and in this case as well his purification does not coincide with the biopolitical one – for if biopolitics wants purification because it attempts to be done with the difference that divides individuals and communities, the purification Badiou has in mind *reveals* such a difference. It "stages," he writes, "a minimal, albeit absolute, difference" – a statement that targets the biopolitical project that Foucault traces back to Hobbes.[97] Like biopolitics, which Foucault famously defines as the power not to kill but to keep alive, Badiou's subtraction is not destructive, but productive; however, it is productive in a wholly different way, staging difference rather than destroying it; and absolutizing it, a project that resonates with Agamben's own statement that the messianic deactivation "absolutizes" the suspension of the state of exception.

Even then, however, a question remains – and here we return to the question of the outside as it was raised in my discussion of Sontag and Steyerl. What happens after this "aesthetic" staging of difference? Badiou notes that the difference is minimal, but absolute, which means that it cannot be processed. In other words: there is no mode of political organization that will enable us to overcome this difference. This is one of the counts on which his work differs substantively from Rancière's. Whereas a theorist like Badiou insists more on the "absolute" character of the minimal difference that such a politics brings into being – it is, indeed, on this count that Badiou's and Rancière's works are more difficult to reconcile[98] – Rancière still has a firm belief in the classic democratic constitutions, a belief that sometimes appears to be lacking in the work of some other contemporary theorists. In a brief discussion of Rancière in *The Time That Remains*, Agamben in fact points out that because Rancière thinks that this difference can be "'processed,'"[99] "the line between democracy and its consensual, or postdemocratic, counterfeit ... tends to dissolve"[100] in his work. So it appears that Agamben, too, is on the side of absolute difference – of a difference that cannot be overcome by whatever political organization we propose. Hence his insistence on a potentiality not-to; his work is crucially not an exploration of actual modes of political organization, and even when he moves toward the articulation of a positive politics in his work, the challenge is precisely to articulate a form of community that would be rooted in the potentiality not-to of whatever being. He argues such a form of community – what he also calls a form-of-life, individual or collective – to be antithetical to the state. But one question that is arguably different is whether such a form-of-life is also antithetical to sovereignty, and the organization, authorship, accountability that it names and that, for example, still characterize the sovereign abbot in the Franciscan form-of-life that Agamben has proposed in response to his criticism of the state of exception.

Rather than once again opposing sovereignty to its other, the track I have chosen in this book is to engage Agamben's criticism of sovereignty's theologico-political articulation, all the while reading this as only one – albeit a dominant one – of several sovereign formations that are part and parcel of sovereignty's capacity to receive form, give form, and explode it – of sovereignty's plasticity. While this is not the way in which Agamben's work has been received – he is generally considered an anti-sovereign thinker who calls for sovereignty's destruction – there are enough instances in his work that warrant a reconsideration of this reception, leading the reader from an all too easy opposition of sovereignty to its negation ("non-sovereignty," as some may put it[101] – sovereignty's "outside," to use the terminology of this chapter) to the pursuit of a "wholly transformed" sovereignty (to recall Benjamin once again) that we could return to after the strike, when we are ready to do politics again. It may ultimately be that this return – which I have theorized in this book as "poetic," a politics at the level of "doing" – is ultimately not in conflict with the potentiality not-to – theorized in this book as "aesthetic," in close proximity with the notion of plasticity – that is the central notion in Agamben's work. For as I see it, whereas potentiality not-to, like the glitch, can exist theoretically as some kind of outside that would be untainted by actualization or form, in practice this outside is always already folded within, as a critical withdrawal or distancing from – a countering to – whatever it exists next to. As such, it can indeed never be processed – even if the history of much political and aesthetic theory has been precisely to do so. But this does not mean that it is antithetical to all political formation: the challenge is, precisely, to perpetually bring political poetics back to its aesthetic difference which I will call here, echoing both Badiou and Steyerl, a "poor difference."

This is the difference of the "flight" that Agamben has talked about in an interview to which I already referred in Chapter 1: "a flight with no elsewhere." "For me," Agamben continues, "it's a question of thinking a flight which would not imply evasion: a movement on the spot, in the situation itself."[102] This is a difficult challenge, to be sure, and one that his work does not always live up to. However, if the task of the critic is in any way similar to the task of the translator as I have discussed it in Chapter 3, it is our task as readers to reactivate the challenge of this flight in our discussion of Agamben's work and mobilize, against the all too easy evasion into an elsewhere, the "movement on the spot, in the situation itself" that he recommends. Doing so means to move from pure to poor so as to discover there what Agamben has theorized as "the highest poverty": a sovereign ("highest") poverty that, still following Benjamin's call, would bring a real state of exception to those other, theologico-political states of exception that otherwise risk saturating the aesthetico-political field.

Notes

1 Kahn, *Political Theology*, 128.
2 Schmitt, *Political Theology*, 5.
3 Badiou, *Century*, 160.
4 Badiou, *Rebirth*, 70.
5 Lacoue-Labarthe et al., "Liminaire," 242ff.
6 Corcoran, "Editor's Introduction," 1.
7 Wright, *Lexicon*, 23. When I asked the author about his use of the verb "suspend," he agreed that it was an error and should be replaced by the verb "deactivate," which I will discuss at the end of this chapter.
8 See Gielen, *Institutional Attitudes*. For two representative texts, see Isabell Lorey's and Mark Fisher's contributions to this volume, which discuss "some misgivings about horizontalism" and insist on "the need for new forms of verticality."
9 Gielen, *Institutional Attitudes*, 2. Note here that the philosopher Peter Sloterdijk, whose work I discussed in the previous chapters, is a prominent figure in Gielen's book because he recuperates verticality in his work. As a result – and Badiou anticipates this in *The Century* – he has sometimes been labeled "fascist," as if every insistence on verticality would necessarily amount to fascism. In such labeling, one finds the forces of horizontalism risking the destruction of politics altogether.
10 See Durantaye, *Giorgio Agamben*, in particular ch. 9.
11 Agamben, *TR*, 104.
12 Taubes qtd. ibid.
13 Agamben, *TR*, 104.
14 It is, I assume, part of Agamben's provocation in this context that one of the other key figures that enables this double understanding in his work is the pornographic actress, whom he theorizes as an example both of the spectacle and of the anti-spectacle. See Agamben, *PR* and Agamben, *N*.

15 Durantaye, *Giorgio Agamben*, 344.

16 Benjamin, *Illuminations*, 257.

17 Ibid.

18 Ibid., 256.

19 Ibid., 257.

20 Düttmann, "Making Poverty Visible," 1.

21 Benjamin, *Selected Works, Vol. 2*, 732.

22 Ibid.

23 Benjamin, *Illuminations*, 83–109.

24 Ibid.

25 Ibid.

26 Ibid.

27 Ibid., 734.

28 Ibid., 735.

29 Sontag, "Looking," 98.

30 Ibid.

31 Ibid.

32 Ibid.

33 Ibid.

34 Ibid.

35 Ibid.

36 Ibid., 97.

37 Ibid.

38 Derrida, *Of Grammatology*, 158.

39 See Agamben, *RA*. Geoffrey Hartman, among others, has taken Agamben to task for this. See Balfour and Comay, "Ethics."

40 Jean-François Lyotard and Marc Nichanian have, each in their respective ways, engaged this issue in their work.

41 Robbins, "Internationalism"; Sontag qtd. ibid., 11.

42 Sontag qtd. Robbins, "Internationalism," 13.

43 Robbins, "Internationalism," 13.

44 Steyerl, *Wretched*, 167.

45 Ibid., 166.

46 Ibid., 167–8.

47 Ibid., 165.

48 Ibid., 169.

49 Steyerl, "Die Gegenwart."

50 Steyerl, *Wretched*, 170.

51 Ibid., 168.

52 Ibid., 163.

53 Ibid., 165.

54 Ibid.

55 Ibid.

56 Ibid., 170.

57 Ibid., 172.

58 Ibid., 173.

59 This is what Daniel Rourke suggests in an interview with Steyerl: "You say we *are* the rubble, or at least, that we should align ourselves with the rubble." Rourke's self-correction – from "are" to "should align ourselves with" – already reveals some hesitation as to who is referred to by Steyerl's notion of "the wretched of the screen." In addition, one needs to ask about the nature of the alignment he mentions: "Spam of the Earth" ends with "love and admiration." I challenge here the politics of such an alignment, which has another "wretched of the screen" – image spam people – substitute for "us." See Rourke, "Artifacts."

60 Ibid. Rourke notes at several points in his interview with Steyerl the Benjaminian overtones of her work.

61 Steyerl, *Wretched*, 161.

62 This is a shift that I have commented on elsewhere. See Boever, *States of Exception*, 100.

63 See <http://www.marxists.org/history/ussr/sounds/lyrics/international. htm>.

64 Fanon, *Wretched*.

65 Boever, "Agamben and Marx."

66 This is a point that should have been given more attention in Srnicek and Williams, *Inventing the Future*.

67 Benjamin, "Critique," 246 / "Kritik," 194.

68 See Simondon, *Du mode d'existence*.

69 In a review of Steyerl's book, Maria Walsh has drawn out another problem with "Spam of the Earth." Noting that the text "ushers in the possibility of freedom from the oppressive normativity of representation and its claims to truth in favour of the liberty of creating new surfaces that are valued in terms of 'velocity, intensity, speed,'" Walsh responds that these tropes "epitomize the forces of neoliberal capitalism that Steyerl exhorts us to join forces against" (Walsh, "Rev."). She thus uncovers what others – most notably the French philosopher of technology Bernard Stiegler – have also called the "pharmakon" of the digital in Steyerl's analysis.

70 Steyerl, "Defense," 1.

71 Ibid.

72 Elsewhere, Steyerl has noted that her work is "not about object-ontologies but image-actions, image-gestures, thing-affinities, changes of reactions of objects, forces, and pixels, that manifest in scars and bruises, but also sometimes in the liquid harmony of the floating world of images." Leaving aside here whether this qualifies as ontology or not – I personally think the list of terms moves from action to ontology – Steyerl's discussion of the poor image assumes different image-ontologies that should be recovered if one wants to assess the politics of poor images. See Rourke, "Artifacts."

73 Steyerl, "Defense," 8.

74 Benjamin, *Illuminations*, 217–51.

75 Steyerl, "Defense," 4.

76 Ibid., 6.

77 Ibid., 8.

78 Ibid.

79 Rourke, "Artifacts."

80 Steyerl, "Defense," 8.

81 Pelenc, "Conversation,"11.

82 Ibid.

83 Ibid.

84 Ibid., 17.

85 Elsewhere, I have argued that Igor Toshevski's "Free Territory" project raises precisely this issue. See Boever, *States of Exception*.

86 Steyerl, "Defense," 1.

87 Rourke, "Artifacts."

88 Agamben, *PR*, 3.

89 Ibid., 77.

90 Agamben, *HP*, xiii.

91 Ibid.

92 Rourke, "Artifacts."

93 Ibid.

94 See Bredekamp, *Thomas Hobbes*.

95 Badiou, *Century*, 55–6.

96 Foucault, *"Society Must Be Defended,"* 62.

97 In a lecture on Hobbes that is part of *"Society Must Be Defended,"* Foucault argues that contrary to what one might think at first sight, Hobbes is not a theorist of war but a theorist against war, a theorist of peace (this is a point I will return to in the final chapter of this book). The point of Hobbes's political theory, as developed in *Leviathan*, was to tell a story:

human beings close a contract, enter into a society, and ultimately found a legal and political order (protected by a sovereign, and called sovereign – for it coincides with the body of the sovereign) that will prevent the "war of all against all" that characterizes the state of nature from ever breaking out again. As Foucault explains, Hobbes's attempt to eradicate war from sovereignty was already heavily contested in Hobbes's time by various sectarian factions who instead insisted on the war-like dimension of sovereignty and resistance. Over the course of the lectures, Foucault suggests that it is the *pacifying* dimension of Hobbes's thought, in other words Hobbes's attempt to *eradicate* war from sovereignty, that ultimately leads into biopolitics and the difference it targets: society must be defended against those alien elements that risk dissolving it – that is the biopolitical motto of state racism that the title of Foucault's course evokes, and that Foucault already finds enacted in Hobbes's theory of peace. This means that what Foucault calls biopolitics historically develops out of Hobbes's attempt to erase war from politics, his attempt to think political society as separate from war. My aim here is to bring some of that war back in – but not at the cost of all sovereignty.

98 Note, however, that in the case of Badiou, there is an insistence on the question of organization – which is not the same, of course, as the "processing" of democracy's absolute difference – that has always also been prominent. Most relevant here is no doubt Badiou's analysis of the Arab Spring. See Badiou, *Rebirth*, 42 (for example).

99 Rancière qtd. Agamben, *TR*, 58.

100 Agamben, *TR*, 58.

101 See my Prologue.

102 Smith, "'I am sure,'" 121.

9

Formations of Infancy

Democratizing emergency means seeking sovereignty, not just challenging it, and insisting that sovereignty is not just a trait of executive power that must be chastened but also potentially a trait of popular power as well, one to be generated and mobilized. Rather than oppose democracy and emergency, then, we might think about democratic opportunities to claim sovereignty even in emergency settings. (Bonnie Honig, "Three Models of Emergency Politics")[1]

Acknowledging the political dimension of critical artistic interventions in an agonistic way supposes challenging the idea that to be political means to offer a radical critique requiring a total break with the existing state of affairs. (Chantal Mouffe, *Agonistics*)[2]

From Philosophy to Literature

At the end of my Prologue, I arrived – via Catherine Malabou's lecture "Odysseus' Changed Soul" – at a theory of "poor sovereignty," of a sovereign disguised as a beggar who for a moment enforces what Malabou understands to be an "ontological displacement" of the risk of abuse that sovereignty carries within it. Odysseus – the poor sovereign – thus becomes a figure of a non-sovereign sovereignty: living his life again, he chooses a normal, uninteresting, boring life of withdrawal from the crowd, and it is from this "private" position that he insists on his kingship – *against* the abuse he is facing upon his return home. Discussing Giorgio Agamben's work toward the end of her lecture, Malabou suggests (correctly, I think) that Herman Melville's scrivener Bartleby operates in Agamben's work as a figure of the non-sovereign or poor sovereignty that she theorizes, and in this chapter I want to develop that suggestion in detail in order to see how it might help us to better articulate a theory of a poverty that would unwork the tyrannical aspects of sovereignty but *without losing sovereignty altogether.*

The argument I want to make is simple: while I agree with Malabou that Melville's Bartleby figures in Agamben's work as a model for such a sovereignty, I think that as such, Bartleby is too close to the destruction of sovereignty that Agamben's work flirts with. He is too close to non-sovereignty in order to still be sovereign, and Malabou seems to be struggling with this precise issue in her lecture. Indeed, I find it very difficult to see the connections between Odysseus the beggar, living a new, uninteresting, normal, boring life in private withdrawal and then reappearing on the scene of abusive sovereignty, and Bartleby, repeating the same nonsensical formula over and over again, and ultimately withdrawing into silent occupation. What future for sovereignty is there in Bartleby's silent withdrawal? It seems to me that there is none, and of course that might be precisely the point, the reason why Agamben is so interested in Bartleby: because he is a figure of the death of sovereignty that I evoked in my Prologue.

However, and going back to the arguments that I have laid out in the previous chapters (particularly in Chapters 1 and 6), I feel that such a withdrawal into silence – as opposed to sovereign speech – does not transform sovereignty but merely opposes it to its opposite, thus participating in the infernal dialectic of silence and a certain kind of speech that much of Agamben's work on sovereignty and language seeks to deconstruct. Indeed, if there is one lesson in Agamben's work, it is that there are other ways of speaking, ways that would carry silence within them without ending speech altogether. If Odysseus the poor beggar is a figure of what could be called the "remains" of sovereignty, it would seem essential here, when dealing with Bartleby, to uncover these "remains" in Melville's story, at some distance from both sovereign speech and Bartleby's progress into silence. Crucially, Agamben proposes "infancy" as a third term in this debate: neither silence nor speech, it names the potentiality not-to-speak. If – big IF – Agamben's work still contains a figure of sovereignty, it will need to be one that is closely linked to infancy. The challenge, then, would be to uncover Bartleby's infancy: neither his silence nor his speech, but his potentiality not-to-speak.

In what follows, and going back to the argument about storytelling that I made in Chapter 2, I propose that *not* Bartleby the scrivener *but* "Bartleby, the Scrivener" – that is: *not* the actual scrivener, *but* the story that Herman Melville or Melville's anonymous narrator, a lawyer, is telling about him – is the figure of that other sovereignty. The story is what I call a "formation of infancy," a sovereign expression of non-sovereignty that in its (still) sovereign expression unworks the silence/speech opposition that reflects the structure of sovereignty (captured by the pair *zoe/bios*), thus pushing that sovereign expression towards non-sovereignty. This develops the aesthetic argument that I have been building over the previous chapters into the region of poetics, of a poetic sovereignty that would – crucially, in its *formation* – supplement the aesthetic sovereignty (focused on challenging a distribution rather than on proposing a formation) that I have theorized.

Malabou and Agamben are thus both right and wrong: while they are right to draw attention to Bartleby in this context, they are wrong to focus so much on the scrivener himself, thus forgetting the very mediation that enables them to know about the scrivener in the first place. Indeed, had it been left up to Bartleby, there likely would not have been a story at all. The scrivener would simply have preferred for it not to be written. That would be the "silence of the law" that I have criticized in Chapter 7 as a naïve conception of freedom, one that perpetuates the structure of sovereignty. As I showed in Chapter 8, this conception of freedom is very well represented in art theory. The true power of the reference to Bartleby, however, lies in the fact that he evokes an impossible story, a story that is told *in spite of* the impossibility of its own telling. Thus, the story marks – like Odysseus the beggar – the entrance of Bartleby's normal, uninteresting, boring withdrawal into privacy *into* the (public) crowd, but without flipping over into sovereignty and its tyrannical abuse (which would mean a complete, total giving in to sovereign speech). And this suspension, this ontological displacement that Bartleby accomplishes, is not temporary: emerging at a time when American (US) democracy was undergoing profound transformations (as Andrew Delbanco in his discussion of the story in his book on Melville has shown[3]), it has lasted until today, establishing itself as a classic – something not temporary but eternal – infecting those who read it, or even just hear about it, with Bartleby's formulaic phrase that haunts the text: "I prefer not to."

What is important about this phrase is not so much whether it says "yes" or "no" or something that is neither (one of the concerns that dominate Gilles Deleuze's reading of the story[4]). What matters is that "I prefer not to" is a kind of speech that in its proximity to silence – for what is Bartleby actually saying when he says "I prefer not to"? – and in its "progress into silence" (as one of the critics of the story puts it),[5] actually seems to become a formation of infancy, and thus a poetic extension of the (aesthetico-political) storytelling and the translatability/communicability that I theorized in Chapters 2 and 3 of this book. However, this claim will have to be nuanced as we go along. For the scrivener thus becomes tied to the formula, which becomes tied to the story, which as an impossible representation comes to mark a non-sovereign sovereignty that, as I will go on to show, also happens to be the story's central thematic concern; at that point, however, we will have taken up quite some distance from the scrivener and his formula, which is – crucially – not a story. If Agamben and Malabou directed their gazes away from the scrivener, and towards the story – and turn from philosophers into literary critics – I think their thoughts would meet, and would yield the notion of a plastic sovereignty of Melville's story that splices together Agamben's and Malabou's work.

A Slip of the Tongue?

In a short essay entitled "Beyond Human Rights," Agamben departs from a paradox he finds in the work of Hannah Arendt: "that the very figure who should have embodied the rights of man par excellence – the refugee – signals instead the concept's radical crisis."[6] He argues, following Arendt, that "[i]n the system of the nation-state, so-called sacred and inalienable human rights are revealed to be without any protection precisely when it is no longer possible to conceive of them as the rights of the citizens of a state."[7] Echoing Karl Marx's position in "On the Jewish Question," Agamben suggests this is implicit in the

> ambiguity of the very title of the 1789 *Déclaration des droits de l'homme et du citoyen*, in which it is unclear whether the two terms are to name two distinct realities or whether they form, instead, a hendiadys in which the first term is actually always already contained in the second.... The status of the refugee has always been considered a temporary condition that ought to lead either to naturalization or to repatriation. A stable statute for the human in itself is inconceivable in the law of the nation-state.[8]

Agamben argues that the refugee should be considered as a "limit-concept that at once brings a radical crisis to the principles of the nation-state and clears the way for a renewal of categories that can no longer be delayed."[9] Industrialized countries today are facing a

> permanently resident mass of noncitizens who do not want to be and cannot be either naturalized or repatriated. These noncitizens often have nationalities of origin, but, inasmuch as they *prefer not to* benefit from their own states' protection, they find themselves, as refugees, in a condition of de facto statelessness [emphasis mine].[10]

Agamben ends by envisioning a community "in which the guiding concept would no longer be the *ius* (right) of the citizen but rather the *refugium* (refuge) of the singular."[11]

It is interesting that Agamben uses the phrase "prefer not to" to describe the refugee's condition of statelessness. Although the phrase is neither quoted nor italicized, "prefer not to" can be read as a reference to Melville's story "Bartleby, the Scrivener," in which a law-copyist brings a crisis to his employer's offices through his repeated use of the phrase "prefer not to." In the same year in which "Beyond Human Rights" was published, Agamben also wrote an extended commentary on Melville's story entitled "Bartleby, or On Contingency."[12] Even though nothing suggests that his use of Bartleby's phrase in "Beyond Human Rights" was intentional – perhaps his contact with the scrivener had simply uncannily "affected [him] in a mental way" and gotten him, as with Melville's narrator and characters, "into the way of involuntarily using the word 'prefer' upon all sorts of not exactly suitable occasions"[13] – I choose to read Agamben's slippage as an invitation to think of Bartleby as a figure who brings a radical crisis to the debates on sovereignty that Agamben's work takes part in.

A revised version of "Beyond Human Rights" was later published in *Homo Sacer: Sovereign Power and Bare Life.*[14] In an article about this book, political scientist and philosopher Andreas Kalyvas points out that "[t]here are two lines of arguments that implicate rights" in Agamben's work, "two readings that coexist uneasily in Agamben's text."[15] While in the one reading, the nation has to "divest" its citizens of their rights in order to reduce them to a life that can be killed without legal consequences, the other argues that the "granting of rights is one of the constitutive operations" by which the nation exercises its "biopower" over the life of its citizens.[16] If we add to this, as Kalyvas does, "Agamben's assertion that the new politics will be a 'nonstatal and nonjuridical politics,' his vision of the coming community comes dangerously close to one of an extralegal, permanent (though sovereignless) exception" that Agamben is trying to criticize.[17] I have engaged this point – the two states of exception in Agamben's work, one positive and one negative – in the previous chapter.

This brings Kalyvas, whose research has focused on the "politics of the extraordinary" (rather than "the exceptional") in the work of Max Weber, Carl Schmitt, and Arendt,[18] to ask two questions. First, whether there is indeed, as Agamben argues, an "intrinsic bond" between sovereign power and what Agamben calls "bare life."[19] In the previous chapters, I have addressed this question by exposing the ontology of sovereignty and unworking it with an ontogenetic conception of sovereignty. And, second (and this is the other question that is central to my project): "[I]s a sovereignless community an adequate and persuasive solution to this problem?"[20] My concern in this chapter will be, specifically, with how Melville's story about Bartleby relates to this second question. Like Agamben, Kalyvas is convinced that "the concept of sovereignty needs to be radically rethought today."[21] Unlike Agamben, however (or unlike Agamben as Kalyvas understands him), Kalyvas does not think sovereignty should be rejected: "To insist on the significance of sovereignty, despite its paradoxes and transgressions, is to insist on its strongly egalitarian and democratic implications."[22] In this, Kalyvas echoes the editors of *Politics Without Sovereignty*, a book I already mentioned in my Prologue. If Bartleby, by his refusal to comply with Melville's narrator's requests – "made according to common usage and common sense"[23] – upsets the community of the law office and forces it to proceed in a way that was "quite out of the common,"[24] how can the "uncommon," "extraordinary" response that Bartleby demands be described? Can Bartleby, like

Agamben's refugee, be considered as a "limit-concept that ... clears the way for a renewal of categories"[25] in our conception of sovereignty? Does such a renewal of categories amount to a destruction of sovereignty? Does it amount to a change within sovereignty? If so, what could such a new conception of sovereignty look like?

Politics of the Story (1)

As I see it, to answer this question it is crucial that one distinguish between Bartleby the scrivener and "Bartleby, the Scrivener": between Melville's actual scrivener and the story that Melville's anonymous narrator writes about him. Let's begin by considering what many philosophers and critical theorists who refer to Bartleby overlook, namely the form of Melville's story, so as to then think through the politics of this form.

As literary critics of the story have pointed out, Melville's account of Bartleby's life is framed by a prologue and an epilogue in which the narrator reflects on the impossibility of writing precisely such an account. "While of other law-copyists, I might write the complete life," the narrator notes at the beginning of the story, "of Bartleby nothing of that sort can be done."[26] This claim is repeated at the end of story, when the narrator regrets that he is "wholly unable to gratify"[27] the reader's curiosity. The prologue and epilogue thus indicate that Melville's story is rethinking its own representative power and specifically its power to represent or write "life." Before the story begins and after it has been completed, its narrator takes care to point out that the story's subject – Bartleby, the scrivener – interrupts the totalizing aspirations of the biographical, life-writing project.

346

Instead of offering its readers the full story of Bartleby's life, Melville's account of the "unaccountable"[28] Bartleby is instituted as an "irreparable loss to literature,"[29] as a life that cannot be written. The prologue and the epilogue realize an "unworking" of the narrator's work (to mobilize the terminology that was developed in the previous chapters, especially in Chapter 6): Bartleby forces the narrator to forgo the biography's promise of fullness and satisfaction and to emphasize instead its limitations. Bartleby's life marks biography's limit.

Interestingly, the crisis that Bartleby brings to the narration reflects the scrivener's subversion of the narrator's law office. There is thus a connection that is established in the story between the biographical project of representing or writing life, and the question of life's relation to law: Bartleby's life not only poses a limit to biography and its attempt to write it; it also poses a limit to the writing of the law (an idea that, via Franz Kafka, takes up an important place in Agamben's work, as I discussed in previous chapters). Here, I want to focus more on the crisis that Bartleby brings to the concept of the political that circulates in Melville's story. For the law office is not only a representative of the law; it is also a space in which different figures live together, and as such it marks a political space to which Bartleby also brings a crisis. How is one to read the story as a dramatization of different conceptualizations of the political?

Although the narrator, a lawyer, belongs to a "profession proverbially energetic and nervous,"[30] he emphasizes that he has never let any of that turbulence invade his peace. His friends and colleagues consider him to be an "eminently safe man" whose first "grand point" is prudence;[31] the second, method. Confronted with the afternoon eccentricities of his employee

Turkey – eccentricities that he is willing to overlook because of Turkey's quick and steady work in the morning – he only occasionally and always "very gently" and "very kindly" remonstrates his employee for the blots he drops on the narrator's legal documents.[32] His other employee Nippers's morning tooth grinding, hissed maledictions, and continual discontent with the height of his working table the narrator is also willing to tolerate: Nippers writes a neat, swift hand and dresses "in a gentlemanly sort of way" that reflects positively on the office.[33]

Bartleby brings a crisis to the easy life of this man of peace. When the scrivener "prefers not to" verify the accuracy of his own copying, the narrator loses his calm: he rises "in high excitement" from behind his desk to "cross the room with a stride."[34] At a later point in the story, when he is calling for Bartleby and receives no answer, he "roars";[35] he also notes that "[h]ad there been anything ordinarily human about [Bartleby], doubtless I should have violently dismissed him."[36] There is something about Bartleby, however, that "not only strangely disarmed me," the narrator notes, "but, in a wonderful manner, touched and disconcerted me."[37] Although the story never makes it explicit what this disarming "something" might be, it seems to be related to the mildness and gentleness of Bartleby's resistance: to the fact that Bartleby, like the narrator, is a man of peace.

Whereas Turkey and Nippers (and also the third employee, Ginger Nut) are noisy and energetic characters, Bartleby appears on the scene as a calm, silent, "motionless young man" who seems to be "of so singularly sedate an aspect" that the narrator hopes "it might operate beneficially upon the flighty temper of Turkey, and the fiery one of Nippers."[38] He expects the scrivener will function as some kind of neutralizer who would save the law office from the eccentricities of its employees by turning their seesaw-performance into a steady excellence. The neutralization, however, happens elsewhere: whereas the narrator by hiring Bartleby had thought to reinforce his authority, the scrivener instead exposes the narrator's impotence. "Indeed," the narrator notes, "it was [Bartleby's] wonderful mildness chiefly, which not only disarmed me, but unmanned me as it were."[39] Nippers and Turkey appear largely unaffected.

The crisis that is found at the level of the narration can be read as a reflection of the story's portrayal of the crisis produced through the confrontation between two men of peace. The difficulty that Melville's story presents lies in the conceptualization of such a dispute. After all is said and done, the narrator and Bartleby can only remain in their state of what Jean-François Lyotard has called a "differend."[40] The differend demands that the law office be rethought not as a space of war but as a space of agonistics (to use a concept that has been most powerfully developed by Chantal Mouffe[41]) – a space of "gaming" in which the aim is not to win but to continuously and collaboratively reinvent the game.[42] The narrator seems to think that such a reconceptualization implies a castration. Although at first, he decides to tolerate Bartleby's subversive behavior, he will ultimately tear himself away from the scrivener, and change his offices. Instead of responding to the demand of the differend by rethinking the law office as an agonistic space, he decides to move his offices. But what power is there in a peace that cannot acknowledge dispute? What concept of the political can such a concept of peace provide? By turning away from the differend, by moving his offices away from the place where a peaceful but ultimately irresolvable conflict exists, the narrator – a "Master in Chancery" at the time when the story is taking place[43] – misses a tremendous opportunity, namely the chance, opened up by Bartleby, to conceptualize peace as a political state that does not exclude conflict: the conflictual peace or "conflictual consensus"[44] of the living, rather than the perpetual peace of the dead evoked by Immanuel Kant at the beginning of "Perpetual Peace."

As I already suggested in my Prologue, the conflict that is staged here – the political antagonism that is played out here – is central to sovereignty and rethinks the friend/enemy distinction that according to Schmitt structures sovereignty. The narrator is stuck in the friend/enemy distinction but cannot bring himself to existentially negate Bartleby: all he can do is to remove himself from the premises of his law office, thus effectively allowing Bartleby to remain (and accomplishing what the story suggests is the castration or unmanning of the narrator's sovereignty). However, a concept of sovereignty could be construed around the "conflictual peace" that Bartleby seems to invite and that presents a concept of the political that obviously neither coincides exactly with the figure of the friend nor with the figure of the enemy. One would need to be able to think a conflictual friend, or an enemy with whom one exists in peace, as sovereignty's central figure. This is precisely the challenge that Melville's story poses.

Let me translate the conclusions I have reached into two closely related points that Melville's story is making. The first one is connected to what Delbanco refers to as Melville's "democratic imagination."[45] By its emphatic attention to the limits that Bartleby poses to representation, Melville's story reveals itself to the reader as a critique of the processes of "naming, enumerating, counting,"[46] and the fragmentation into closed identities that take place in representative democracies.

Within the context of a much older and larger debate on representation, multiculturalism has led to a contemporary political situation (intensified, one could argue, by a digital culture of surveillance) in which it has become increasingly difficult to remain indeterminate – to withdraw from representation (to recall Hito Steyerl's work on this issue, discussed in Chapter 8). The "unaccountable" scrivener, however, demands precisely that: he wants to be present without letting himself be defined, accounted for, explained. His "peace" is, unlike the narrator's, close to Agamben's "Idea of Peace," as I discussed it at the end of Chapter 2: "Not the appeal to guaranteed signs, or images, but the fact that we cannot recognize ourselves in any sign or image: that is peace."[47]

However, it is crucial to see that although the politics of Bartleby the scrivener can perhaps be allied with such a project of withdrawing from representation, Melville's story "Bartleby, the Scrivener" cannot: for it is, after all, a representation, one that carries the impossibility of representation within it but remains a representation nevertheless. Agamben's "Idea of Peace," in this context, would not so much have to be read as a complete giving up on signs or images but as a call for *another use* of signs or images, in the same way that a critique of multiculturalism or representative democracy's identity politics does not necessarily add up to a call for the destruction of identity or representation. The politics of the story is decidedly different from Bartleby's politics.

Both Nippers, who thinks of Bartleby's position as a temporal condition, "a passing whim,"[48] and the narrator, who would like to return Bartleby to "his native place,"[49] are unable to conceive of the scrivener as a person beyond the dichotomy of naturalization and repatriation that also dominates the condition of Agamben's refugee, and that challenges (according to Agamben) the conception of human rights. In other words: they are incapable of rethinking representation outside of the silence (repatriate)/speech (naturalize) binary. In this context, it is worthwhile noting that Melville's story performs a humanization of the scrivener that runs parallel to the attempt at naturalizing him/bringing him into speech. Whereas at the beginning of the story, the narrator observes that there is nothing "ordinarily human"[50] about Bartleby, his figuration of the scrivener changes over the course of the story and leads him to exclaim at the very end "Ah! Bartleby! Ah! humanity!"[51] – the use of parataxis possibly suggesting that for him, Bartleby somehow represents humanity as such.

It is interesting to see, however, and this is a second point I want to make, how this shift from the inhuman to the human is established. In a passage that is written very much in the same tone as the exclamations I just quoted, Melville's narrator suggests that it was "the divine injunction: 'A new commandment give I unto you, that ye love one another'"[52] that saved him. The reference to the commandment to "love your neighbor as yourself" allows us to situate Melville's story in the debates on the theologico-political in which Agamben's work, and the dialogue it stages between Walter Benjamin and Carl Schmitt, takes up an important position. In the end, after all attempts to rationalize the scrivener's behavior have failed, it is religiously inspired "charity" that makes the narrator "indulge" Bartleby and allows the narrator to let Bartleby remain in the law office "for as long as [he] see[s] fit."[53] The narrator's final decision to remove his offices is taken only under the pressure of "the constant friction of illiberal minds," he writes, "that wears out at last the best resolves of the more generous."[54] The story shows how the inhuman Bartleby is slowly but surely molded into a figure of humanity as such. This molding is achieved by figuring Bartleby as our neighbor, whom we should – according to the divine injunction – love as ourselves.

Whereas the inhuman Bartleby could have allowed the narrator to turn Bartleby into a figure not just of human rights, but rather of inhuman rights, of the rights of those who are not considered human, he instead decides to appropriate Bartleby's being as the very figure of our common humanity. What we see happening here, and what we may want to resist, is a version of what Slavoj Žižek has referred to as "the ethical 'gentrification' of the neighbor."[55] It is useful to also recall at this point Agamben's critique of the concept of dignity in the second chapter of *Remnants of Auschwitz: The Witness and the Archive*. Shouldn't human rights first and foremost aim to protect those who have lost all humanity, those who are considered to belong to the community-without-community of the inhuman? Bartleby resists both the multiculturalist logic of "naming, counting, enumerating" and the ethico-theological gentrification that still dominates the contemporary political climate.

Here too, however, and before I am misunderstood, I must add a caveat. By casting Bartleby as a figure of what today is being called the "posthuman," I do not seek to throw out the humanizing impulse that would seek to recognize Bartleby as human. Posthumanism never sought to entirely abandon the notion of the human, in the same way that postmodernism never sought to entirely abandon the notion of the modern: why else would these terms – post-X – keep the term they seek to abandon (X) as part of their name? Instead, post-X marks a critical intensification of X that, in the case of posthumanism, draws out the politics of inclusion and of exclusion that have constituted the category of the human. In this sense, post-humanism is precisely about drawing attention to those who, when it comes to figuring the human, have been thought to be "in" or "out." My criticism of Bartleby's humanization, then – of the way the human operates in Melville's story as a condition for the narrator to treat the scrivener in a certain way – does not intend to abandon the notion of the human, but to show precisely how it operates in the story as a condition for care. And it is in this context that I wonder whether, in response to the denial of one's humanity, it is most productive, politically, to insist on one's humanity. For doing so would merely keep the notion of the human intact, without unworking its politics. "No, you are not human!" / "Yes, I am human!" – *ad infinitum.*

As an aside, let me offer this example: Art Spiegelman's *Maus*, a graphic novel about the Holocaust, begins with a motto by Adolph Hitler. It says: "The Jews are undoubtedly a race, but they are not human."[56] In response, one could insist on the humanity of the Jewish people: "You are wrong: the Jewish people are human!" But that is not what happens in Spiegelman's book: the Jewish people are represented as mice. However, they are not the only "race" that is represented as animals. The Germans too, are animals (cats). In other words: Spiegelman's response is not to insist on the humanity of the Jewish people, but to represent *everyone* as animals. His project is thus to rethink humanity through this becoming-animal. I have always thought there was more value to this approach than to approaches that keep intact the standard of the human, and merely add more and more groups of people to the family of humans. Whereas the latter always create further exclusions of non-humans, the former simply equalizes everyone at the level of animals, and starts again from there.

In her work on these issues, Judith Butler has written insightfully about the "differential norm" of the human.[57] Holding on to the notion of the human as a category, she nevertheless reconfigures it as a "differential" notion, that is: as a notion that is filled with meaning in the different contexts in which it is being used. It is, therefore, not a stable value, but one that is perpetually shifting and it seems to me that whatever humanistic politics we adhere to – whether it is the humanism of the Enlightenment, or the so-called black humanism or other humanisms that are critical of it – will need to confront this fact.[58] This does not mean that the norm of the human is left behind. It merely means that it becomes, in Butler's terminology, a norm infused with difference. This is, indeed, precisely what Michel Foucault in his essay on the Enlightenment tried to point out, when he worked hard to disentangle the Enlightenment from humanism. In order for humanism to become "enlightened" in Foucault's sense of the term, that is: in order for humanism to adopt the philosophical attitude, ethos, or life that he theorizes in his text – an attitude of perpetual questioning – it would need to disentangle itself not just from certain understandings of the Enlightenment, but precisely also from any stable value of the human that would ultimately interfere with such a critical project. It is to such a reading of Bartleby as a figure of the posthuman that I seek to contribute by challenging the narrator's humanization of the scrivener as a condition for care.[59] I challenge that condition by rethinking our motivations to care from the bottom up: not by lifting those who deserve our care into the realm of precious humanity, but by bringing down our own precious humanity to the level of those who are supposedly outside of it, in order to begin to care again from those other grounds.

Politics of Language (1)

Melville's story has thus revealed itself, starting from a consideration of its peculiar form, as a literary text that mobilizes many of the concerns central to the debate on "sovereignty" that drive Agamben's work. If what sets Agamben's work apart is to a certain extent his tying of these political concerns to linguistic issues, this dimension too can be pursued in Melville's story.

Indeed, the story problematizes the politics of communication and specifically language in the context of the political reflection it develops. In his book *Just Gaming*, the already mentioned Lyotard suggests that language for us is first and foremost someone talking. He argues, however, that there are language games in which the important thing is to listen, in which the rule deals with audition. And he suggests that such a game is the game of the just.[60] Bartleby, who is ultimately forced to quit the narrator's premises and is imprisoned in a section of the Tombs called the Halls of Justice,[61] invites a game of listening rather than of talking. It is precisely this listening that the narrator in the story fails to achieve. When Bartleby arrives at the office, the narrator "procure[s] a high green folding screen" which is meant to "isolate Bartleby from [his] sight, though not remove him from my voice."[62] While this is a move in the right direction, an important change still needs to be made: it is the narrator, and by extension the reader, who must try – even though there is a screen (of time, space, text) blocking Bartleby from view – not to be removed from *the scrivener's* voice.

So what is it that Bartleby is saying? On the third day of his new job, after Bartleby has already done "an extraordinary quantity of writing," the necessity arises for "having [Bartleby's] writing examined."[63] When the narrator calls out to Bartleby "to verify the accuracy of his copy," Bartleby replies in a "mild, firm voice" that he "would prefer not to."[64] It is worthwhile emphasizing, in this context, that Bartleby's first refusal is not a refusal to copy. Instead, he is refusing to verify the accuracy of his copy – he simply prefers not to verify whether his copy is identical to the original. To him, it does not matter whether the copy is accurate. By giving back a copy that he refuses to verify, one could argue that Bartleby interrupts the communication of the copy. He interrupts the sign of the copy and turns it into pure value instead: it no longer needs a symbolic life – meaning – to be added to it in order to be of value. Symbolic meaning doesn't matter; all that matters is the materiality of the copy.

It is not a coincidence that Gilles Deleuze has characterized Bartleby's phrase as a "formula" and that Tom Cohen's text on Bartleby is the centerpiece of the "material" readings collected in his book *Anti-Mimesis from Plato to Hitchcock*.[65] For Bartleby, language is not transparent but material. During his first days in the law office, the narrator writes, "Bartleby did an extraordinary quantity of writing. As if long famishing for something to copy, he seemed to gorge himself on my documents. There was no pause for digestion."[66] There is a kind of letter-eating going on here, perhaps even (if we recall the association between Bartleby and the dead letter office) a kind of auto-cannibalism. Bartleby consumes the documents that he is asked to copy, as if the letters of the documents are something material, cakes that can be eaten. Bartleby's interruption of the copy should not be read as an interruption against the copy. What is interrupted is not so much the copying as the sign of the copy, its *exchange* of the meaning of the original. Thus, Bartleby establishes a shift from communication to what I will call here, recalling Chapters 1 and 3, "the vulgar materiality of language." *But that is only the first step.*

Once again, Bartleby's subversion of the space of the law office becomes particularly interesting when it is articulated legalo-politically. In the end, the problem that Bartleby poses to the narrator is a magnified version of his invitation to go beyond the horizon of communication. He would like to remain within the protective realm of the law office without giving the office anything in return other than his mere being. Bartleby's demand, an appeal to an extraordinary generosity on the side of the narrator, is to be allowed to remain unconditionally within the protective space of the law office. Bartleby thus interrupts the political economy of the law office, not in order to destroy it but to invite *another use of it*. In his recent discussion of Benjamin's reading of Kafka, Agamben suggests something along similar lines: he argues that for Benjamin, "[w]hat opens a passage toward justice is not the erasure of the law, but its de-activation and inactivity [inoperosità] – that is, another use of the law."[67] Although the narrator may not have learned Bartleby's lesson as a lawyer, I would argue that he *did* learn it as a narrator: the prologue and epilogue to the story push the text precisely toward the kind of deactivation and dereliction that Benjamin is talking about.

The question is, however, whether – from an Agambenian point of view – this "material" turn of the story is "enough" to capture the story's politics, and its engagement with sovereignty. My concern is that in the *zoe/bios* pair, where *zoe* stands for the mere materiality of language and *bios* for the symbolic meaning added to it, the materialist reading of the story – focused on the formula and the scrivener, who mean "nothing" other than their material existence – comes down entirely on the side of *zoe*, thus effectively doing violence to Melville's story, which is a great story not so much because it is limited to Bartleby's formula but because that formula becomes part of a story that does more than "preferring not to" (the story is not simply an accumulation of "I prefer not to"-s). While Melville's story certainly moves towards that materialist dimension, I would argue that as a story, it contracts the symbolic dimension of language into language's material dimension in a new way, practicing the symbolic such that it carries this material dimension within it as its unworking – rendering the material symbolic without fully flipping over into it. Turning the story into a form-of-life, which thus stands as an answer to the production of bare life that the story problematizes.

If the story represents law as a dimension of the broader field of investigation called "sovereignty," and if Bartleby represents the life that "escapes" sovereignty – a limit that this life shares with the Schmittian sovereignty that decides on the exception and that thus is always partly within, partly outside the law – then the value of Melville's story is not so much that it enforces the law or comes down entirely on the side of life's escape from it but that it offers its readers a new law within which Bartleby's life finds refuge – in-between Bartleby's progress into silence, and the law's tendency towards speech. A new kind of speech is indeed being invented in the story: I agree with many of the story's commentators on that. But that new kind of speech is not Bartleby's "material" formula. Instead, it is the way in which this materiality of language, linked to Bartleby's simple fact of living, is contracted into the symbolic life of language – and by implication the structure of the law office – that surrounds it.

The tragedy of the story, at the level of its engagement with sovereignty, is that *the law office* turns out to be incapable in the story of contracting Bartleby into its protective space in this way. Bartleby is ultimately locked away in the Tombs prison to die.

However, Melville's *story* does manage to contract Bartleby into its limits and in this way it succeeds where the law office does not. Literature brings something to sovereignty here that exceeds the ontology of *zoe/bios* – and its inevitable generation of bare life, as I discussed in the previous chapters – that displaces this ontology outside of the silence/speech, material/symbolic binaries of the concept, and that thus accomplishes – quite like Odysseus the beggar in Malabou's reading – a renewal of categories within the sphere of sovereignty (and as I indicated in my discussion of *The Highest Poverty* in Chapter 4, I do consider form-of-life to be a form of sovereignty). *The story* "Bartleby, the Scrivener" is a figure of the poor sovereignty that Malabou advocates: the non-sovereign sovereignty that she pleads for in her lecture "Odysseus' Changed Soul." In Agamben's terms, Melville's story is a formation of infancy that, in-between silence and speech, practices a different kind of speech that would be able to provide refuge for the silence of life. *Zoe* and *bios*, material and symbolic life thus become contracted in an entirely new way, beyond the two bodies of sovereignty, into what I have called here a plastic sovereignty that in Melville's story finds its poetic articulation. The actual Bartleby merely marks the explosive limit of sovereignty: bare life, which, in its coupling with sovereignty, risks being confused with sovereignty as such.

Politics of the Story (2)

In closing, and in order to draw out these conceptual distinctions a little more clearly, I want to consider the plastic form of sovereignty that I argue Melville's story is offering next to another conceptualization of sovereignty with which Melville's story, and the enigmatic scrivener around which it revolves, arguably has much in common. This will involve a detour through a text of political *anthropology* that I would like to begin to consider here as offering a possible answer to the problems of political *theology* that plague the concept of sovereignty. What might a political anthropology of sovereignty look like, a sovereignty that would truly contract the human being into a form of life, into an *anthropolitical* form-of-life on the far side of the *zoe/bios* distinction that informs the two-body problem of the *theologico-political* king? The aesthetico-political approach to sovereignty that I have developed in this book intends to provide such a political anthropological position against that of political theology.

After Andrew Delbanco, whose Melville biography offers a reading of Melville's work in close dialogue with the political situation of both his *and our* time,[68] I have been trying to show that there is something politically significant about the recurring references to "Bartleby, the Scrivener" in critical theory today. I began by commenting on Agamben's use of the phrase "prefer not to" to describe the position of the refugee between assimilation and repatriation: I overheard, you could say, Agamben's understanding of Bartleby as a political figure. For this, however, I took my cue from Melville's story. For such an overhearing also takes place in Melville's story. Early on in the story, when the narrator is walking in the street and debating the probabilities pro and con his assumption that the scrivener finally will have left his offices, he encounters "an excited group of people standing in earnest conversation" and overhears the following line: "'I'll take odds he doesn't,' said a voice as I passed."[69] "'Doesn't go? – done,'" the narrator replies, "'put up your money,'" only realizing afterwards that "[t]he words I *overheard* bore no reference to Bartleby, but to the success or non-success of some candidate for the mayoralty [emphasis mine]."[70] With the narrator, and because of the half rhyme of the words "mayoralty" and "Bartleby," we nevertheless overhear the suggestion that the scrivener is a political figure. But the key question I want to address here is, of course: what kind of political figure? Offering what concept of the political? What politics?

Michel Foucault's 1975–6 lectures at the Collège de France, collected in the book *"Society Must Be Defended,"* offer Foucault's engaging discussion of (among other things) Karl von Clausewitz's assertion that "war is politics continued by other means." After the September 11 terror attacks, von Clausewitz's statement – and in particular Schmitt's reversal of it: "politics is war continued by other means" – gained a new importance in contemporary conceptualizations of the political. In 1974, just before Foucault began his inquiry into what he considered to be a new understanding of war as the basis of all institutions of power, Pierre Clastres published *Society Against the State*, a book that argued against the "unquestioned conviction" in ethnological inquiries "that political power is manifested within a relation that ultimately comes down to coercion."[71] To Clastres, it is not at all evident "that coercion and subordination constitute the essence of political power at all times and in all places."[72] On the basis of his study of the concept of the political in Indian groups in Paraguay and Venezuela, Clastres argues that it is possible to speak of power when there is neither coercion nor violence. He makes reference to a "vast constellation of [archaic] societies in which the holders of what elsewhere would be called power are actually without power"[73] and suggests that the Indian groups' "radical rejection of authority" may have been "formed in terms of an intuition that power is essentially coercion."[74] Political power is universal, Clastres argues, but it exists in (at least two) particular modes: coercive and non-coercive. And the latter is still a form of power. The Western conception of power as coercive only applies to one particular mode of power. My suggestion here will be that Melville's story can be read through the lens of this conceptual distinction as well as others that are operative in Clastres's text. I want to ask, specifically, about whether the two modes of power between which Clastres distinguishes – coercive and non-coercive – can help us think two modes of sovereignty. In the same way that Clastres destabilized the conception of power as essentially coercive, I want to destabilize the conception of sovereignty as essentially theologico-political. In the same way that Clastres's project does not go against power, mine does not go against sovereignty. Both accomplish, rather, a shift within our conceptions of power and sovereignty. Naturally, and following Clastres's suggestion, what is most relevant here are Clastres's remarks about the Indian chief. However, those will only turn out to constitute one side of my analysis.

In the second chapter of his book, Clastres recalls Robert Lowie's analysis of three distinctive features of the Indian chief: the chief is a peacemaker, a moderating agency; he must be generous with his possessions, and cannot allow himself, without betraying his office, to reject the incessant demands of those under his administration; only a good orator can become a chief.[75] These three features recall the relation between Melville's narrator and Bartleby. The narrator is a "man of peace" who tries to moderate Bartleby's subversive presence in the law office; in his struggle with the scrivener, he proves to be a very generous person, who does not easily allow himself to reject the demands of the copyists under his administration; as the story demonstrates, he has a way with words.

Clastres points out that to be a peacemaker means to be a "moderator of differences."[76] It is "the multiplicity of divergent trends [in the society of the group] that legitimates the unifying activity of the main chieftainship."[77] These descriptions recall Kalyvas's alternative conception of sovereignty. Starting from Plato's dialogue *The Statesman*, he proposes to conceive of sovereignty as a kind of "weaving" (hence, the title of his article, "The Sovereign Weaver"): "Like weaving," he writes, "politics is an art of combining different elements into a unified fabric, the fabric of the *polis*, and like the weaver, the genuine sovereign-statesman fashions the multiple webs that constitute the political community."[78] He concludes: "The weaver, in other words, creates unity out of plurality."[79] The chief as an alternative figure of sovereignty, then.

The unity accomplished by such an alternative sovereign would not be a unity that is opposed to plurality. In light of what I wrote above when I suggested Melville's story invites us to conceptualize peace as a position that does not exclude conflict, Clastres's observation that the "equilibrium" of the Indian group "should not be confused with the homogeneity of a whole"[80] becomes particularly interesting. Homogeneity would be "more appropriate to a geometrical arrangement of parts," he writes, "than the inventiveness immanent to culture."[81] This moves us towards the description of the community as a space of agonistics, of gaming that I proposed earlier on. Thus, Clastres continues, "we see disclosed the lateral and somewhat furtive presence of differences and their ultimate potential for open conflict."[82] For these Indian groups, conflict is a "dimension of collective life engendered by the social culture itself."[83] "Like Western societies," Clastres optimistically continues, "archaic societies are perfectly capable of handling the possibility of difference within identity, of otherness in homogeneity."[84] "Although they function as units, they nonetheless allow their elements a certain 'play'"[85] – the word "play" recalls, once again, the culture of gaming. In this context, I should also point out that for the Indian groups, the non-coercive concept of power still includes the possibility of war. The chief has not only civil power, but also military power: in times of war, the tribe adopts a coercive model of power that is dropped again after the war has ended. So this alternative conception of sovereignty is hardly power-*less*.

To understand better the figure of Bartleby in Melville's story – the figure that Agamben and others consider to present the biggest challenge to traditional conceptions of sovereignty – I want to have a closer look at one of the most brilliant chapters of Clastres's book, in which he offers an analysis of what he interprets to be the masculine and the feminine space in the society of the Guayaki Indians: "the forest where the men do their hunting and the encampment where the women reign."[86] Clastres is interested specifically in the stories of two men, both of whom bring a crisis to this strict distribution of space. The first, Chachubutawachugi, is a widower who is pané, that is: who has bad luck in hunting. The second, Krembegi, is a homosexual who lets his hair grow "conspicuously longer" than that of the other men, and does only "a woman's work."[87] Whereas Krembegi "conceived of himself as a woman," Clastres writes, "and had adopted the attitudes and behavior peculiar to that sex," Chachubutawachugi "had remained a man," even though he had been "forced to give up in part his masculine attributes [his bow]."[88] In other words: whereas Krembegi follows the logic of the tribe and "becomes a woman," Chachubutawachugi "refus[es] the movement of the same logic."[89] As a consequence, he is "expelled from the circle of men, but without being assimilated into that of the women."[90] "This meant," Clastres continues, "that … *he literally was nowhere.*"[91] Whereas Krembegi occupied a "well defined though paradoxical place," Chachubutawachugi "constituted in his very person a kind of logical scandal."[92]

This is not too far removed from Agamben's description of the refugee and from the analysis that I offered above of the crisis Bartleby brings to the narrator's law office. Consider the spatial distribution in Melville's story, which recalls that of the Indian group. At the beginning of the story, just before the narrator introduces his employees to the reader, he offers a short description of his chambers, noting that "[a]t one end, they looked upon the white wall of the interior of a spacious sky-light shaft" and offer, on the other, "the view … of a lofty brick wall, black by age."[93] This contrast between white and black sets the tone for the narrator's opposition of Turkey and Nippers: whereas Turkey works swiftly in the morning and gets too energetic in the afternoon, it is the other way round with Nippers. The narrator hopes that Bartleby will rid the office of these eccentricities by working steadily all through the day. But the scrivener's effect turns out to be quite different: he doesn't just break down the binary opposition of Turkey and Nippers, but puts a stop to work altogether – all the while demanding to be allowed to remain within the space of the office. Read in comparison with Clastres's description of Krembegi and Chachubutawachugi, Bartleby clearly resembles the latter. Like Chachubutawachugi, he is literally nowhere: there is no place for him on Wall Street. By remaining "unemployed" and "idle" in a law office, the scrivener constitutes a logical scandal. Like Chachubutawachugi, he introduces an "element of disorder"[94] – in Malabou's terms: an ontological displacement – into the community in which he has no part. Like Bartleby,

Chachubutawachugi is a kind of refugee, someone who falls between "assimilation" ("becoming a woman") and "repatriation" ("becoming a hunter again").

Politics of Language (2)

> Ways should be found to enable the singular, the exceptional, the rare to coexist with a State structure that is the least burdensome possible.... There is a proverb "the exception proves the rule", but the exception can just as easily deflect the rule, or even recreate it. (Félix Guattari, *The Three Ecologies*)[95]

Until now, Clastres's book has enabled me to get a better sense of the narrator's role as "chief" of the law office, as well as of Bartleby's role as the element within the office that poses a radical, irresolvable challenge to its distribution of the sensible. The narrator is thus aligned with what Jacques Rancière, theorist of the politics of aesthetics, would call "the police" (even if it is a police that, in this case, exercises a non-coercive power and thus challenges, politically, the Western conceptualization of power) and Bartleby with "politics" (even if it is a politics that, to Rancière's taste, would no doubt be too passive).[96] But what happens when language is considered as part of this configuration, a key component not only in Melville's story and of Clastres's analysis, but also in Agamben's understanding of theologico-political sovereignty?

To answer that question, let me begin by having a look at Clastres's discussion of the chief's speech. Clastres notes that for the chief, "speaking is more than a privilege, it is a duty."[97] "It can be said not that the chief is a man who speaks, but that he who speaks is a chief."[98] One could argue, of course, and this would confirm what I wrote earlier, that since the narrator is telling the story, it is he who is the chief of the story. But I would like to push things a bit further at this point, and emphasize Clastres's indication of the chief's particular kind of speech. Clastres explains that the chief's speech "falls outside of the province of communication.... Reciprocity ceases to regulate [its] circulation."[99] Hence, he concludes, "it is in the negative relation maintained to the group [the Indian tribe] that the impotence of the political function is rooted."[100] Clastres's analysis of the "marginal position" of the chief's speech as resulting from "the rupture that power injects into the ... cycle of ... exchange"[101] recalls my analysis of *Bartleby's speech* (rather than the narrator's speech) as an interruption of communication. So it seems that Bartleby *also* bears features of the Indian chief. From the perspective of a linguistic analysis, it seems that Bartleby may be closer to Clastres's understanding of the chief than Melville's narrator.

And there is more. Upon closer reflection, the narrator arguably also bears features of Chachubutawachugi (associated with Bartleby in the first reading of the story that I offered). As I indicated above, Bartleby exposes the narrator's impotence. "Indeed," the narrator notes, "it was [Bartleby's] wonderful mildness chiefly, which not only disarmed me, but *unmanned* me as it were [emphasis mine]."[102] Thus, the narrator's power becomes haunted by Bartleby's *chiefly* silhouette: the scrivener's "wonderful mildness chiefly" denaturalizes the phallocentric community of the law office. This denaturalization, which the narrator seems to experience as a castration, ultimately leads the narrator into a self-inflicted state of exile: under the pressure of "the constant friction of illiberal minds"[103] − people are gossiping about him on Wall Street − he decides to remove his offices. Note that he doesn't expel Bartleby from his premises; rather, he expels his offices from Bartleby's premises. It could be argued that the roles are thus reversed here: Bartleby becomes the chief, and it is the narrator who no longer fits within the tribe that Bartleby establishes.[104]

The story thus accomplishes something that I have already laid out above, namely the contraction of the narrator – symbolic life – and Bartleby – material life – into a single entity, with both carrying aspects of each other. While it seems obvious that Bartleby is closer to the logical scandal of Chachubutawachugi, in the same way that the narrator is obviously closer to the chief in Clastres's discussion, Melville's story also contracts these two figures in Clastres's book – a suggestion that in fact lies already contained in Clastres, who notes their affinity – and this requires some further reflection on the concept of the political and the politics that are being accomplished here.

The key question, then, turns out to be the following: what understanding of the "chief" emerges from the *double* reading I have offered – from a reading that splices the narrator and Bartleby together into the reality of Melville's story, which encompasses both and exists at the uneasy but politically promising crossroads of an "impossible story"? The chief is a man of peace, exercising a non-coercive power that can become coercive in times of war (that is: it is not without muscle), and such a position is – through the meaningless speech that the chief practices, and via the connection of Bartleby in Melville's story – associated with the logical scandal of Chachubutawachugi. This presents us with the case of a chief who participates in the ontological displacement of his own chiefhood. Alternatively, it presents us – again, via the intermediary of Bartleby – with a Chachubutawachugi who is a figure of sovereignty: it reveals Bartleby and Chachubutawachugi to us as figures of an alternative conception of power (rather than as mere figures of "silence"). Following Clastres's analysis, it would be crucial that these chiefs are poor. They represent a poor kind of sovereignty that unworks the sovereignty familiar from the Western tradition. Crucially, such a sovereignty could not come about through the chief or Chachubutawachugi alone, or through the narrator or Bartleby alone: it is realized by both of them, through their combination, and in the case of Melville's story it is the story that brings the narrator and Bartleby together into some new contract. Literature may be able to accomplish something, when it comes to poetic formations built on the aesthetic politics I have theorized, that the legalo-political order of theologico-political sovereignty cannot.

I suppose that, given the reference to Delbanco that I already included above, it might not come as a surprise if I present the literary challenge to theologico-political sovereignty here in "democratic" terms. For indeed, and building on the work that has been done by scholars like Dimitris Vardoulakis and Stathis Gourgouris in this context,[105] I think of this challenge as democratic. But what is too often forgotten when it comes to thinking this challenge as democratic, even if Gourgouris certainly doesn't do so, is that such a challenge remains a "cracy," that is: a political rule, power or force (one could even say, "violence" – though Clastres might contest this), and that such a rule is an essential component of political organization. Even if democracy has no foundation other than self-organization, even if it requires an imaginary of a rule without beginning or end/aim, even if it has no a priori principles (as Gourgouris in a recent text summarizes[106]), it is not *without* organization, rule, and principle and these are essential features of what has traditionally been called "sovereignty." To surgically separate "democracy" from those elements would mean, as I see it, to render democracy powerless and it risks producing precisely the political ineffectiveness that we are suffering from today. Indeed, in his recent work on governmentality (rather than sovereignty) Gourgouris has been calling for what he refers to as a "left governmentality,"[107] suggesting there is a need to explore practices of governance from the left. I couldn't agree more, and I have presented Foucault's late work on the care of the self here (and elsewhere) as taking part in such a project. Pushing Gourgouris's argument on this count, I want to ask: if there can be a left governmentality, can there be left sovereignty? Why couldn't there be? Couldn't there be such a thing as a left state? If not, what are the consequences of this negation, specifically of the separation it inserts between leftist politics and state formation, sovereign power?

Chantal Mouffe has in this context taken on the left's negative attitude towards the state, reading the ongoing development of both the Occupy Movement and the transformations in the Arab world as "a call for a radicalization of liberal democratic institutions, not for their rejection."[108] She argues that "[t]o effectively challenge neo-liberal hegemony," one should not reject representative democracy or any kind of "hegemonic" order (to recall a term that she theorized with Ernesto Laclau). As she sees it, and I put myself in line with her reflections, the multitude will not "auto-organize itself, avoiding taking power and becoming the state";[109] the left will remain weak as long as it places its hope in such a phantasy. Instead, "[w]hat needs to be challenged is the lack of alternatives offered to citizens, not the very idea of representation."[110] She criticizes in this context the "horizontalism" of the Occupy Movement, arguing – and Naomi Klein does the same in her book on climate change[111] – that Occupy or any other leftist movement could do with some verticalism if it wants to be politically efficient. When Mouffe explains that her approach "acknowledges the constitutive character of social division and the impossibility of final reconciliation,"[112] she evokes – insists even – on the radical negativity of silence *but without giving up on speech altogether* (as is evidenced by the words "constitutive character," "reconciliation" versus "*final* reconciliation"). Indeed, with her notion of agonistics – a politics in which "the antagonistic dimension is always present, since what is at stake is the struggle between opposing hegemonic projects which can never be reconciled rationally, one of them needing to be defeated" (she opposes herself to Habermas and Rawls on this count, who continue of course the Kantian heritage that I've already criticized above), in other words: a politics of "real confrontation, but one that is played out under conditions regulated by a set of democratic procedures accepted by the adversaries" – Mouffe develops in my view a theory of plastic sovereignty, even if she would probably never agree to this term. Sovereignty, in her work, appears to be closely associated with hegemony. However, note that she does not give up on hegemony altogether: indeed, she argues that one needs to counter hegemony with other hegemonies, and that agonistic politics consists of pluralizing hegemonies. As for sovereignty: *idem ditto.*

This enables me to return, in closing, to an essential element of my title, namely the fact that "sovereignty" becomes pluralized when it is paired with "plasticity." While I have spoken of "plastic sovereignty" throughout this book, it should by now be clear that while I have used the notion in the singular, I have sought to think it in the plural: pluralization is one of the key dimensions of sovereignty's plasticity, the way in which plasticity challenges the theologico-political construction of a sovereignty of the one.

As is clear from Mouffe's book, this argumentation also affects our understanding of the state. The agonistic project is not so much about a radical rejection of the state in the name of, say, the radical negativity of freedom. It would be, rather, a project of pluralizing the state, opposing to whatever is the hegemonic state formation alternative counter-hegemonic formations, and counter-states. That is what Mouffe calls politics. Interestingly, she has developed this argument in part in a contribution she wrote for an art-theory book titled *Institutional Attitudes: Instituting Art in a Flat World*.[113] Edited by sociologist Pascal Gielen, this book extends work that Gielen has done elsewhere by criticizing the neoliberal, flat world in which we have landed – echoed, I would argue, by the flat ontology that is increasingly becoming popular in critical theory[114] – and considering whether, and what kind of, verticalism may be needed if we want to remain politically autonomous and self-referential. Institutions have a major role to play in this and to ignore them, reject them, withdraw from them is, in Mouffe's view, "profoundly mistaken."[115] One of the risks in this context is, as I have demonstrated in Chapter 8, art's association with the kind of freedom – total escape from law – that in fact reinforces the exceptionalist sovereignty that we are suffering from today.

If the challenge, in a world where "flatness rules" is "to stand up and get some air," it seems extremely important, before such a position reinforces the old verticality of sovereignty once again, to reflect carefully about the particular dynamics of such a stance. Reinstating the vertical in a flat world that came about in response to a verticality gone rogue, the call for verticalism that also informs my book can clearly not simply be a return to the old verticality of sovereignty: instead, it rethinks the horizontal and the vertical as tendencies that, in tandem, unwork both horizontalism's and verticalism's excesses and would seek to bring about other kinds of institutions – which are, ultimately, versions of what I am calling here sovereignty and the state. How much more meaningful, and true to actual practices, would it be to associate art not with the genius-like romanticism of breaking the law, escaping it, constituting an exception to it, but with what Guattari in the epigraph to this section of the chapter calls "deflecting" the law or "recreating" it? As Mouffe points out,

> [t]oday, artists can no longer pretend to constitute an avant-garde offering radical critique. But this is not a reason to proclaim that their political role has ended; they have an important role to play in the hegemonic struggle. By constructing new practices and new subjectivities, they can help subverting the existing configuration of power.[116]

Was there really ever any artist who "escaped" the law in a kind of sovereign gesture of suspension, actualizing a freedom that would stand entirely separate from the legalo-political order? (According to Mouffe, this is an illusion that must be abandoned.[117]) If there was, I doubt that we would know about such a Bartleby-like figure, for the reality is that without any organization, rule, or principle, there simply cannot be either artist or art. The entire history of art needs to be rewritten, then, not as a history of law-breaking, but as a history of law-making, considering how artists and art over time have contributed to at the very least deflecting, and probably also recreating sovereignty.

This final plea may not sit well with readers familiar with Agamben's work. Recall, they might object, that in the closing section of *The Coming Community*, Agamben writes that

> [t]he novelty of the coming politics is that it will no longer be a struggle for the conquest or the control of the State, but a struggle between the State and the non-State (humanity), an insurmountable disjunction between *whatever* singularity and the State organization [emphasis mine].[118]

Whatever singularity against the state: this is the conflictual formula that seems to dominate Agamben's concept of the coming politics. It seems to be entirely in line with the post-operaismo politics of Michael Hardt, Antonio Negri, and Paolo Virno whose work Mouffe sharply criticizes.

However, I think it's worth pointing out that Agamben's book doesn't end with this disjunction and the destruction of the state or state organization that it seems to imply. Importantly, the section from which I have been quoting is followed by an appendix entitled "The Irreparable": a series of "fragments" that, according to their author, should be read as a commentary on the philosophies of Martin Heidegger and Ludwig Wittgenstein.[119] Prefaced by Agamben's explicit acknowledgment of "their obvious shortcomings,"[120] these bits and pieces actually deconstruct the conflictual binary of state/humanity that dominates the closing section of the book – and one should perhaps not have expected anything less from a thinker that, more than some others writing about these issues, has continuously been inclined to the literary in his thought. The question that emerges in this appendix seems to be, rather, how we can think whatever singularity and state organization *together*, as another kind of state (which is a different project from "trying to gain control of the State").

It seems to me that this question, although originally formulated in 1990, just after the fall of the Berlin Wall, is still extremely relevant today. If the terror attacks from 11 September

2001 arguably brought a return to the binary oppositions of the Cold War, this time suggesting a clash of civilizations between the Judeo-Christian West and the Muslim East, and if the theologico-political sovereignties that those oppositions have tended to reinforce are evidently responsible for the political conflicts that have dominated the world since – political conflicts that, according to many, may actually be more economic than political in kind and be traced back to sovereignties of the 1 percent that seek to increase their wealth – it would seem petty to allow those tyrannical abuses of the power of organization, rule, principle, accountability, authorship, and such to take all those politically effective notions down with them. It would mean, ultimately, to give up on politics simply because it carries the possibility of abuse within it. But such – possibility of abuse – is, precisely, the tragic nature of politics: that it has no guarantee, and certainly not one that would be established elsewhere, for example through a transcendental, heteronomous agency. Instead, it leaves the world squarely up to us as something that can receive form, that gives form, and might also – it must be said, and plenty of scholars have been saying it – explode when stretched beyond its limits. Given this plastic nature of the world, one that is perhaps becoming increasingly clear as the world's "nature" is being pushed to its limit, would it be any wonder that the mode of government such a world requires is a power that would be attuned to such a liminal state: a plastic sovereignty or, if you will, governmentality that would bring organization, rule, principle, accountability, authorship to the abyssal condition of human existence, not to exploit such a power into its tyrannical abuse, but to theorize and practice it into more effective forms of living together, beyond the "sovereign" distinction between the simple, material fact of life and symbolic life – between *zoe* and *bios*, the two-body distinction that always inevitably produces the explosive, limit-form of life that Agamben, after Benjamin, calls "bare life"?

For this, I have argued, a new contract theory is necessary: a new contraction of the symbolic into the material and vice versa, and in this book I have proposed the notion of plastic sovereignty as accomplishing such a contract – beyond the theologico-political ban of bare life, and with the muscle to be politically effective. This is a project, I have argued, that takes place not only in the political realm that has been central to the third and final part of this book; it started, at least in this book, in the realm of aesthetics, and more particularly linguistics, moving from an alternative conception of language (and the related storytelling and translation) toward an alternative conception of politics. Along the way, and in view of the particular linguistic and political situation today, I have drawn out some crucial economic aspects of theologico-political sovereignty and the ontology it assumes, thus revealing that the way in which we are in language is immediately relevant for a contemporary thinking of economy as well.[121] Finally, if much of my efforts here have been dedicated to the thinking of an aesthetic politics that would expose the distributions that prevent us from uncovering the new contract in language, ontology, and politics that I propose, I have in closing also insisted on the poetic extension of such a project, exploring how actual formations of the aesthetico-political infancy that is central to Agamben's project – in particular, literary formations that take political theology to task – can help us think future formations of sovereignty, beyond a renewed call to cut off the head of the king.

The fact of the matter is that the king will never die. We have always already been living in the realm of the king's survival: it is, indeed, precisely the call for the king's death that reproduces the two-body problem that guarantees sovereignty's continued life (hence, the cry "the king is dead, long live the king"). It was never a particularly revolutionary thing to proclaim the king's death. It simply fortified the king's survival. The problem is, however, that such a survival has seemed to be outside of our reach, unchangeable, the continued operator of an order from which there is no escape. The real issue, therefore, is how to arrive at another king: not simply an other king, one that would continue the symbolic life through her or his material body, but another king, one that would mark an ontological displacement of that two-body order – a king, otherwise.

In their different ways, both Catherine Malabou and Giorgio Agamben put us on the track of such a political thought and practice, the former by thinking a tripartite operation of plasticity, and the latter by proposing the *zoe–bios*–bare life triad as the matrix of sovereignty. Matching the one onto the other, it becomes possible to see that the true challenge here is in fact to proclaim the king's life: not the same one as before, but a new one – boring, uninteresting, at a remove from the public eye. Poor and in withdrawal, such a life would neverthe-less still mark a form of power, would maintain the qualities of authorship, accountability, organization that characterize sovereignty, and would be able to turn coercive whenever threatened: it would combine the characteristics of what I called (in Chapter 6) its "retirement" with the exercise of politics that requires engagement. It would mark a political life of peace that does not exclude conflict: Mouffe's agonistic, "conflictual consensus." It would be a sovereignty that dismantles those aspects of its life that, by now, we should have been done with. But to accomplish this, we had to see that to be done with something does not mean to call for its death: it means in fact to call for its life – but a wholly different kind of life.

Living, which is from the beginning living together and therefore politics, should have taught us at least that much.

Notes

1   Honig, "Three Models of Emergency Politics," 48.
2   Mouffe, *Agonistics*, 104.
3   Delbanco, *Melville*.
4   Deleuze, "Bartleby."
5   Lebowitz, *Progress*.
6   The essay "Beyond Human Rights" was published in *MWE*. The quotation here is taken from a revised version of the essay that was published in *Homo Sacer* as the chapter "Biopolitics and the Rights of Man": *HS*, 126–35; here 126.
7   Agamben, *MWE*, 19–20.
8   Ibid., 20.
9   Ibid., 23.
10 Ibid.
11 Ibid., 24.
12 Agamben, *P*, 243–71.
13 Melville, "Bartleby," 27.
14 See n. 6.
15 Kalyvas, "Sovereign," 116.
16 Ibid.
17 Ibid.
18 Kalyvas, "Politics."
19 Kalyvas, "Sovereign," 118.
20 Ibid.
21 Ibid.
22 Ibid.
23 Melville, "Bartleby," 15.
24 Ibid., 16.
25 Agamben, *MWE*, 23.

26 Melville, "Bartleby," 3.

27 Ibid., 46.

28 Ibid., 35.

29 Ibid., 3.

30 Ibid., 4.

31 Ibid.

32 Ibid., 6.

33 Ibid., 8.

34 Ibid., 13.

35 Ibid., 19.

36 Ibid., 13.

37 Ibid., 14–15.

38 Ibid., 11.

39 Ibid., 21.

40 Lyotard, *Differend*.

41 Mouffe refers to Lyotard in this context: Mouffe, *Agonistics*, 11.

42 Lyotard and Thébaud. *Just Gaming*. See in particular Sam Weber's afterword to this translation.

43 Melville, "Bartleby," 4.

44 Mouffe, *Agonistics*, 8. It is worth noting in this context that Andrew Arato has considered how Mouffe's, and especially Ernesto Laclau's, concepts of the political continue political theology, for instance in their attachment to the friend/enemy distinction. On this count, see in particular Laclau, *On Populist Reason*. I want to thank Martín Plot for drawing my attention to Arato's criticism.

45 Delbanco, *Melville*, 119.

46 See Derrida, "Oligarchies."

47 Agamben, *IP*, 82–3.

48 Melville, "Bartleby," 18.

49 Ibid., 25.

50 Ibid., 13.

51 Ibid., 46.

52 Ibid., 34.

53 Ibid., 34–5.

54 Ibid., 35.

55 Žižek, "Neighbor," 163.

56 Spiegelman, *Maus*, 4.

57 Butler, *Frames*, 76.

58 I am engaging here, implicitly, with Weheliye, "'Feenin.'"

59 On the particular importance of care in this context, see also Boever, *Narrative Care*.

60 Lyotard, *Just Gaming*, 71.

61 Melville, "Bartleby," 46.

62 Ibid., 12.

63 Ibid.

64 Ibid., 13.

65 Cohen, "Letters."

66 Melville, "Bartleby," 12.

67 Agamben, *SE*, 64.

68 Delbanco, *Melville*.

69 Melville, "Bartleby," 31.

70 Ibid.

71 Clastres, *Society*, 11.

72 Ibid., 13.

73 Ibid., 11.

74 Ibid., 43.

75 Ibid., 29.

76 Ibid., 60.

77 Ibid.

78 Kalyvas, "Sovereign," 124–5.

79 Ibid., 125.

80 Clastres, *Society*, 60.

81 Ibid.

82 Ibid.

83 Ibid.

84 Ibid., 60–1.

85 Ibid., 61.

86 Ibid., 104.

87 Ibid., 108.

88 Ibid., 110.

89 Ibid.

90 Ibid.

91 Ibid.

92 Ibid.

93 Melville, "Bartleby," 4–5.

94 Clastres, *Society*, 110.

95 Guattari, *Three Ecologies*, 34–5.

96 Rancière, *Dis-agreement*.

97 Clastres, *Society*, 41.

98 Ibid.

99 Ibid.

100 Ibid.

101 Ibid., 42.

102 Melville, "Bartleby," 21.

103 Ibid., 35.

104 This mutual infection was arguably already contained in the idea of a powerless chief, and in the fact that Chachubutawachugi poses such a powerful challenge to the tribe's distribution of the sensible.

105 See Vardoulakis, *Sovereignty*; Gourgouris, "Democracy"; Gourgouris, "The question."

106 Gourgouris, "Democracy."

107 Gourgouris, "The question." Gourgouris has referred to the government elected in Greece in January 2015 as an example of such "left governmentality."

108 Mouffe, *Agonistics*, 119–20.

109 Ibid., 125.

110 Ibid.

111 See Klein, *This Changes*, 158.

112 Mouffe, *Agonistics*, 15.

113 Gielen, *Institutional Attitudes*.

114 I am thinking here of the work of Manuel DeLanda, Levi Bryant, and Ian Bogost. While I think this work is crucial in flattening, or horizontalizing, some of the problematic aspects of an enlightened, humanistic thought that has tended to verticalize (following an anthropological measure that is based in reason), I wonder if "flat" or "horizontal" is really a useful adjective in this context to describe what DeLanda et al. are aiming for. I would propose they adjust the adjective flat to "flattening" to draw out the *tendency* of the horizontalizing move they propose, and also – and this is more closely related to my own project – to preserve a verticalizing tendency that has, in spite of the problems to which it has led, its virtues. "Flat" resonates, to my ear (but I am hardly the only one to have pointed this out), with a neoliberal world in which politics no longer has any response to the economy.

115 Mouffe, *Agonistics*, 100.

116 Ibid., 105.

117 Ibid.

118 Agamben, *CC*, 85.

119 Ibid., 89.

120 Ibid.

121 I hope to be able to return to this point in a book tentatively titled *Finance Fictions*.

Bibliography

Abbott, Matthew. *The Figure of this World: Agamben and the Question of Political Ontology*. Edinburgh: Edinburgh University Press, 2014.

Adorno, Theodor. "Commitment." In: Adorno, Theodor, Walter Benjamin, Ernst Bloch, Bertolt Brecht, and Georg Lukács. *Aesthetics and Politics: The Key Texts of the Classic Debate Within German Marxism*. New York: Verso, 2002.

—. *Prisms*. Trans. Samuel Weber and Shierry Weber. Cambridge: MIT Press, 1967.

Anderson, Benedict. *Imagined Communities: Reflections on the Origin and Spread of Nationalism*. New York: Verso, 1991.

Arendt, Hannah. *Eichmann in Jerusalem: A Report on the Banality of Evil*. New York: Penguin, 1994.

—. *The Human Condition*. Chicago: University of Chicago Press, 1998.

Aristotle. *The Nicomachean Ethics*. Trans. David Ross. New York: Oxford University Press, 1998.

Asad, Talal. *On Suicide Bombing*. New York: Columbia University Press, 2007.

Attell, Kevin. *Giorgio Agamben: Beyond the Threshold of Deconstruction*. New York: Fordham University Press, 2014.

Badiou, Alain. *The Century*. Trans. Alberto Toscano. Cambridge: Polity, 2007.

—. *The Rebirth of History: Times of Riots and Uprisings*. Trans. Gregory Elliott. London: Verso, 2012.

Balfour, Ian and Rebecca Comay. "The Ethics of Witness: An Interview with Geoffrey Hartman." In: Comay, Rebecca, ed. *Lost in the Archives*. New York: Distributed Art Publishers, 2002. 492–509.

Barthes, Roland. "Zazie and Literature." In: Barthes, Roland. *Critical Essays*. Trans. Richard Howard. Evanston: Northwestern University Press, 1972. 117–23.

Benjamin, Walter. "Critique of Violence." In: Benjamin, Walter. *Selected Writings, Volume 1: 1913–1926*. Ed. Marcus Bullock and Michael W. Jennings. Cambridge: Belknap/Harvard University Press, 1996. 236–52. / "Zur Kritik der Gewalt." In: Benjamin, Walter. *Gesammelte Schriften, Vol. 2.1*. Ed. Rolf Tiedemann and Herman Schweppenhäuser. Frankfurt am Main: Suhrkamp, 1997. 179–203.

—. *Illuminations: Essays and Reflections*. Trans. Harry Zohn. New York: Schocken, 1985.

—. *Selected Writings, Volume 1: 1913–1926*. Ed. Marcus Bullock and Michael W. Jennings. Cambridge: Belknap/Harvard University Press, 1996. / *Gesammelte Schriften, Vol. 2.1*. Ed. Rolf Tiedemann and Herman Schweppenhäuser. Frankfurt am Main: Suhrkamp, 1997.

—. *Selected Writings, Volume 2: 1927–1934*. Ed. Michael W. Jennings, Howard Eiland, and Gary Smith. Trans. Rodney Livingstone and Others. Cambridge: Belknap/Harvard University Press, 1999.

—. "The Storyteller: Observations on the Works of Nikolai Leskov." In: Benjamin, Walter. *Selected Writings, Volume 3: 1935–1938*. Ed. Howard Eiland and Michael W. Jennings. Cambridge: Harvard University Press, 2002. 143–66. / "Der Erzähler: Betrachtungen zum Werk Nikolai Lesskows." In: Benjamin, Walter. *Gesammelte Schriften, Vol. 2*. Ed. Theodor Adorno. Frankfurt am Main: Suhrkamp, 1955. 229–58.

—. "The Task of the Translator." In: Benjamin, Walter. *Illuminations: Essays and Reflections*. Trans. Harry Zohn. New York: Schocken Books, 1985. 69–82. / "Die Aufgabe des Übersetzers." In: Benjamin, Walter. *Gesammelte Schriften, Vol. 4.1*. Ed. Tillman Rexroth, Rolf Tiedemann, and Herman Schweppenhäuser. Frankfurt am Main: Suhrkamp, 1972. 9–21.

Bennett, Jane. *Vibrant Matter: A Political Ecology of Things*. Durham: Duke University Press, 2010.

Berardi, Franco "Bifo." *Precarious Rhapsody: Semiocapitalism and the Pathologies of the Post-Alpha Generation*. Trans. Arianna Bove, Erik Empson, Michael Goddard, et al. London: Minor Compositions, 2009.

Berman, Antoine. *The Experience of the Foreign: Culture and Translation in Romantic Germany*. Trans. S. Heyvaert. Albany: SUNY, 1992.

Bickerton, Christopher J., Philip Cunliffe, and Alexander Gourevitch, eds. *Politics Without Sovereignty: A Critique of Contemporary International Relations*. New York: University College London Press, 2007.

Boever, Arne De. "Agamben and Marx: Sovereignty, Governmentality, Economy." *Law and Critique* 20.3 (2009), 259–70.

—. "Bio-Paulitics." *Journal for Cultural and Religious Theory* 11.1 (2010), 35–51. Available at: <http://www.jcrt.org/archives/11.1/boever.pdf>.

—. "La traduction de l'opération d'individuation." Paper delivered at: "Gilbert Simondon et l'Invention du Futur," Centre Culturel International de Cerisy, Cerisy-la-salle (France), Summer 2013.

—. "Losing Face: Francis Bacon's *25th Hour*." *Film-Philosophy* 16 (2012), 85–100. Available at: <http://www.film-philosophy.com/index.php/f-p/article/view/240>.

—. *Narrative Care: Biopolitics and the Novel*. New York: Bloomsbury, 2013.

—. "Politics and Poetics of Divine Violence: On a Figure in Giorgio Agamben and Walter Benjamin." In: Clemens, Justin, Nicholas Heron, and Alex Murray, eds. *The Work of Giorgio Agamben: Law, Literature, Life*. Edinburgh: Edinburgh University Press, 2008. 82–96.

— "Rev. Watkin, William. *The Literary Agamben: Adventures in Logopoièsis*. New York: Continuum, 2010." *Bryn Mawr Review of Comparative Literature* 10.1 (2012). Available at: <http://www.brynmawr.edu/bmrcl/BMRCLFall2012/TheLiteraryAgamben.htm>.

—. *States of Exception in the Contemporary Novel: Martel, Eugenides, Coetzee, Sebald*. New York: Continuum, 2012.

Bosteels, Bruno. *The Actuality of Communism*. New York: Verso, 2011.

Bredekamp, Horst. *Thomas Hobbes Visuelle Strategien*. Berlin: Akademie Verlag, 1999.

Brown, Wendy. *Regulating Aversion: Tolerance in the Age of Identity and Empire*. Princeton: Princeton University Press, 2006.

Buck-Morss, Susan. "Hegel and Haiti." *Critical Inquiry* 26.4 (2000), 821–65.

Butler, Judith. *Frames of War: When Is Life Grievable?* London: Verso, 2009.

—. "Indefinite Detention." In: Butler, Judith. *Precarious Life: The Power of Mourning and Violence*. New York: Verso, 2004. 51–100.

—. *Notes Toward a Performative Theory of Assembly*. Cambridge: Harvard University Press, 2015.

—. *Precarious Life: The Powers of Mourning and Violence*. New York: Verso, 2004.

Calarco, Matthew and Steven DeCaroli, eds. *Giorgio Agamben: Sovereignty and Life*. Stanford: Stanford University Press, 2007.

Campbell, Timothy. *Improper Life: Technology and Biopolitics from Heidegger to Agamben*. Minneapolis: University of Minnesota Press, 2011.

Castells, Manuel. *Communication Power*. New York: Oxford University Press, 2009.

Clastres, Pierre. *Society Against the State*. Trans. Robert Hurley and Abe Stein. New York: Zone Books, 1989.

Coen, Joel and Ethan Coen. *No Country for Old Men*. Film. USA: Miramax, 2008.

Cohen, Tom. "The Letters of the Law: 'Bartleby' as Hypogrammatic Romance (Letters)." In: Cohen, Tom. *Anti-Mimesis from Plato to Hitchcock*. Cambridge: Cambridge University Press, 1994. 152–78.

Collins, George. "Petit annonce pour un sous-groupe de travail sur les cultures de soi." Available at: <http://www.arsindustrialis.org/petite-annonce-pour-un-sous-groupe-de-travail-sur-les-cultures-de-soi>.

Combes, Muriel. *Gilbert Simondon and the Philosophy of the Transindividual*. Trans. Thomas LaMarre. Cambridge: MIT Press, 2013.

Cooper, Melinda. *Life as Surplus: Biotechnology and Capitalism in the Neoliberal Era*. Seattle: University of Washington Press, 2008.

Corcoran, Steve. "Editor's Introduction." In: Rancière, Jacques. *Dissensus: On Politics and Aesthetics*. New York: Continuum, 2010. 1–24.

Crary, Jonathan. [Untitled]. *Artforum* (December 2009), 77–8.

Danner, Mark. "After September 11: Our State of Exception." *The New York Review of Books* (13 October 2011). Available at: <http://www.nybooks.com/articles/2011/10/13/after-september-11-our-state-exception/?pagination=false>.

Dean, Jodi. *Blog Theory*. Cambridge: Polity, 2010.

Delbanco, Andrew. *Melville: His World and Work*. New York: Alfred A. Knopf, 2005.

Deleuze, Gilles. "Bartleby, ou la formule." In: Deleuze, Gilles. *Critique et Clinique*. Paris: Éditions Minuit, 1993. 89–114.

Derrida, Jacques. *The Death Penalty: Volume I*. Trans. Peggy Kamuf. Chicago: University of Chicago Press, 2014.

—. *Dissemination*. Trans. Barbara Johnson. Chicago: University of Chicago Press, 1981.

—. *Of Grammatology*. Trans. Gayatri Chakravorty Spivak. Baltimore: Johns Hopkins University Press, 1997.

—. "Oligarchies: Naming, Enumerating, Counting." In: Derrida, Jacques. *Politics of Friendship*. Trans. George Collins. New York: Verso, 1997. 1–25.

—. *Sovereignties in Question: The Poetics of Paul Celan*. Ed. Thomas Dutoit and Outi Pasanen. New York: Fordham University Press, 2005.

Deutsches Wörterbuch von Jacob Grimm und Wilhelm Grimm. Bd. 12, 2. Leipzig: Hirzel, 1951.

Durantaye, Leland de la. *Giorgio Agamben: A Critical Introduction*. Stanford: Stanford University Press, 2009.

Düttmann, Alexander García. "Making Poverty Visible – Three Theses." Trans. Arne De Boever. *Parrhesia* 4 (2008), 1–10.

Esposito, Roberto. *Bíos: Biopolitics and Philosophy*. Minneapolis: University of Minnesota Press, 2005.

Etymologisches Wörterbuch des Deutschen. Bd. Q–Z. Berlin: Akademie, 1989.

Fanon, Frantz. *The Wretched of the Earth.* Trans. Richard Philcox. New York: Grove Press, 2004.

Foucault, Michel. *The Birth of Biopolitics: Lectures at the Collège de France 1978–1979.* Trans. Graham Burchell. Ed. Michel Senellart. New York: Palgrave, 2008.

—. *The Care of the Self: The History of Sexuality,* Vol. 3. Trans. Robert Hurley. New York: Vintage, 1988.

—. *The History of Sexuality. Vol. 1: An Introduction.* Trans. Robert Hurley. New York: Vintage, 1990.

—. *Le Gouvernement de soi et des autres: Cours au Collège de France 1982–1983.* Ed. François Ewald, Alessandro Fontana, and Frédéric Gros. Paris: Gallimard, 2008.

—. *The Politics of Truth.* Los Angeles: Semiotext(e), 2007.

—. *Security, Territory, Population: Lectures at the Collège de France 1977–1978.* Trans. Graham Burchell. Ed. Michel Senellart. New York: Palgrave, 2007.

—. *"Society Must Be Defended": Lectures at the Collège de France 1975–1976.* Trans. David Macey. Ed. Mauro Bertani and Alessandro Fontana. New York: Picador, 2003.

—. *Technologies of the Self: A Seminar with Michel Foucault.* Ed. Luther H. Martin, Huck Gutman, and Patrick H. Hutton. Amherst: University of Massachusetts Press, 1988.

—. *This is Not a Pipe.* Trans. and ed. James Harkness. Berkeley: University of California Press, 1983.

Freud, Sigmund. "The Moses of Michelangelo." Trans. James Strachey. In: Freud, Sigmund. *Writings on Art and Literature.* Stanford: Stanford University Press, 1997. 122–50.

—. "The 'Uncanny.'" Trans. James Strachey. In: Freud, Sigmund. *Writings on Art and Literature.* Stanford: Stanford University Press, 1997. 193–233.

Frost, Tom. "Agamben and the Possibilities of Tradition." In: Frost, Tom, ed. *Giorgio Agamben: Legal, Political and Philosophical Perspectives.* London: Routledge, 2013. 54–71.

Frost, Tom, ed. *Giorgio Agamben: Legal, Political and Philosophical Perspectives.* London: Routledge, 2013.

Gielen, Pascal, ed. *Institutional Attitudes: Instituting Art in a Flat World.* Amsterdam: Valiz, 2013.

Godard, Jean-Luc. *Notre Musique.* Film. France: Avventura, 2004.

Gourgouris, Stathis. "Democracy is a Tragic Regime." *PMLA* 129.4 (2014), 809–18.

—. "The Question is: Society Defended Against Whom? Or What?" *The New Philosopher*, 25 March 2014. Available at: <http://www.newphilosopher. com/articles/the-question-is-society-defended-against-whom-or-what-in-the-name-of-what/>.

Guattari, Félix. *The Three Ecologies*. Trans. Ian Pindar and Paul Sutton. London: Continuum, 2008.

Han, Sora Y. "Strict Scrutiny: The Tragedy of Constitutional Law." In: Clough, Patricia Ticineto and Craig Willse, eds. *Beyond Biopolitics: Essays on the Governance of Life and Death*. Durham: Duke University Press, 2011. 106–35.

Haraway, Donna. *Simians, Cyborgs, and Women: The Reinvention of Nature*. New York: Routledge, 1991.

Hardt, Michael and Antonio Negri. *Commonwealth*. Cambridge: Harvard University Press, 2009.

—. *Empire*. Cambridge: Harvard University Press, 2000.

—. *Multitude*. New York: Penguin, 2005.

Heller-Roazen, Daniel. *The Fifth Hammer: Pythagoras and the Disharmony of the World*. New York: Zone Books, 2011.

Hobbes, Thomas. *Leviathan*. New York: Oxford University Press, 1998.

Honig, Bonnie. "Three Models of Emergency Politics." *boundary 2* 41.2 (2014), 45–70.

Kahn, Paul W. *Political Theology: Four New Chapters on the Concept of Sovereignty*. New York: Columbia University Press, 2012.

Kalyvas, Andreas. "The Politics of the Extraordinary: Max Weber, Carl Schmitt, Hannah Arendt." Dissertation. Columbia University, 2001.

—. "The Sovereign Weaver: Beyond the Camp." In: Norris, Andrew, ed. *Politics, Metaphysics, and Death: Essays on Giorgio Agamben's* Homo Sacer. Durham: Duke University Press, 2005. 107–34.

Kant, Immanuel. *Groundwork of the Metaphysics of Morals*. Trans. Mary Gregor. Cambridge: Cambridge University Press, 2007.

—. "Perpetual Peace: A Philosophical Sketch." In: Kant, Immanuel. *Political Writings*. Trans. H. B. Nisbet. Cambridge: Cambridge University Press, 1983. 93–130.

—. "Was ist Aufklärung?" In: Foucault, Michel. *The Politics of Truth*. Trans. Lysa Hochroth and Catherine Porter. Los Angeles: Semiotext(e), 2007. 29–37.

Kishik, David. *The Power of Life: Agamben and the Coming Politics*. Stanford: Stanford University Press, 2012.

Klein, Naomi. *The Shock Doctrine: The Rise of Disaster Capitalism*. New York: Picador, 2007.

—. *This Changes Everything: Capitalism vs. the Climate*. New York: Simon & Schuster, 2014.

Klossowski, Pierre. *Tableaux Vivants: Essais Critiques 1936–1983*. Paris: Gallimard, 2001.

Kotsko, Adam. "What Saint Paul and the Franciscans Can Tell Us About Neoliberalism." Available at: <http://itself.wordpress.com/2013/05/22/what-st-paul-and-the-franciscans-can-tell-us-about-neoliberalism/>.

Laclau, Ernesto. *On Populist Reason*. New York: Verso, 2007.

Lacoue-Labarthe, Philippe, Jacques Rancière, Jean-François Lyotard, and Alain Badiou. "Liminaire sur l'ouvrage d'Alain Badiou 'L'être et l'évènement.'" *Le Cahier* (*Collège international de philosophie*) 8 (1989), 201–25, 227–45, 247–68.

Lagarde, François. *Simondon du désert*. Film. France: Hors oeil, 2012.

Lebowitz, Alan. *Progress into Silence: A Study of Melville's Heroes*. Bloomington: Indiana University Press, 1970.

Lévi-Strauss, Claude. *The Savage Mind*. Trans. [not listed]. Chicago: University of Chicago Press, 1966. / *La pensée sauvage*. Paris: Plon, 1962.

Locke, John. *Second Treatise of Government*. Indianapolis: Hackett, 1980.

Lotringer, Sylvère and Christian Marazzi. *Autonomia: Post-Political Politics*. Los Angeles: Semiotext(e), 2007.

Lyotard, Jean-François and Jean-Loup Thébaud. *The Differend: Phrases in Dispute*. Trans. Georges Van Den Abeele. Minneapolis: University of Minnesota Press, 1988.

—. *Just Gaming*. Trans. Wlad Godzich. Minneapolis: University of Minnesota Press, 1985.

McCarthy, Cormac. *No Country for Old Men*. New York: Knopf, 2005.

Malabou, Catherine. *Changing Difference: The Feminine and the Question of Philosophy*. Trans. Carolyn Shread. Cambridge: Polity, 2011.

—. "Darwin and the Social Destiny of Natural Selection." *theory@buffalo* 16 (2012), 144–56.

—. *The Future of Hegel: Plasticity, Temporality and Dialectic*. Trans. Lizabeth During. London: Routledge, 2005.

—. *The New Wounded: From Neurosis to Brain Damage*. Trans. Steven Miller. New York: Fordham University Press, 2012.

—. "Odysseus' Changed Soul." Unpublished ms. 1–17.

—. *Ontology of the Accident: An Essay on Destructive Plasticity*. Trans. Carolyn Shread. Cambridge: Polity, 2012.

—. "Sovereignty and Biology." Unpublished ms. 1–10.

—. *What Should We Do With Our Brain?* Trans. Sebastian Rand. New York: Fordham, 2008.

—. "Who's Afraid of Hegelian Wolves?" In: Patton, Paul, ed. *Deleuze: A Critical Reader*. Oxford: Blackwell, 1996. 114–38.

Man, Paul de. "'Conclusions' on Walter Benjamin's 'The Task of the Translator.'" *Yale French Studies* 97 (1985), 10–35.

Marx, Karl. *Capital: A Critique of Political Economy*. Vol. 1. Trans. Ben Fowkes. London: Penguin, 1990.

Melville, Herman. "Bartleby, the Scrivener; A Story of Wall Street." In: Melville, Herman. *Billy Budd, Sailor and Other Stories*. New York: Penguin, 1986. 3–46.

Mills, Catherine. *The Philosophy of Giorgio Agamben*. Montreal: McGill-Queen's University Press, 2009.

Moore, Alan. *V for Vendetta*. New York: DC Comics, 2005.

Mouffe, Chantal. *Agonistics: Thinking the World Politically*. London: Verso, 2013.

Murray, Alex. "Beyond Spectacle and the Image: The Poetics of Guy Debord and Agamben." In: Clemens, Justin, Nicholas Heron, and Alex Murray, eds. *The Work of Giorgio Agamben: Law, Literature, Life*. Edinburgh: Edinburgh University Press, 2008. 164–80.

—. *Giorgio Agamben*. London: Routledge, 2010.

Murray, Alex and Jessica Whyte. *The Agamben Dictionary*. Edinburgh: Edinburgh University Press, 2011.

Nealon, Jeffrey. *Foucault Beyond Foucault*. Stanford: Stanford University Press, 2008.

—. *Plant Theory: Biopower and Vegetable Life*. Stanford: Stanford University Press, 2015.

Negri, Antonio. "Giorgio Agamben: The Discreet Taste of the Dialectic." In: Calarco, Matthew and Steven DeCaroli, eds. *Giorgio Agamben: Sovereignty and Life*. Stanford: Stanford University Press, 2007. 109–25.

Nelson, Dana D. *Bad for Democracy: How the Presidency Undermines the Power of the People*. Minneapolis: University of Minnesota Press, 2008.

Nietzsche, Friedrich. *On the Genealogy of Morals and Ecce Homo*. Trans. Walter Kaufmann and R. J. Hollingdale. New York: Vintage, 1989.

Nolan, Christopher. *The Dark Knight*. Film. USA: Warner Brothers, 2008.

Norris, Andrew, ed. *Politics, Metaphysics and Death: Essays on Giorgio Agamben's Homo Sacer*. Durham: Duke University Press, 2005.

Noudelmann, François. *The Philosopher's Touch: Sartre, Nietzsche, and Barthes at the Piano*. New York: Columbia University Press, 2012.

Parsley, Connal. "'A Particular Fetishism': Love, Law and the Image in Agamben." In: Frost, Tom, ed. *Giorgio Agamben: Legal, Political and Philosophical Perspectives*. London: Routledge, 2013. 31–53.

Pelenc, Arielle. "Arielle Pelenc in Conversation with Jeff Wall." In: Duve, Thierry de, Arielle Pelenc, Boris Groys, et al. *Jeff Wall*. London: Phaidon, 2003. 8–23.

Rajchman, John, "Enlightenment Today." In: Foucault, Michel. *The Politics of Truth*. Los Angeles: Semiotext(e), 2007. 9–27.

Rancière, Jacques. *Dis-agreement: Politics and Philosophy*. Trans. Julie Rose. Minneapolis: University of Minnesota Press, 2004.

—. *The Emancipated Spectator*. Trans. Gregory Elliott. New York: Verso, 2009.

—. *The Future of the Image*. Trans. Gregory Elliott. New York: Verso, 2007.

—. *The Ignorant Schoolmaster: Five Lessons in Intellectual Emancipation*. Trans. Kristin Ross. Stanford: Stanford University Press, 1991.

—. "Who is the Subject of the Rights of Man?" In: Balfour, Ian and Eduardo Cadava, eds. *And Justice for All? The Claims of Human Rights. The South Atlantic Quarterly* 10.2/3 (Spring/Summer 2004). 297–310.

Reiss, Benjamin. "Sleep's Hidden Histories." *Los Angeles Review of Books* (15 February 2014). Available at: <http://lareviewofbooks.org/review/sleeps-hidden-histories>.

Robbins, Bruce. "Comparative National Blaming." Available at: <http://www.columbia.edu/~bwr2001/papers/comp_national_blaming.pdf>.

—. "Internationalism in Distress." In: Robbins, Bruce. *Feeling Global: Internationalism in Distress*. New York: New York University Press, 1999. 11–37.

—. "Orange Juice and Agent Orange." *Occasion: Interdisciplinary Studies in the Humanities* 2 (2010), 1–14. Available at: <http://arcade.stanford.edu/sites/default/files/article_pdfs/Occasion_v02_Robbins_122010_0_0.pdf>.

Rockhill, Gabriel. "The Janus-Face of Politicized Art: Jacques Rancière in Interview with Gabriel Rockhill." In: Rancière, Jacques. *The Politics of Aesthetics: The Distribution of the Sensible*. Trans. Gabriel Rockhill. New York: Continuum, 2004.

Rourke, Daniel. "Artifacts: A Conversation Between Hito Steyerl and Daniel Rourke." *Rhizome* (March 2013). Available at: <http://rhizome.org/editorial/2013/mar/28/artifacts/>.

Ruda, Frank and Jan Voelker, "The Necessary Critique of Divine Violence: Notes on Agamben, Benjamin and Sorel." In: Frost, Tom, ed. *Giorgio Agamben: Legal, Political and Philosophical Perspectives*. London: Routledge, 2013. 75–96.

Rutsky, R. L. "The Spirit of Utopia and the Birth of the Cinematic Machine." In: Rutsky, R. L. *High Technè: Art and Technology from the Machine Aesthetic to the Posthuman*. Minneapolis: University of Minnesota Press, 1999. 23–47.

Santner, Eric. *The Royal Remains: The People's Two Bodies and the Endgames of Sovereignty*. Chicago: University of Chicago Press, 2011.

—. "Terri Schiavo and the State of Exception." Available at: <http://www.press.uchicago.edu/Misc/Chicago/05april_santner.html>.

Schmitt, Carl. *Political Theology: Four Chapters on the Concept of Sovereignty.* Trans. George Schwab. Cambridge: MIT Press, 1985.

Seymour, David M. "The Purgatory of the Camp: Political Emancipation and the Emancipation of the Political." In: Frost, Tom, ed. *Giorgio Agamben: Legal, Political, and Philosophical Perspectives.* London: Routledge, 2013. 97–118.

Sherman, Cindy. *The Complete* Untitled Film Stills. New York: Museum of Modern Art, 2003.

—. "The Making of *Untitled.*" In: Sherman, Cindy. *The Complete* Untitled Film Stills. New York: Museum of Modern Art, 2003. 4–16.

Shread, Carolyn. "The Horror of Translation." *theory@buffalo* 16 (2012), 77–95.

—. "Translator's Preface." In: Malabou, Catherine. *Ontology of the Accident: An Essay on Destructive Plasticity.* Trans. Carolyn Shread. Cambridge: Polity, 2012. vii–ix.

Simondon, Gilbert. *Du mode d'existence des objets techniques.* Paris: Aubier, 1989.

—. *L'individuation psychique et collective, à la lumière des notions de Forme, Information, Potentiel et Métastabilité.* Paris: Aubier, 2007.

—. "Technical Mentality." Trans. Arne De Boever, *Parrhesia* 7 (2009), 17–27.

Sloterdijk, Peter. "*Rules for the Human Zoo*: A Response to the *Letter on Humanism,*" *Environment and Planning D: Society and Space* (2009), 12–28.

Smith, Jason. "'I am sure that you are more pessimistic than I am': An Interview with Giorgio Agamben." *Rethinking Marxism* 16.2 (2004), 115–24.

Sontag, Susan. *Against Interpretation and Other Essays.* New York: Delta, 1966.

—. "Looking at War: Photography's View of Devastation and Death." *The New Yorker* (9 December 2002), 82–92.

—. *Regarding the Pain of Others.* New York: Farrar, Straus, and Giroux, 2003.

—. "'There' and 'Here.'" In: Sontag, Susan. *Where the Stress Falls.* New York: Picador, 2001.

Spiegelman, Art. *Maus: A Survivor's Tale, Vol. I.* New York: Random House, 1986.

Spivak, Gayatri Chakravorty. *An Aesthetic Education in the Era of Globalization.* Cambridge: Harvard University Press, 2012.

Srnicek, Nick and Alex Williams, *Inventing the Future: Postcapitalism and a World Without Work.* New York: Verso, 2015.

Steyerl, Hito. "Die Gegenwart der Subalternen." In: Spivak, Gayatri Chakravorty. *Can the Subaltern Speak? Postkolonialität und subalterne Ar-*

tikulation. Trans. Alexandar Joskowicz and Stefan Nowotny. Vienna: Turia+Kant, 2008. 7–16.

—. "In Defense of the Poor Image." *e-flux* 10 (2009). Available at: <http://www.e-flux.com/journal/in-defense-of-the-poor-image/>.

—. *The Wretched of the Screen*. Berlin: Sternberg Press, 2012.

Stiegler, Bernard. *Ce qui fait que la vie vaut la peine d'être vécue: De la pharmacologie*. Paris: Flammarion, 2010.

—. *La télécratie contre la démocratie: Lettre ouverte aux représentants politiques*. Paris: Flammarion, 2008.

—. "The Proletarianization of Sensibility." Trans. Arne De Boever. *Lana Turner* 4 [no date], 124–40. Available at: <http://www.lanaturnerjournal.com/archives/prolsensestiegler>.

—. *Taking Care of Youth and the Generations*. Trans. Stephen Barker. Stanford: Stanford University Press, 2010.

—. *Technics and Time, 1: The Fault of Epimetheus*. Trans. Richard Beardsworth and George Collins. Stanford: Stanford University Press, 1998.

Stiegler, Bernard and *Ars Industrialis. Réenchanter le monde: La valeur esprit contre le populisme industriel*. Paris: Flammarion, 2006.

Vande Veire, Frank. "I Love Art, You Love Art, We All Love Art, This is Art – Een pamflet over de kunstwereld." Available at: <http://www.network54.com/Forum/113844/thread/1054633068/last-1061224920/I+Love+Art---+Een+pamflet+over+de+kunstwereld>.

—. "Men neemt de kunst haar crisis af." Available at: <http://www.dewitteraaf.be/artikel/detail/nl/2725>.

Vardoulakis, Dimitris. *Sovereignty and Its Other: Toward the Dejustification of Violence*. New York: Fordham University Press, 2014.

Walsh, Maria. "Rev. Steyerl, Hito. *The Wretched of the Screen*. Berlin: Sternberg Press, 2012." *Art Monthly* (April 2013), 35.

Watkin, William. *Agamben and Indifference: A Critical Overview*. London: Rowman & Littlefield, 2014.

—. *The Literary Agamben: Adventures in Logopoièsis*. London: Continuum, 2010.

Weber, Samuel. *Benjamin's -Abilities*. Cambridge: Harvard University Press, 2010.

—. "Taking Exception to Decision: Walter Benjamin and Carl Schmitt." In: Kunneman, Harry and Hent de Vries, eds. *Enlightenments: Encounters Between Critical Theory and Contemporary French Thought*. Kampen: Kok Pharos, 1993. 141–61.

Weheliye, Alexander G. "'Feenin': Posthuman Voices in Contemporary Black Popular Music." *Social Text* 71 20.2 (2002), 21–47.

Whyte, Jessica. *Catastrophe and Redemption: The Political Thought of Giorgio Agamben*. Albany: SUNY Press, 2014.

—. "'The king reigns but he doesn't govern': Thinking Sovereignty and Government with Agamben, Foucault and Rousseau." In: Frost, Tom, ed. *Giorgio Agamben: Legal, Political and Philosophical Perspectives*. London: Routledge, 2013. 143–61.

—. "Use." In: Murray, Alex and Jessica Whyte. *The Agamben Dictionary*. Edinburgh: Edinburgh University Press, 2011. 194–6.

Wood, Michael. "Rev. Nolan, Christopher. *The Dark Knight* (Warner Brothers, 2008)." *The London Review of Books* 30.16 (2008). Available at: <http://www.lrb.co.uk/v30/n16/michael-wood/at-the-movies>.

Wright, Stephen. *Toward a Lexicon of Usership*. Eindhoven: Deltahage, 2013.

Zabala, Santiago and Gianni Vattimo. *Hermeneutic Communism: From Heidegger to Marx*. New York: Columbia University Press, 2011.

Žižek, Slavoj. "The Neighbor and Other Monsters: A Plea for Ethical Violence." In: Žižek, Slavoj, Eric L. Santner, and Kenneth Reinhard. *The Neighbor: Three Inquiries in Political Theology*. Chicago: University of Chicago Press, 2005. 134–90.

Index

text
    and image, 121–4
    and life, 178
theological economy, 152–3, 204,
    282
theologico-political sovereignty, 6
theology, 99, 282; *see also* political
    theology
theory, 108n
"Theses on the Philosophy of History,"
    73n, 298
This is not a Pipe, 117–21
Time That Remains, The, 100, 295,
    330–1
Toward a Lexicon of Usership, 292–3
Transborder Immigrant Tool, 46
translatability, 111, 113, 125–30,
    131–5, 136, 139
translation, 111–14, 123, 124–30,
    131–3, 197–9
translational ontogenesis, 113, 143n
two-body problem, 34
tyrannical sovereignty, 34

uncanny, 60–4, 95
unconditional translatability, 129, 133,
    134, 135
unforgettable, 222–3n
Untitled Film Stills, 137–9
US
    Civil War, 267
    executive power, 271
    political history, 266–9
    presidency, 251, 252, 263, 267–8
    visa regulations, 43
use, 225, 226–7, 320, 322, 326

Valéry, Paul, 77
Vande Veire, Frank, 56–60, 62–3
Vardoulakis, Dimitris, 17, 38n, 219n,
    370, 382n

verticality, 67, 123, 294, 323, 373–4
*Vibrant Matter: A Political Ecology of
    Things*, 38n
violence
    divine, 48, 96, 98, 99–100, 169–71
    educative, 48
    and law, 81–9, 96, 97–8, 99–100,
        232–3
    mythical, 88
    sovereign, 89
visa regulations, 43, 44
vogelfrei, 161–2
von Clausewitz, Karl, 362

Wall, Jeff, 78, 79–80, 230–4, 302–3,
    305, 318–20
waltende, 89, 106n
war, 302–6, 365
"What is an Apparatus?," 183, 202–4,
    206–10, 212, 219n
"What is Enlightenment?," 68–9,
    193–7, 355
What Should We Do With Our Brain?,
    28
whatever being, 296
Whyte, Jessica, 19–20
will to power, 185
work, 225–7, 233–4, 238
"Work of Art in the Age of
    Mechanical Reproduction, The,"
    77–8
*Work of Giorgio Agamben: Law,
    Literature, Life, The*, 50
"Work of Man, The," 226
Wretched of the Screen, The, 306–14
Wright, Steven, 292

Zabala, Santiago, 75n
zoe, 7, 24–5, 27, 30, 154, 360
    separation from *bios*, 7–8, 9–10,
        11–12, 13, 22, 358